GROCERY ACTIVISM

# GROCERY ACTIVISM

## The Radical History of Food Cooperatives in Minnesota

*Craig B. Upright*

UNIVERSITY OF MINNESOTA PRESS

MINNEAPOLIS | LONDON

Published by the University of Minnesota Press
111 Third Avenue South, Suite 290
Minneapolis, MN 55401-2520
http://www.upress.umn.edu

Printed in the United States of America on acid-free paper

The University of Minnesota is an equal-opportunity educator and employer.

27 26 25 24 23 22 21 20          10 9 8 7 6 5 4 3 2 1

Library of Congress Cataloging-in-Publication Data
Names: Upright, Craig B., author.
Title: Grocery activism : the radical history of food cooperatives in Minnesota / Craig B. Upright.
Description: Minneapolis : University of Minnesota Press, [2020] |
Includes bibliographical references and index. |
Identifiers: LCCN 2019053484 (print) | ISBN 978-1-5179-0072-4 (hc) | ISBN 978-1-5179-0073-1 (pb)
Subjects: LCSH: Food cooperatives—Minnesota—History—20th century. |
Natural foods industry—Minnesota—History—20th century.
Classification: LCC HD3286.A3 M687 2020 (print) | DDC 334/.5—dc23
LC record available at https://lccn.loc.gov/2019053484

# CONTENTS

# FROM NICHE MARKETS TO MAINSTREAM MEALS

In June 2017, Amazon announced that it was purchasing the national organic retail giant Whole Foods. In a deal worth $13.7 billion (to be paid in cash), the former online-only mail-order department store of the Internet acquired more than 450 physical stores and 87,000 additional employees. The acquisition addressed a growing limitation that Amazon encountered as it continually expanded into markets traditionally serviced by local merchants with brick-and-mortar operations. While the shipping of smaller, denser products (such as books, Amazon's original raison d'être) was a rather straightforward and imminently calculable proposition, the efficient delivery of larger and more valuable products necessitated a nationwide network of secured distribution centers. Amazon wanted a set of storefront operations where customers could pick up their orders and consumers would feel more comfortable purchasing high-end electronics such as flat-screen television sets knowing these wouldn't be left on one's front porch all afternoon waiting to be picked up by a random passerby. The grocer chain had also spent years establishing an elaborate distribution system, and Amazon wanted to break free of its reliance on national shipping firms such as FedEx and UPS.

But Whole Foods offered alluring fruits beyond its national presence and preexisting distribution system. If the online retailer wanted to quickly procure a national set of storefront operations, it could have purchased one of the national drugstore companies such as Walgreen's or CVS. If it were interested in not just placing its products within reach of every neighborhood but also acquiring a fleet of delivery trucks, it could have made a pitch to acquire the United States Postal Service. Whole Foods, however, had something even more valuable: a loyal and relatively elite consumer base that regularly shopped at its stores several times a week.

Amazon's acquisition of Whole Foods was just the latest piece of evidence that organic food has become a mainstream consumer item, but it certainly was not the first. The contemporary existence of a green, circular "organic" label—indicating that the underlying product has been certified to meet national standards—is easily taken for granted these days. Organic food, once the subject of derision among agricultural executives, professional scientists, and federal officials, is no longer seen as an antiestablishment challenge to mainstream grocery stores. One can find the organic label on food products in every imaginable outlet, from our nation's largest food chains to truck stops across the land.

The project of providing a single, coherent national definition of the term "organic" at the end of the twentieth century, however, took several decades of persistent lobbying and was undertaken by the U.S. Department of Agriculture (USDA) only after an act of Congress in 1990. When the first proposed standards were unveiled in 1997, they provoked more than 275,000 comments—the largest input of individual comments on any regulatory matter exposed to a public comment period. Most of these comments were negative, suggesting the proposed standards did not go far enough to protect the integrity of the organic label. In the end, it took five more years for the USDA to put its national

*Figure 1.* The U.S. federal "certified organic" logo. The final rule of the National Organic Program was published in 2000, ten years after Congress passed the Organic Foods Production Act, which required the Department of Agriculture to create a set of national standards.

organic standards program in place (as long as it had taken the nation's founding fathers to craft the United States Constitution following its declaration of independence from England). The final document weighed in at 507 pages.[1]

In the second half of the twentieth century, the concept of "organic" underwent a tremendous transformation in terms of its public awareness, social image, and acceptance by the larger agricultural industry. First coined in the 1940s by the magazine publisher and health guru J. I. Rodale, the term was relegated to a small set of practitioners during the next two decades and practiced mainly in home gardens. During the rising countercultural movements of the late 1960s into the 1970s, it was embraced by activists who rejected institutional structures and by hippies who sought a greater connection to Mother Nature. From the 1980s on, organic food gradually developed as the fastest-growing niche market and found ever-increasing shelf space in conventional grocery stores and supermarkets. Originally seen as a marker of checking out from American consumerism, the preference for organic food is now often associated with individuals who have higher status and greater affluence.

Whole Foods, of course, is more than just an upscale grocery store. Founded in 1978, the retailing of organic food has formed the central core of its identity throughout its expansion into a national chain, and it is often credited with the mainstreaming of "organic" foods in the American market. Whole Foods Market opened its second Austin store in 1982, expanded to Houston in 1984, and opened a third Austin store in 1985. Its first acquisition of an existing natural foods store took place in 1986, when it bought the Bluebonnet Natural Foods grocery in Dallas. During these early years, Whole Foods created a subsidiary, named the Texas Health Distributors, a wholesaler of organic and natural foods products that included customers outside its corporate umbrella. Over the next ten years it began a pattern of expansion by acquiring previously established independent natural foods retailers throughout the country, targeting North Carolina (two Wellspring Groceries, 1991), New England (five Bread & Circus stores, 1992), and California (six Mrs. Gooch's outlets, 1993). During this first phase of the Whole Foods Market expansion project, one principle emerged that guided its continued dominance into the twenty-first century: entry into markets with a demonstrated market demand for organic products. The easiest way to identify such markets? The presence of a cooperative grocery store, most likely one that was founded during the 1970s, in areas such as Berkeley, Chicago, Boston, and St. Paul, Minnesota. Those cooperatives' origins are where the history of this book begins.

This book explores one key period in the history of organic food, when the product was in its infancy and dedicated groups of activists promoted two separate but essential enterprises: the production of organic food and its distribution to the consuming public. While its proponents originally spoke of the "organic food movement," it eventually became an industry. Organic food slowly developed into a marketable product available even to those in both rural and urban areas who were not avid gardeners but who wanted to help create a more sustainable landscape. The emergence of organic food as a commodifiable comestible began in the 1970s, and the primary vendors for these products was a new type of cooperative store staffed and stocked by activists who were engaged in a quixotic project of social change.

The development of the organic food industry—including the farmers, distributors, markets, and retailers—is a story that was unfolding across the country. But the events taking place in Minnesota during this time did more than simply reflect national trends. In the 1970s, Minnesota was witness to the formation of a significant population of cooperative stores, most of them founded by countercultural organizers who wanted their fellow Americans to wake up and take an active role in their communities. Natural and organic food, free from unnecessary processing and packing, became the principle product sold in these stores. The motivations of these stores' founders, both passionate and varied, were based on challenging existing power structures. The debates that took place during this time helped influence the perceptions of and attitudes toward organic food for decades to come. The cooperatives in Minnesota took advantage of a unique opportunity to create a dialogue among different groups: Vietnam War protesters, Marxist agitators, commune members, intellectuals, back-to-the-land hippies, urban dwellers, and rural farmers. This microcosm of the national landscape did not interact simply due to geographic proximity. The cooperators during this time very consciously institutionalized centers for debate and distribution, and they promoted an ethos of "cooperation among cooperatives" to a degree rarely seen during this time. The creation of the

"People's Warehouse" and, later, the "All Cooperating Assembly" helped all of these organizations define their purpose, refine their strategies, and (eventually) pursue a commonly held set of goals.

It is important to study these stores and their stories because it is difficult to understand what "organic" means today without knowing what it could have been, without exploring how this new product, sold in these unconventional settings, attracted the passions of those who wanted to make their world a better place. The origins of organic food embedded within this product a set of social and political values that have endured, affecting not just how (and where) these products are sold but why people buy them and how people's personal decisions about what

*Figure 2*. When the Seward Cooop opened in 1971 at its corner lot on Franklin Avenue in Minneapolis, it primarily sold nonperishable food items in bulk out of a variety of plastic tubs and bins. The lack of excessive packaging could be as appealing as the products themselves, and this also helped reduce the cost of the wares. Dairy products were sold in the rear of the store; cutting and wrapping cheese has long been a staple chore of volunteer labor in worker-owned food cooperatives. Perishable produce was gradually introduced into these stores, but every used refrigerated cooler prone to breaking down could be a liability as well as an asset. Courtesy of the Minnesota Historical Society; photographer unknown.

they buy can truly affect the community around them. The events taking place in Minnesota during this time provide a rare if not a singular window into the debates, uncertainties, challenges, and triumphs within both organic and cooperative communities.

I began this study wondering why grocery cooperatives have continued to thrive in spite of the greater availability of organic foods in conventional supermarkets. We can explain why these co-ops *emerged* by pointing to their status as the primary suppliers of these products during the 1970s. When this new generation of cooperative stores began their mission to provide wholesome, natural food in a consumer- and worker-oriented retail environment, organic food existed mostly as a concept, a work in progress whose formal definitions were being refined by growers and consumers alike. These organizations first helped to create the distribution infrastructure for these goods and then demonstrated the continued viability of selling them in a competitive market. Organic and natural foods still maintain a prominent presence in the produce bins and dry goods shelves of contemporary cooperatives, but these stores by no means retain a monopoly on this product. The introduction of greater competition, especially in stores that already appealed to a wider mainstream consumer base, would appear to make these older, smaller, local stores irrelevant, since most consumers can now more conveniently obtain the goods elsewhere. But these cooperative grocery stores didn't go away. In fact, they have continued to grow—in both size and number—and they still play important roles in their communities. The reasons for their resilience and the rationales for examining them closer, I suggest, have three components.

First, cooperatives did not emerge primarily to serve as a vendor for organic and natural foods. Cooperatives formed to promote social change. Cooperative (as well as organic) activists often proclaim that "food is power" and speak of themselves as participating in a movement. At first, selling natural or organic foods was an extension of other activities and interests, all directed toward critiquing the mainstream institutions of the day.

Promoting "social change" is an admittedly broad and somewhat vague goal. The second reason that cooperatives have not only survived but thrived in today's diversified grocery market is related to the specific ways they wanted to improve society. Social movements often have to choose between addressing the structure of society—the laws and social arrangements by which we organize our lives—and the culture of society. Each has a profound influence on the other, of course, but it is difficult to address both at the same time. As these cooperatives matured in the 1970s, they embraced an ideology of "intentional consumerism," encouraging members of society to more thoughtfully consider both the origins and the implications of their food purchases. Organic food had a natural affinity with cooperatives not because of the specific practices associated with its production but because those who farmed organically demonstrated a more conscious approach to these practices. While never being able to completely escape the realm of commodification, all members in the cooperative food chain sought to raise awareness of those responsible for the creation of these nutritional necessities. Seen in this light, the cooperatives' embrace of the United Farm Workers' call for a boycott of grapes in the early 1970s, for example, makes perfect sense— the UFW sought to win rights and recognition of the laborers in California's grape industry by demonstrating support from the wider American public. Although the contemporary corporatized organic food market presents myriad contradictions, the fact that organic and cooperative consumers discuss and debate these issues points to one level of success: many shoppers *have* become more aware and conscious of their purchasing decisions. Co-ops survived, and they remain relevant today because they made a deliberate attempt to change the culture of society.

Finally, I suggest that the story of Minnesota cooperatives mirrored changes in the larger organic food industry, illustrating a forty-year process of changing social values in the United States. As each of these two movements progressed toward mainstream acceptance in society, they created more stable market infrastructures that could both attract and satisfy a larger consumer base. The public perception of organic food in the United States has been transformed: once considered the marginalized haven of antiprogress liberals supporting alternative lifestyles, the organic food industry is now associated with progressive "green" ideologies and elite consumerism. Such transformations, which happen as industries pursue new markets for existing products, occur regularly in the capitalist marketplace—where manipulating perception has become a multimillion-dollar business in itself. Transformations within the cooperative grocery sector have garnered less scrutiny, in part because they took place at lower levels of social structure. As organic food came to be produced and distributed nationally—as in the rise of franchised retailing operations such as Whole Foods and Wild Oats—local, independent cooperatives had to react.

One explanation for the success of these cooperatives counterintuitively points to one of their unique limitations: grounded in local economies, relying on local support (for their members, workers, and

---

### WHAT'S IN A BOYCOTT?

An Upcoming article in FAMINEWS will include information on present national boycotts. The hows and whys, questions and answers regarding certain products will be discussed. Four boycotts will be covered:
* Nestle's (Bottlefed Babies in Third World Countries)
* Lettuce and Grapes (United Farmworkers in California, Arizona and Mexico)
* Tuna Fish (Let's save the whales and dolphins)
* Wine Producers (Gallo and other Modesto California gangs)

These companies/products are not carried at Famine Foods, but there is a need to raise consciousness to food and drink that we purchase elsewhere. Hopefully, these articles will provide a forum for discussions on exploitation of land, people, and labor, with suggestions as to what each of us can do.

— CORN & BEANS

Ken Maly  * Karen Smaby  * Deb Stellpflug
*  Annie Young  *

---

*Figure 3*. With the wider availability of photocopying technology available in the 1970s, food cooperatives produced a variety of newsletters for their members. In the 1977 edition of FAMINEWS, published by the Famine Foods Co-op in Winona, Minnesota, the contributors promised to help explain the rationale behind several ongoing food boycotts promoted by activists across the world. Courtesy of Bluff Country Co-op, Winona, Minnesota.

customers) to survive, cooperatives had to pay more attention to the needs and wants of their communities. As these practices developed over three decades, cooperatives situated themselves perfectly for the emerging "locavore" movement that emphasized supporting regional food-sheds and independent businesses. As two economic trends accelerated in the twenty-first century—the rise of antichain sentiments and the fetishization of locally produced food products—cooperatives stood as one business model perfectly poised to appeal to a clientele that sought economic justice or social status (or both) through the purchase of limited-availability food products. Similarly, organic food has emerged as a product embedded with social values, no matter where it is purchased, and it retains an aura of enlightened self-interest that provides personal benefits while still promoting projects of environmental social change.

These cooperatives responded to challenges that were specific to their particular social, political, and economic contexts. Their collective success stemmed in large part from a recognition that people are not just willing but also very interested in promoting a healthier environment. In many cases, people are willing to make a small sacrifice when they feel it serves a larger good; they're willing to forgo some of the conveniences of our modern economy when they feel it makes a difference. These preferences can be observed in more recent sustainability trends, such as the increased popularity of farmers' markets, community-supported agriculture, and local foodsheds. Similar patterns exist in other nonfood-related projects related to environmental protection: the growth of recycling and freecycling, reductions in carbon footprints, the development of alternative and renewable fuels. The successful deployment of strategies to address the results of industrialization often does not make strict economic sense when one considers the short-term costs and benefits. But all of these projects, both within and outside the agricultural realm, have required a multiplicity of actors in public and private arenas, pursuing individual goals for personal gain in harmony with larger social goals striving for social change. The population of cooperatives serves as a microcosm of these processes, and, though they may not indicate the path that others will follow, they do help demonstrate the range of available options.

As with all social movements and capitalist transformations, this sector involved many different individuals and organizations motivated by a variety of interests. I am not suggesting that the cooperative grocery movement was independently responsible for the eventual success of the organic food industry. However, the cooperatives did emerge at a crucial moment in this history, at a time when both the federal government and larger agricultural concerns had a vested stake in refuting the critiques associated with organic production methods. Despite attempts to discredit the science, integrity, and politics associated with this new approach to sustainable agriculture, the cooperatives persisted in advancing the cultural values of organic food as well as the increasing availability of these products.

I should, however, also point out what this book is *not* about. I will intentionally avoid one topic I know would interest many readers. I will not make any attempt to formally define what "organic" means as a certified label in the contemporary market, nor will I discuss in any detail the specific practices associated with organic farming. (And because the term was not used as a reference to regulated practices during these early years, I will often use the term "natural" or "eco-foods" as rough synonyms on occasion.) Instead, I am initially taking the term as something of a known quantity, however imprecise that shared understanding might be. I treat it not merely as an abstract social construct, however, but as a construct based on broad principles of growing food in a sustainable manner using a minimum of input substitutions. My own personal understanding of these principles can be summed up with the phrase "feed the soil, not the plant." There are readily available volumes written by brilliant scholars on the specific regulations associated with the National Organic Standards Program, adopted in 2002. I am much more interested in how the cultural understanding of this term has impacted social movements and economic markets. Back in the early 1970s, there was a group of consumers that *wanted* the term to be meaningful—not just in terms of production standards but as an expression of political ideals and social values. And they wanted to purchase those foods in a store that was similarly aligned with their beliefs: committed to egalitarian principles of democratic governance and sustainable economic communities. I contend that even after several decades of regulatory definitions of the term, in the public consciousness organic food is still a product that appeals to individuals' preferences for changing their world in some meaningful way. Organic is still an oppositional term, one that suggests a break from the traditional, mainstream practices of contemporary society—even when it is purchased from Whole Foods, now owned by one of the richest men on the planet.

While co-ops do not deserve sole credit for the ultimate embrace of organic food in mainstream, middle-class society, they did help create the infrastructure that demonstrated the market viability of organic foods. Repeatedly emphasizing that "food is power," the activists promoting the sale of this type of product in this type of venue sought to elevate the practice of sustainable farming as a responsibility we all share to promote the health of consumers, farm laborers, and all citizens of the earth. These organizations also helped illuminate the issues of federation, decentralization, and—yes—cooperation that helped define organic food as a hybrid public-private good in the marketplace. In particular, the often-unseen interactions among these organizations promoted the definition of organic food as a product that belonged to a community rather than as a commodity subject to control by competing actors.

Perhaps the most important factor that allowed the co-ops to endure and become stable members of their communities involves their adherence to one of the founding principles suggested by the nineteenth-century Rochdale Pioneers: cooperation among cooperatives. When the early cooperatives encountered challenges sourcing products, they created a nonprofit distribution arm to serve the entire organizational community. Because they wanted to help ensure the success of each independent organization, they formed a loose federation to help resolve disputes and maintain communication among themselves. They assisted one another with financing, shared best practices, discussed the legal ramifications of organizing and operating in compliance with state statutes, cheered on the creation of new organizations, and bemoaned the fall of those that disbanded. Cooperative activists also sought out those producers most likely to provide them with goods created with a conscious ideology, celebrated their sources by promoting their individuality, and created an infrastructure to better ensure that all members of this growing network could survive.

The remainder of this introductory chapter previews the six that follow, outlining the major currents of discord and harmony revealed by a closer examination of the population of new-wave cooperatives in Minnesota. An explanation of the success of the new-wave cooperative requires us to look beyond the initial appeal of organic food by considering what participation in these organizations represented for those who spent countless hours nurturing the environments in which to sell it.

Chapter 1 traces the development of natural/organic foods through the twentieth century as a response to concerns about global agricultural transformations. Most historical accounts of the agricultural sector in the United States center on the rising industrialization of the nation's farms, as their products became not only the foundations for nutritional sustenance but also the basis for a much larger economic trade based on commodity exchange. Several leaders of a movement we would later term "sustainable agriculture" raised objections in the first two-thirds of the twentieth century along various lines: spiritual, economic, health. The arguments against the increasing industrialization of our global agricultural systems stemmed from a variety of concerns. Rudolph Steiner raised spiritual concerns, encapsulated by his philosophy of Anthroposophy and his endorsement of biodynamic growing methods. Sir Albert Howard was inspired by economic concerns for peasant farmers, resulting in his Indore methods for preserving soil nutrients without the need for costly fertilizers. And J. I. Rodale promoted growing methods that would result in better physical health for those who consumed food produced by those methods. Each sought to apply correctives to some negative result of the modernization of agriculture, both to articulate and to address the social ills that they perceived. The natural/organic production regimes that developed during the twentieth century accommodated all of these concerns, and they were an ideal fit for an idealistic group of reformers who wanted to challenge power in the political and economic arenas.

The development of organic production regimes was a part of larger sustainability movements. Chapter 2 demonstrates that, although a new wave of cooperative grocery stores arose in the late 1960s and early '70s to sell organic products, this organizational form has a much longer history. Since the founding of the nation, "cooperation" has been a recurring theme in American organizational forms as a civil society response to satisfy social needs. Consumer cooperatives have often formed to supply goods that are unavailable elsewhere or to provide goods at a cheaper price. Contemporary theorists suggest that the cooperative represents a solution to improve market efficiency, but a quick survey reveals that most of the groups that formed cooperatives did so in order to advance a particular social agenda. Groups associated through labor, ethnicity, and religion, as well as others with elective or ascriptive affinities, chose this organizational form to advance their personal/professional interests or to promote their own projects of social change. In every era of cooperative development, some proponents have hoped that these organizations would replace capitalist economic systems. But many others (including the federal government during the 1930s) viewed them as useful correctives to address specific market failures. Though cooperatives do not inherently represent a radical threat to traditional for-profit enterprises, the new-wave cooperators of the 1970s did attempt to use their organizations to resist societal power structures. In this chapter, we can observe how the "hot cause" of eco-foods joined with the "cool mobilization" of the cooperative grocery store, and I consider the challenges associated with operating a social movement organization within a capitalist environment.

Chapter 3 takes a closer look at the population of new-wave co-ops operating in Minnesota, a state with a long history of cooperative formation. The state of Minnesota presents a unique and ideal bounded geography in which to study the transformations of both the organic food industry and new-wave cooperatives. While the success of one did not necessarily depend on that of the other, both found their institutional footings in the wake of larger countercultural movements, and both shared underlying principles that sought to reform some aspect of the capitalist agricultural landscape. Minnesota, with its long history of progressive politics—tied to farming—has played host to activists from both camps: agricultural activism and cooperative organizations. In the 1930s, it elected the socialist-populist Floyd B. Olson as its governor on the Farmer-Labor ticket. (This state's current Democratic Party is formally referred to as the Democratic–Farmer–Labor Party, or DFL, resulting from a coalition formed in the 1940s by Hubert Humphrey.) With more than forty new-wave food cooperatives currently in operation, it has the highest number of any state in the nation. Finding information on organizations that have gone out of business—many of which maintained only minimal records—often presents a daunting challenge to organizational sociologists. Fortunately, the Minnesota History Center houses an excellent archive of such materials.

From 1970 to 1980, sixty cooperative grocery stores opened in forty-two of Minnesota's eighty-seven counties. In the first half of the decade, most of these co-ops were in the Twin Cities of Minneapolis and St. Paul; in the second half, most of the new co-ops formed in much smaller, often rural communities. While the product (natural/organic food) and the retail venue (cooperatives) did not have to come together in the 1970s, both shared common cultural and ideological principles. Each movement helped cover deficiencies in the other: co-ops provided a welcoming and forgiving outlet, while organic food helped cement a market identity for the new stores. While many of the principles and practices of organic food lay in sympathy with these projects, we have no reason a priori to assume that the activists in these two movements would become as strongly linked as they did. Most of these cooperatives promoted the sale of natural/organic foods, but this posed a lot of challenges since these products were in short supply.

The next chapter explores the first phase of cooperative formation in Minnesota, between 1970 and 1975, in order to contrast it with those that developed over the next five years. At first glance, the different patterns of formation reflect an urban-rural divide. However, the early co-ops were not limited to the Twin Cities; they also formed in much smaller communities, and there were also many larger cities where co-ops did not form. During the first wave of formation, communities that demonstrated progressive political attitudes—expressed by spikes of support for the antiwar candidate George McGovern, who challenged President Richard Nixon in the 1972 presidential election—were most likely to develop a co-op. The early history of Minnesota new-wave cooperatives centers on the creation (and eventual dissolution) of the People's Warehouse, the primary distributor for the new co-ops in the early 1970s. The activities surrounding the mission, ownership, and takeover of the People's Warehouse illustrate a few key features of this cooperative community: cooperation, tension, and the importance of provisioning to the success of this growing network of organizations. This first phase came to an end with an episode known as "the Co-op Wars," in which a group of Marxist agitators attempted to take over these stores and imbue them with a more revolutionary purpose. The resolution of this conflict helped solidify the co-ops' commitment to organic foods. To better understand why these hostilities took place, we can examine

*Figure 4.* Tensions flared across ideological lines on January 17, 1976, as members of the Co-op Organization attempted to take over the Mill City Co-op but were rebuffed by neighborhood supporters. The Minnesota Historical Society has both an excellent set of photographic archives from the state's newspapers and a well-informed staff of reference librarians to locate them. Courtesy of the Minnesota Historical Society; photograph by Pete Hohn for the *Minneapolis Tribune.*

different approaches to challenging power in the structure and the culture of society.

In chapter 5, we examine the patterns of cooperative formation between 1975 and 1980, after the Co-op Wars had helped these organizations more clearly articulate their missions and their commitments to one another. In the wake of the People's Warehouse controversy, the cooperative community formed the All Cooperating Assembly (ACA), representing a loose federation of co-ops in this region of the Upper Midwest that they referred to as "the North Country." The formation of new cooperatives in the state continued at a fast pace, rising from seventeen storefront operations in 1975 to fifty-eight by 1980. However, a closer examination reveals that most of this growth took place outside the Twin Cities metropolitan area, in contrast to the trend from the earlier period. Though relative levels of neighborhood political engagement—as measured by electoral support for George McGovern in his 1972 presidential campaign—help explain most of the initial formations, this factor had no bearing in the later years. Nor is this a simple case of an urban phenomenon diffusing to more rural areas, because co-ops did not develop evenly throughout the state. Previous experience with the cooperative organization form provides the best explanation for why they formed in some cities and towns in Minnesota but not others.[2] These organizations participated in a larger project to transform the culture of society by more explicitly promoting the consumption of sustainable foods. Embedding social values in the products they sold, they gave their members and patrons opportunities to enhance basic economic transactions through ethical and political consumerism.[3] Because their survival was still tenuous and relied on selling food products that existed beyond mainstream distribution systems, they helped create an organizational infrastructure to stabilize their market, and many of the stores matured well beyond their original minimalist formations.

The final chapter considers the contemporary legacies of the early cooperatives, many of which remain in operation to this day. As increased competition within the organic sector removed any special status they enjoyed as the sole purveyors of organic food, they have continued to refine and express the value of cooperatives within a community. As organic food has become more common in conventional grocery retailers, issues of local provisioning have gained new attention. New-wave co-ops have excelled in this from their outset, in large part because they had to; when organic food was not widely available, they often had to forge relationships with local growers to provide it. If cooperatives continue to pursue one of the primary Rochdale principles—education—they might convince future potential patrons that it is not just what you buy that matters but where.

My interest in the distribution networks of organic food began when I was employed as the purchasing agent for a fine-dining restaurant in Minneapolis, Minnesota. During the summer of 1994, before arriving at work each day, I stopped by a neighborhood farmers' market to supplement our produce cooler with the freshest seasonal fruits and vegetables that I could find. My chef was committed to purchasing food from local farmers and to serving organic food whenever possible. Unfortunately, most of the items proffered for sale satisfied only one of these two criteria. The central dilemmas I faced every day, more than twenty-five years ago, form the primary motivation for this academic inquiry. They are similar to the questions that were raised when the cooperative movement was first getting started, and they are still relevant even as organic food has become more widely available.

When presented with the choice between purchasing local and purchasing organic, which is more important? Who is more deserving of the limited resources in my food budget: the local farmer from the county next door who uses conventional growing methods or the conglomerate shipping organic carrots more than a thousand miles from California? How will the relative differences in products' appearance and quality affect these calculations? At what price point does my desire for a local and/or organic tomato go unfulfilled? I found that, try as I might to reconcile our political, economic, and culinary rationales to make the most responsible market decision, there was no easy formula as I filled my boxes for work. From my personal experience, I know there are additional factors—such as convenience, alluring marketing, existing relationships—that also affect purchasing decisions.

Ultimately, this examination of the emerging organic food market is itself a testament to the success of the social movement. When I was deciding what to buy, organic had become as important a criterion as price and quality. The fact that this term still has relevance among both activists and mainstream agricultural concerns also points to a tremendous change in modern society: as a precursor to contemporary green movements, the organic food industry demonstrates that new social values can be incorporated into preexisting institutions. Cooperatives remain relevant because they presented themselves as social movement organizations, even if they no longer have loftier aims of restructuring the American economy by replacing free-market capitalism with cooperative business ventures. In fact, those two concepts are not mutually exclusive, as the cooperatives have very well demonstrated for the past forty years. In the following chapters, I hope to demonstrate that projects centered on social change at the community level can promote a collective effort to raise awareness of how individual market decisions have a global impact.

# 1

## THE CAUSE OF
## ORGANIC FOOD

My brother is a blacksmith. Using his forge, hammer, arc welder, and a variety of machines that pound, cut, and drill holes into masses of steel, he makes his living by transforming metal bars into functional and aesthetically pleasing products. It seems like an archaic profession, especially since Philadelphia, where he lives, has several large home-supply stores in which you can purchase a mass-produced version of most of the items he makes. If, however, you want to repair rather than replace your iron fence or gate, you must employ a craftsman; if you want a custom-made piece of steel rather than a facsimile made of plastic, you have to contract with an artisan who works on a smaller scale than do the national chains of big-box stores. My brother also specializes in creating specialty window grates and entrance gates, ornamental yet imposing barriers to protect the inhabitants and the goods within their homes. Given Philadelphia's economically diverse urban core, in which the processes of gentrification and decay often take place simultaneously in the same neighborhood, his skills are in demand. Today, he has the relative luxury of choosing which jobs to take. When we walk the streets around 45th and Baltimore, it always seems he has an endless supply of work within striking distance of his home.

During a visit several years ago, Andy took me to the back door of the Mariposa Co-op in West Philadelphia, showing off one of his most recent window grates. After unlocking the door of a narrow, long storefront nestled between a modest Laotian-Thai café and an empty, boarded-up building, he guided me through the aisles, past the bulk bins and the dairy cooler, to open the back door. The window grate he created had a simple design with an industrial feel: a heavy diamond border surrounding a set of two-inch-diameter rings touching one another and attached to the door by way of four bicycle sprockets. As *mariposa* means "butterfly" in Spanish, the central motif was a pair of large butterfly wings that landed on either side of the central vertical division.

In many ways, the Mariposa Food Co-op felt as anachronistic as the art of blacksmithing. Founded in 1971, at the start of the new-wave cooperative trend in the United States, Mariposa was, until 2012, one of the few cooperative grocery stores in the country that still sold products only to its members. Though many cooperatives started with this policy, over the past four decades most have expanded their charters to allow nonmembers to shop, while providing discounts and dividends to members as incentives for joining the organization. Mariposa's members, on the other hand, had exclusive buying privileges. Each member received a key to the store, and, when they engaged in after-hours shopping, they recorded their purchases in a log at the front counter. There was no cash register—a policy that reduced opportunities for theft from both outside and within the membership.

When new members joined the Mariposa Food Co-op, they purchased a share in the organization; they could pay the necessary $100 investment in $20 annual installments, and they could be reimbursed for this "fee" should they end their membership. Members also agreed to volunteer at least two hours every four weeks—again, a common requirement of newly formed cooperatives in the 1970s and '80s but one that has gradually disappeared from contemporary organizations. Most cooperatives have transitioned from this "worker cooperative" model to a consumer cooperative operation; with that change, most cooperatives have shifted from relying on volunteer efforts of members to employing workers at prevailing wages. At Mariposa, though, no member could substitute personal wealth for sweat equity. In fact, in the spring of 2008, even the privilege of volunteering didn't come easy: the cooperative had reached its membership cap of 700 and required prospective members to join a waiting list.[1]

In St. Paul, Minnesota, where I have lived for the past twenty-five years, I can walk to the grocery store at the end of my block. That store, the Mississippi Market, is also a cooperative, although it in no way resembles the Mariposa storefront I had visited in Philadelphia.

When this second branch of the Mississippi Market opened, in 1999, it moved into a brand-new, 7,000-square-foot building that had required an investment of $4.2 million. In some ways, the store had helped to bring the Twin Cities cooperative movement back to its roots. Almost three decades earlier, the Selby Food Co-op, the first of Minnesota's "new-wave" storefront co-ops, had opened in the same neighborhood, only two blocks away. Back in 1971, Selby Avenue was a neighborhood in transition and decline, still suffering from the recent construction of the nearby freeway, which had ripped apart the social fabric of an African American community along Rondo Avenue known since the late nineteenth century as "Oatmeal Valley." In the 1970s, the intersection of Selby and Dale Avenues was notable for the presence of a bar on each corner and for its association with minor drug trafficking. Twenty-five years later, the gentrification of the nearby Summit Hill neighborhood had extended to Selby past Dale, and today the parking lot of the new branch of the co-op harbors far more late-model minivans than beat-up Volkswagen Beetles.

### *"The Co-op Wars"*

The Mississippi Market is but one of more than a dozen cooperative grocery stores currently doing a brisk business in the Twin Cities of Minneapolis and St. Paul. Most provide discounts to other cooperatives' members, and they operate as partners pursuing similar missions rather than as competitors. Several claim membership in a loose federation administered by the National Co+op Grocers, a business services organization that is, itself, a cooperative. The image presented by these stores is one of harmony and teamwork. Their guiding principle, "cooperation among cooperatives," was articulated more than 160 years ago by one of the first "modern" cooperatives, the Rochdale Pioneers in England. One of their mottos is "Stronger Together."

This seemingly tranquil coexistence belies a more contentious past. In May 1975, several members of a Marxist group known as the Co-op Organization took over the People's Warehouse in Minneapolis, taking control of its financial records and its checkbook. Their goal was to curtail the sale of organic food. This small distribution center, supplying dry goods to more than a dozen small cooperative grocery stores in the area, became one of the principal fronts in a year-long battle to control the focus and mission of these organizations. What prompted this band of activists to arm themselves with baseball bats and attempt to forcibly take over member-owned cooperative stores?

During the winter of 1975–76, the confrontation prompted by the Co-op Organization forced many cooperative activists to define their purpose more clearly. The CO sought to use the emerging grocery cooperatives as the literal and figurative front for a proletarian army meant to challenge the capitalist imperialistic state and reform the structure of society. They proclaimed that "natural" and especially "organic" food was a product for the bourgeoisie that worked against the coming workers' revolution. But in its simplest formulation, the issue really centered on what types of beans should be stocked on the co-ops' shelves. Canned beans, while usually full of preservatives and marketed by large agricultural concerns, provided cheap and fast nutrition for revolutionaries. Dried beans, sold in bulk and requiring a long soaking period before they could be boiled and transformed into something edible, symbolized a purity that helped the natural food cooperative members make a stronger connection to the land on which the beans were grown.

The CO believed the stores should win over members of the working class by selling only the food they wanted and were able to buy, even if it was overprocessed and overpackaged and even if it wasn't healthy. As one CO member told a newspaper reporter, "The poor people in the community want foods they can get elsewhere but at cheaper prices. If a co-op is truly to serve the community, it'd look like a 7–11 store with cheaper prices."[2]

The Co-op Wars were eventually resolved on the side of the activists who promoted natural and organic foods, a watershed moment in this history. As we show in chapter 4, the CO presented an existential threat to this community of organizations, forcing them to more forcefully articulate their goals and the strategies that would align with their larger values. The supporters of organic food helped to create a stronger distributor network and a loose federation that promoted both the cooperative cause and the sale of organic foods in co-ops. Deeply immersed in changing the dynamics of food consumption, co-ops wanted the label "organic" to matter.

After the Co-op Wars, these Minnesota co-ops primarily aimed to transform the culture rather than the structure of society. We could even say that Karl Marx had this same aim: to change the structure of economic life, Marx believed, one must first change the cultural values of the oppressed. The cooperatives formed in the late 1960s and early 1970s helped promote awareness of larger sustainability issues, and joining a co-op provided a way for individuals to participate in a project of social change. Throughout this history, however, we can see a continuing tension between competing goals of smashing social institutions and practices and creating new organizations and value systems. Is that hammer in your hand to be used to break something old or build something new? It is nearly impossible to do both at the same time.

But in many ways, all of this is getting ahead of the story. Before we look further at the cooperatives' embrace of organic and natural foods, we must first see how these products emerged as critiques of an industrializing society that treated food as a mass-produced commodity. Before we had co-ops acting as social movement organizations, organic foods emerged as a social movement cause.

## The Origins of Organic Food

"Organic food" is a thoroughly modern concept. It emerged in response to the midcentury, post–World War II industrial landscape that transformed nearly every aspect of contemporary society. The term is an abstraction that encompasses both an acknowledgment and a critique of mainstream agricultural practices. It was first coined in the 1940s by J. I. Rodale, a Pennsylvania magazine publisher who had been searching for a dietary regimen to address his many physical ailments. Rodale used this label to describe a new relationship between production and consumption, one that required a more conscientious approach that emphasized cooperation with the natural environment while minimizing the use of external inputs such as pesticides and fertilizers.[3]

The larger public awareness of organic and natural foods began to coalesce in the 1960s, and cooperative stores that opened to supply them began to emerge en masse in the '70s. In order to understand how these movements swept across the nation, however, it is necessary to consider a much longer history of dissent along two fronts: concerns about changing production methods for the food we consume and efforts to ensure a fair marketplace that served the common good. In this chapter, I examine the growth of the major alternative paradigms that developed during the twentieth century, and then in chapter 2 I describe how the cooperative grocery store developed as an ideal venue for these activists in the 1970s.

## The Rise of Industrial Agriculture

In his work *Market Rebels*, Hayagreeva Rao provides several examples of consumer movements that helped introduce radical innovations to economic markets. These include the cultural acceptance of the automobile in the United States, the rise of craft brewers, and the development of contemporary "fusion" cuisines. In the case of eco-foods, consumers began to *resist* changes that had degraded not only the quality of foods available for purchase but also the lands on which they were grown. The technological advances they promoted resided in the realm of knowledge—in some cases rediscovering forgotten or abandoned knowledge—related to the ability to produce food in ways that did not rely on excessive fertilizers, pesticides, or the machinery that characterized modern industrial agriculture. The industrialization of agriculture had, of course, already spawned critiques among small groups of individuals concerned with the ecological, economic, and social ramifications of these processes. When several crises in these areas drew growing national attention in the 1950s and 1960s, the stage was set for activists' wider and deeper mobilization. But to understand how eco-food became a hot cause when it did, it is important to first examine how agriculture had changed over the preceding one hundred years.

Throughout most of the history of human agriculture, "organic farming" would have been a redundant phrase. Assuming for the moment a very basic definition of "organic" as a set of production methods that ensures soil viability for future harvests, the underlying principles simply involve different methods to restore nutrients to the soil lost during the growing season: rotate crops, compost all plant refuse, and avoid monocropping to help prevent massive pest infestations. The agricultural goal is to stabilize soil inputs, reducing the damage that might jeopardize continued use of the land. For example, corn plants leach nitrogen from the soil, rendering it unusable over time unless it is repaired by the cultivation of nitrogen-fixing legumes on that land during the off-season, an alternative to using a chemical fertilizer. Over the course of many centuries in countless cultures, these practices have been tested, optimized, and passed down from one generation to the next. The social goal of the practices is to routinize and minimize the amount of human labor required to maintain soil viability. The most successful farming cultures have treated an agricultural settlement as a self-sustaining environment, producing all of the required soil inputs as close to their final application target as possible and creating a multitude of large-scale terrariums across the land, converting sunlight into a surplus of nutritional food products.

The past 150 years, however, have seen tremendous change in these systems' social, economic, and political organization. The nineteenth-century laboratory work of Justus von Leibig, regarded as the father of agricultural chemistry, laid the foundation for the first chemical interventions in agriculture. Von Leibig demonstrated that pure chemical inputs could be substituted for composting plants and manure and that scientific management of these chemical inputs could maximize short-term crop production. This early work on fertilizers, coupled with later advances in pesticides, would be applied to commercial agricultural enterprises via a second technological advance—the internal combustion engine of the John Deere tractor. Together, these developments dramatically changed the ecosystem of farming as it had been practiced for thousands of years, not only because they required the input of materials that could only be produced off-site but also because the most efficient delivery method for these inputs necessitated mono-cropping (farming large areas with a single type of plant).

The practices and ideologies of what we now consider organic or sustainable farming arose in response to the industrialization of agriculture. Various individuals and organizational efforts stood as challenges to emerging mainstream practices, critiques of a status quo we would later term "conventional" farming. The scale of the transformations helps us better understand the critiques offered by the advocates of sustainable agriculture.

## Input Substitutions: Fertilizers

The history of technological innovation in American agriculture from 1750 through 1950 describes a series of input substitutions, replacing inherited knowledge and manual toil with mechanical processes that foster increased productivity and standardization. In eighteenth-century America, land was abundant and fertile, but labor was relatively scarce; most of the technological innovations and changes that sought to replace labor with machines were developed in the United States. Across the Atlantic, years of farming had worn out the native soils, but labor was plentiful, and this is where most of the research into soil fertility took place. Throughout the nineteenth century, English and European scientists in the fledgling field of agricultural chemistry began isolating the elements required for plant growth, and industrialists sought the natural resources that could be used in place of traditional composts and manures. Though the early scientists often poorly understood the chemical and biological processes, industrialists and manufacturers quickly disseminated and promoted the empirical results of increased output in the spirit of scientific management.

A fertilizer is any natural or manufactured material that is added to soil to increase its fertility and enhance its potential to promote plant growth. Plants cannot live without three primary nutritional elements: nitrogen, phosphorus, and potassium (often referred to by their symbols in the periodic table of elements, NPK). With the exception of legumes' ability to obtain nitrogen from the atmosphere, all plants must obtain these elements from chemical compounds in the soil. The soil's natural supply of these elements decreases over time because of natural conditions, leaching, or intensive crop cultivation.[4]

Increased adoption of artificial fertilizers was in large part the result of historical events and industrial innovations as nonfarming concerns sought to create a consistent supply of nitrogen, phosphorus, and potassium. Technological advances often occur during periods of national hostility. For example, during World War I, chemists devised means to process nitrogen industrially to produce nitrates and nitrites. The salts of nitric acid include saltpeter, one of the principle components of gunpowder. Nitrating glycerol forms nitroglycerin, which (as perfected by Alfred Nobel) provides the explosive potential of dynamite and other munitions. The German scientist Fritz Haber (1868–1934) received the Nobel Prize in Chemistry in 1918 for his work (collaborating with Carl Bosch) on synthetically produced nitrogen. In the awards presentation, the president of the Royal Swedish Academy of Sciences declared that

Haber was "the first to provide the industrial solution and thus to create an exceedingly important means of improving the standards of agriculture and the well-being of mankind. We congratulate you on this triumph in the service of your country and the whole of humanity." Of course, this synthetically produced nitrogen was also of enormous value to Germany during World War I for making munitions such as gunpowder and grenades.[5]

The application of fertilizers produced off the farm increased steadily in the United States throughout the nineteenth and early twentieth centuries, from 53,000 tons in 1850 to 7,296,000 tons in 1920. The domestic fertilizer industry experienced a period of rapid expansion and innovation, employing more than 38,000 people and producing products valued at $300 million annually just a few years after the end of World War I.[6]

## Input Substitutions: Pesticides

In addition to the challenge of (re)supplying nutrients to the soil, agriculturalists have always contended with pest control. The farmer is engaged in a race to harvest before the output is damaged or destroyed by other plants (weeds), insects, birds, mammals, and/or microbes that share the same goals as the human consumers: to extract the requirements for sustaining life from a limited amount of natural resources. Though some cultures have resorted to excommunicating caterpillars or trying grasshoppers in court, more conventional practices of pest control have focused on making the agricultural environment less inviting to the invaders.[7] Rotating crop fields is one such method, for this requires pests that favor one type of plant to migrate to the new location, distant from where eggs have been laid. Destroying crop residues after harvest also reduces pest habitats, and growing crops in rows, a practice adopted in Northern Europe during the 1730s concurrent with new innovations in plow design, made the removal of weeds a much simpler task.

The term "pesticides" includes not only the class of chemicals that destroy weeds and insects but also various avaricides (mites), avicides (birds), molluscicides (snails), nematicides (roundworms), rodenticides, bactericides, fungicides, and virucides. It was not until the chemical industries in the United States introduced synthetic pesticides in the 1940s that the domestic and international pesticide industry became a major factor in industrialized agriculture. Though mineral pesticides (based largely on lead, arsenic, and sulfur) had been used on agricultural fields since at least the 1860s, concerted research on pest control did not occur until the production of surplus food products began in earnest at the start of the twentieth century. In 1913, the first issue of the journal *Review of Applied Entomology* appeared with 629 pages of abstracted articles from more than 700 other publications; at the time, there were 124 technical journals on pest control in the United States alone. For the next thirty years, however, because of their high cost, the use of pesticides was reserved for high-value crops.[8]

The poster child for the dangers of pesticide use is the chemical compound dichlorodiphenyltrichlorethan, better known as DDT. It was synthesized in 1874 by Otto Ziedler of Strasbourg University, but its potential as an insecticide was not discovered until the 1930s by a Swiss doctor named Paul Müller. The production of DDT stepped into high gear during World War II, when it was used as an insecticide to protect troops from the transmission of disease such as typhus and malaria. Full-scale production began in 1944, when 91,600,000 pounds were produced. In the same year, the Du Pont corporation started producing DDT for commercial uses. DDT was found to be an effective pesticide for many different agricultural applications, controlling pests such as pea aphids, cabbage caterpillars, onion thrips, tuber flea beetles, potato leafhoppers, and tobacco budworms. A year later, DDT was recommended to federal agencies and industry to combat clothes moths and carpet beetles. Following the war, DDT was used to fumigate airplanes (to prevent the migration of Japanese beetles and other pests) and to protect carpets from insect damage; it was sprayed on seeds in storage silos and distributed aerially over forested areas. As DDT-resistant flies and mosquitoes developed, new variants of DDT were introduced, combined with other pesticides to combat them. By 1955, more than 200 million pounds of DDT were produced annually in the United States.[9]

Input Substitutions: Capital

The industrialization of American agriculture often lagged behind technological innovations and scientific discoveries, but over time new industries formed to take advantage of emerging economic opportunities presented by exploiting natural resources and replacing traditional agricultural input regimes. Some of the main features of industrialization are easily observed: commodity surplus production versus subsistence farming; the use of machines to perform tasks of hand labor; increased dependence on related industries and reduced independence for individual farms. Business interests as well as governmental agencies encouraged farmers to reject the seed or fertilizer or labor that previously existed on the farm and to substitute for them resources produced off-site. It is difficult not to see a pattern in each project of agricultural "advance." Those substitutions create dependency relationships with nonfarming business interests, and each transition further removes some of the profits from the previously self-sufficient farm. As Deborah Fitzgerald explains in *Every Farm a Factory*,

> In American agriculture, industrialization began as a logic of production, almost a philosophy. For some it was a principle that unified a disparate collection of observations, practices, and problems. For others it was a road map that offered directions from old-fashioned traditionalism to modernity.[10]

We observe this transition through the decreasing reliance on manual labor in farming operations, as well as the increased need for capital and land. Table 1 shows that from 1850 to 1950 the amount of land devoted to agriculture in the United States increased steadily, peaking at 1,161 million acres. However, the overall number of farms began decreasing after 1920, falling from 6.4 million to 3.7 million operations as their average size grew. During this same time period, the expenses associated with farming operations shifted dramatically from costs for manual labor to the cost of capital equipment. In 1870, more than two-thirds of all farming expenditures were for labor, but this fell to one-fourth by 1957. At the same time, the amount of money invested in equipment rose from one-fifth to more than half of all expenses. Throughout the twentieth century, American farming interests produced more food on fewer (but larger) farms through the substitution of fertilizers, chemicals, and mechanical technology for labor.

The industrialization of American agriculture did not result from an economically based decision on the part of any central committee;

*Table 1.* Farm Numbers, Land in Farms, Farm Costs, 1850–1957

| Year | Number of Farms[a] | Land in Farms[b] | Average Farm Size[c] | Labor Costs (%) | Land Costs (%) | Capital Costs (%) |
|---|---|---|---|---|---|---|
| 1870 | 2.7 | 408 | 153 | 65 | 18 | 17 |
| 1880 | 4.0 | 536 | 138 | 62 | 19 | 19 |
| 1890 | 4.6 | 623 | 137 | 60 | 18 | 22 |
| 1900 | 5.7 | 839 | 146 | 57 | 19 | 24 |
| 1910 | 6.4 | 879 | 138 | 53 | 20 | 27 |
| 1920 | 6.4 | 956 | 148 | 50 | 18 | 32 |
| 1930 | 6.3 | 987 | 157 | 46 | 18 | 36 |
| 1940 | 6.1 | 1,061 | 174 | 41 | 18 | 41 |
| 1950 | 5.4 | 1,161 | 216 | 40 | 15 | 45 |
| 1957 | 3.7 | 1,124 | 303 | 27 | 15 | 54 |

*Sources:* U.S. Census Data, 1850–1969; Loomis and Barton (1961, 11).

[a] Measured in millions.
[b] Measured in millions of acres.
[c] Measured in acres.

the United States did not experience the collectivization of farming, and no governmental agency mandated these changes. Instead, there was a shift toward an industrial logic of organization supported and often actively promoted by economic and governmental institutions. Writing in 1961 on the history and trends of U.S. agricultural output for the USDA, the agricultural economists Ralph Loomis and Glen Barton promoted this ideology in glowing terms:

> Increased productivity in the agricultural sector has released resources and facilitated industrialization. Industrialization, in turn, has fostered and facilitated technological developments adaptable to agriculture and thereby has stimulated increased productivity in agriculture.... Of fundamental importance to economic development are the cultural, social, legal, and economic institutions that form a sympathetic atmosphere for growth. These institutions reflect a conscious promotion of material well-being.[11]

This increased productivity, however, resulted from increased standardization of farming practices that produced multiple social, economic, and environmental consequences. We've already observed the increased consolidation of farming operations in the United States that coincided with a decrease in the number of individual laborers required to harvest the crops. In 2007, a mere 5,541, or 0.3 percent of the more than two million farms in this country, accounted for 27.9 percent of agricultural product sales. The top 55,509 farms (1.8 percent of the total number) were responsible for 59.2 percent of the $297 billion of sales. Though 116,286 farms (5.3 percent) had sales exceeding $500,000, more than 1.5 million operations cleared less than $25,000.[12] Most food produced in this country today comes from a small number of very large farms that rely heavily on mechanization and standardization, resulting in increased mono-cropping and a loss of biodiversity.

## Emergence of Alternative Paradigms

Most of the major technological changes that occurred in twentieth-century American agriculture emerged as scientifically managed solutions to specific problems concerning the vitality and yield of particular crops. The perspective of the organic farming social movement—which emphasizes healthy soils as much as it does productive plants—provides a unique vantage point from which to observe large-scale social changes in one of the most important segments of our economy. This industrial transformation took place over several generations. It was so gradual that we consider "organic" the oppositional term to "conventional" farming. The story of organic agriculture began with a critique of industrial farming practices and the political climates that allowed them to take place. The term "organic" and its precursors had to be introduced into the agricultural, political, and cultural lexicons only because few people recognized the "new" practices as deviant behaviors. What we refer to now as "conventional" farming represents nothing less than a complete reorganization of both the macro agricultural economic market and the micro ecosystem found within an individual farming enterprise.

The basic premise of sustainable agriculture is fairly simple: farming systems should seek to supply as many of their required inputs from within, maintaining soil fertility by replacing what is taken away and growing surplus crops to feed others while preserving the ability to feed future generations. Though proponents recognize the scientific foundations of agricultural biology and the role that essential minerals such as N, P, and K play in plant growth, they also believe that the biological methods for extracting these nutrients from decaying organic matter are complex processes that provide additional benefits. Sustainable agriculture has been practiced for several thousand years. Contemporary activists acknowledge the need to fertilize plants and control pests, but they wish to learn from the past before replacing the labor and skills of the trained farmer with factory-produced products developed in a research laboratory.

The more specific principles of sustainable agricultural practice are relatively few. One of the primary considerations involves fixing nitrogen levels to maintain soil fertility. In the nineteenth century, agricultural chemists demonstrated that the application of nitrogen-based fertilizers (as opposed to manures) yielded increases in crop production. In the 1880s, researchers at the newly formed state Agricultural Experimental Stations verified that years of poor soil management had exacted a heavy toll: mineral nutrients had been extracted without replacement in surplus-oriented crop production. The two primary methods for reducing nitrogen depletion in soil—use of green manuring and rotation of fields with nitrogen-fixing legumes—were known to agricultural scientists even at the start of the twentieth century. These methods had also been known to peasant farmers for millennia, of course, but industrialization and scientific management had dismissed these practices in favor of obtaining higher annual yields through industrial fertilization. Scientists "rediscovered" these practices in response to concerns over soil depletion.

Two heads of the Agricultural Experimental Stations wrote treatises on the subject. Cyril George Hopkins at the University of Illinois wrote a volume titled *Soil Fertility and Permanent Agriculture* in 1910. At Kansas State University, R. I. Throckmorton coauthored a 1918 report on soil fertility, and its summary stated:

> Kansas soils have decreased rapidly in productivity during the past 50 years. The yield of corn has decreased 40 percent and the yield of wheat has decreased 17 percent during this period. . . . The organic content of the soil may be maintained by applications of barnyard manure and by plowing under green manure crops, straw, and other crop residue. A rotation containing a hay or grass crop will also aid.

> Straw is an important source of organic matter and should be utilized
> as far as possible.

The use of synthetic fertilizers continued to increase, though. Advocates
of sustainable agriculture chose to form nongovernmental organizations
to expand the work of experimental stations and create new research
programs to show the long-term benefits of replenishing the soil the
"old-fashioned" way.[13]

The organic movement arose in response to these continuing projects of the industrial revolution taking place in the agrarian sector of
the economy. The formal articulation of and the public reaction to the
social problems associated with the industrialization of agriculture took
longer to develop. The most active social critics of the agricultural industrial revolution were not urban social scientists but activists promoting
specific programs of social change within these communities. Rudolph
Steiner (1861–1925) and his philosophical/religious practice of Anthroposophy urged his followers to adopt a new, harmonious relationship to
the earth, particularly with the production of food products. Sir Albert
Howard (1873–1947) sought to address not only the soil degradation he
observed in the farming communities of Indore, India, but also the economic livelihood of the native growers who could not afford off-farm
fertilizer inputs. Inspired by Howard's 1940 thesis in *An Agricultural
Testament* but primarily concerned with the health issues posed by modern agriculture, J. I. Rodale (1898–1971) encouraged farmers and home
gardeners to forgo the use of chemical fertilizers and pesticides. Each
sought to apply correctives to perceived negative social ills resulting from
the modernization of agriculture.

### Rudolph Steiner and the Biodynamic Movement

In 1875, Madame Helena Petrovna Blavatsky (1831–91) founded the
Theosophical Society in New York City. Theosophy emerged as a belief
system based on Eastern philosophies of Hinduism and Buddhism; it
seeks a better understanding of the relationship of humans to the universe in which they reside. In 1900, Blavatsky invited Steiner to present a
series of lectures to the German Theosophical Society. Born in Kraljevec,
Croatia, Steiner was familiar with both the most recent technological

developments of the Industrial Age and the workings of a peasant community that had changed little since the Middle Ages. In 1912, Steiner formed his own society, based on an alternative belief system he termed Anthroposophy, with 3,000 initial members in Cologne, Germany.

One goal of the Anthroposophists was to reconnect humans to the rhythmic nature of the cosmos. In 1924, Steiner delivered lectures to a group of farmers in Poland. These lectures formed the basis of an agricultural philosophy and practice later to be known as "biodynamic" production. Steiner outlined the basic Theosophical (and now Anthroposophical) relationships involving humans, the planet, and the cosmos, with the planet conceived as a spiritual entity that sustains life through its interactions with the creative energies and rhythms of the eternally evolving universe. A general orientation of biodynamic cultivation rests on the principle that the immediate environment as well as all life on earth results from the positive flow of cosmic forces streaming from other planets and fixed stars. It encompasses a holistic view of life and views each farming enterprise as an individual entity. In more logistical terms, biodynamic farming suggests that soil fertility is maintained through composting, green manuring, crop rotation, and diversification. All farm inputs must be sourced from living materials, produced directly on the farm itself in a project of continual reparation of the damage caused by human interactions.

Steiner did not base his critique of artificial fertilizers on any deep-seated mistrust of industrialization. Rather, he saw the need for these off-farm inputs as a symptom that the soil had been damaged, that the farmer was not in tune with the cosmic forces that would properly regulate plant nutrition. If the farm-organism was healthy, he argued, artificial inputs would simply be unnecessary. They would disappear. The alternative farming practices Steiner proposed, however, were predicated on the view of industrialized or mainstream agriculture as inherently unsustainable. For Steiner, the main fault of modern agriculture lay in its reliance on scientific rather than on peasant knowledge; he said, "I have always considered what the peasants and farmers thought about things far wiser than what the scientists were thinking." The remedies he proposed were based on treating the individual farm as a single, self-sustaining unit that requires nurturing of its spiritual and biological life. The biodynamic system of agriculture relies on composting, but it also encourages the use of homeopathic "activators" and medicines to heal the damaged soil.

The Bio-Dynamic Farming and Gardening Association officially formed in the United States in 1938. That same year, the Anthroposophic Press (a New York subsidiary of London's Rudolph Steiner Publishing Company) printed the thesis of Ehrenfried Pfeiffer, Steiner's most prominent U.S. disciple, on soil fertility renewal and preservation. Titled *Bio-Dynamic Farming and Gardening*, the book in its first line offers a singular proclamation: "Every agricultural enterprise is a self-contained biological unit." Though Steiner's belief in planetary harmony and the proper scheduling of farming activities in accordance with the lunar cycle have been downplayed as biodynamic methods have become more secularized, the relationship between biodynamic agriculture and Anthroposophy has remained strong.[14]

### Sir Albert Howard and the Indore Process

The same year that Steiner delivered his famous lectures to the Anthroposophic farmers in Poland, the British botanist Sir Albert Howard (1873–1947) was promoting another set of sustainable agriculture practices in Indore, India. Born in an English farming community to a family that practiced mixed farming, Howard received an agricultural diploma from Cambridge University in 1897. In 1905 he accepted the post of Imperial Economic Botanist at the Agricultural Research Institute in Pusa, India. Lord Curzon (1859–1925), who had been the governor general and viceroy of India since 1899, had initiated an experiment the previous year to explore how the soils of India could be increased and improved. The plan involved educating India's peasant farmers in modern agricultural methods. Howard had previously performed agricultural research in university laboratories, but in India he obtained a seventy-five-acre farm "on which I could grow crops in my own way and study their reaction to insect and fungous pests and other things. My real education in agriculture then began."[15]

Howard had ample opportunity to study the native Indian agricultural practices, paying particular attention to those that promoted healthy and sustainable crop productions without the use of artificial inputs. The two main practices he observed were composting and crop rotation, both of which involved returning waste to the soil. In 1924, he was appointed

Director of the Institute of Plant Industry, Indore, and Agricultural Adviser to States in Central India. He was no stranger to agricultural chemistry, having received honors in chemistry as an undergraduate. In his 1924 report *Crop Production in India: A Critical Survey of Its Problems*, he described the increasingly common condition of nitrogen depletion. Well aware that the best natural sources of nitrogen were found in cow dung, Howard wrote that the shortage of timber had resulted in burning dung for fuel, removing it from the agricultural circle of production. Other causes of nitrogen depletion included the annual monsoons, which washed away many of the soil's nutrients. Applying nitrogen-based fertilizers was one remedy, but it was not economically feasible for cash-poor Indian farmers.

Howard proposed what seems a rather novel approach, given the emphasis on technological advances so common at the time:

> The first step in the consideration of the problem is to ascertain whether any of the losses can be avoided or reduced. We cannot advise the cultivator to give up burning cow-dung for fuel without providing some substitute. So far, no one has succeeded in accomplishing this. The export of seeds and other products must obviously go on, otherwise the cultivator will soon find himself without money with which to pay his dues and purchase the necessaries of life.

Howard had analyzed the problem of nitrogen depletion by examining its cause and had proposed a structural solution that took into account the economic realities of the indigenous farming community.[16]

Howard went on to propose improved manuring practices and the cultivation of nitrogen-fixing legumes. His description of the nineteenth-century scientific debates concerning the biological processes involving nitrogen stands in stark contrast to the characterization of farmers as crude practitioners of the "rudest of the arts" as suggested by founders of the Rothamsted Experimental Station (RES). Established in 1843 in Rothamsted, England, the RES focused its research on the benefits of commercial artificial fertilizer. Its studies began with the premise that previous systems of agriculture, those that had sustained social groups and nations for centuries, lacked the proper scientific footing required to maximize yields. Howard refuted these notions: "Although it was not till 1888, after a protracted controversy lasting thirty years, that Western science finally accepted as proved the important part played by these crops in enriching the soil, nevertheless centuries of experience had already taught the cultivators of the Orient the same lesson."[17]

In *The Waste Products of Agriculture* (1931), Howard and his assistant Yeshwant D. Wad further described how the fertility of soil was lost by intensive methods of crop production, and they began outlining a program to restore fertility by changing those practices without the use of artificial manures.

In Howard's writing, we see a sustained critique of the industrialization of agriculture, particularly the role that research laboratories and experimental stations played in the destruction of soil fertility. In *An Agricultural Testament* (1940), he wrote:

> Agricultural science began by fragmenting this potato problem into a number of parts. Potato blight fell within the province of the mycologist; a group of investigators dealt with eelworm; a special experiment station was created for virus disease; the breeding and testing of disease resistant varieties was again a separate branch of the work; the manuring and general agronomy of the crop fell within the province of the agriculturist. The multiplication of workers obscures rather than clarifies this wide biological problem. *The fact that these potato diseases exist at all implies that some failure in soil management has occurred.*[18]

Howard spent thirty-five years in India. His experimental station in Indore continued to adapt Chinese methods of composting, which would eventually be referred to as the Indore Process. In many ways, Howard anticipated the major arguments that activists would use more than fifty years later to promote organic and sustainable farming, pointing out not only the environmental degradation but also the economic, health, and social costs associated with industrialized agriculture.

## J. I. Rodale and Organic Agriculture

Howard's masterwork, *An Agricultural Testament*, attracted the attention of enthusiastic activists throughout England. Across the Atlantic, the work also inspired a struggling magazine publisher named Jerome Irving Rodale to purchase a sixty-acre farm near Emmaus, Pennsylvania, to test Howard's theories. Rodale had made several failed attempts to publish journal-digests before finding a successful topic. In 1935,

*Health Digest* was a modest success, and the Rodale Publishing House was soon producing *Fact Digest, Everybody's Digest, Health Guide, You Can't Eat That, You're Wrong about That, True Health Stories,* and *Modern Tempo.* With a staff consisting of a single assistant, Rodale edited each journal himself from an office in Allentown, Pennsylvania.[19]

It was during his voracious reading that Rodale had run across a work by Howard in *Health for All,* a British health journal. Rodale began corresponding with Howard and formulated a plan to purchase the farm to demonstrate the efficacy of Howard's "new" practices of cultivation. In the early 1940s, he began to sell or discontinue all of his journals to focus on his new passion; when Rodale referred to this as "organic" agriculture, Howard accepted and endorsed the use of this term. The first issue of *Organic Farmer* went to press in 1942. Despite sending out thousands of brochures, Rodale received fewer than two dozen requests and quickly renamed his publication *Organic Gardening and Farming (OGF)* to expand his potential audience. Howard was soon listed as an associate editor.[20]

Over the next two decades, Rodale modified the name and format of his publication several times, each iteration operating at a loss. *OGF* was split in 1949—*Organic Farmer* was designed to appeal to moderate-size farms, while *Organic Gardening* was aimed at urban dwellers—and rejoined as *OGF* again in 1954. Rodale's attempts to attract gardeners rather than farmers met with greater success in part because of the economic and political situation. Though the number of Americans working on farms had been steadily decreasing for thirty years, nonfarmers were encouraged to grow their own vegetables in garden plots during the Great Depression, and the federal government promoted home "Victory Gardens" during World War II. Household gardeners were not concerned with the profit/loss calculations of farming surplus crops for market, and hobbyists had the luxury of experimentation. Another major factor influencing the reception of Rodale's message was his emphasis on the individual health aspects of organic food, rather than on the economic or environmental effects of industrial agriculture.

Rodale's reputation underwent a transformation in the late 1960s, as organic farming received renewed attention in the budding environmental movement. In June 1971, the *New York Times* would hail the seventy-two-year-old Rodale as the "Guru of the Organic Food Cult." He died one week later while taping an interview on the *Dick Cavett*

*Show* television program, only minutes after joking, "I've decided to live to be a hundred. . . . I never felt better in my life!" Even so, of all the twentieth-century proponents of sustainable agriculture, Rodale had perhaps the largest impact through his publishing empire. Following his death, his son, Robert, took over the company and began writing a regular column in the *Washington Post* on the topics of organic gardening, recycling, and creating healthier diets through the consumption of natural foods. Rodale Press remains a major and profitable presence in the publishing world. In addition to the continued publications of *Organic Gardening* and *Prevention* magazines—both dating back more than sixty years—the company published Vice President Al Gore's *An Inconvenient Truth: The Planetary Emergency of Global Warming and What We Can Do about It* in 2006 in conjunction with the successful documentary film release. J. I. Rodale's lasting legacy, however, remains not only coining the term "organic" thirty-five years before the concept achieved national recognition but also helping to sustain the growing desire for consuming foods produced with a conscience.[21]

## *Rise of Environmental Issues as a Hot Cause in the 1960s*

Steiner, Howard, and Rodale all helped to establish research programs to promote the production of agricultural foodstuffs that addressed social, economic, and nutritional concerns. In the late 1950s and early 1960s, two events helped crystallize growing worries about the pesticides that had helped industrialized agriculture achieve many of its productivity gains. The first major food scare and the specter raised by Rachel Carson of a nature devoid of songbirds each helped to elevate debates about government oversight of spreading poison on the earth to the national level, eventually resulting in the creation of a new federal agency. Concerns about pollution in the environment helped focus attention on how some of those chemicals had entered our food stream as well as the water and air.

On November 9, 1959, Secretary of Health, Education and Welfare Arthur S. Flemming made the following announcement:

> The Food and Drug Administration today urged that no further sales be made of cranberries and cranberry products produced in Washington

and Oregon in 1958 and 1959 because of their possible contamination by a chemical weed killer, aminotriazole, which causes cancer in the thyroids of rats when it is contained in their diet, until the cranberry industry has submitted a workable plan to separate the contaminated berries from those that are not contaminated.

After this announcement, just two weeks before Thanksgiving, sales of the fruit plummeted. With this statement, Flemming ushered in the modern age of national food scares. In the late 1950s, government-sponsored projects aimed at eradicating nuisance insects had begun to receive attention from the mainstream media. A widespread incidence of wildlife mortality took place soon after a mosquito-control program was implemented near Duxbury, Maine, and, in 1957, after DDT was sprayed over all of eastern Long Island in an attempt to eliminate gypsy moths, environmentalists sought court action to stop such widespread, indiscriminate application of pesticides. Pesticide use started to become the focus of those interested in both the well-being of the natural world and the health and safety of the consumer as championed by Rodale.[22]

Three years later, Carson's 1962 tome, *Silent Spring*, opened a new chapter in sustainable agriculture and the modern environmental movement. Carson (1907–64), a former editor for the U.S. Fish and Wildlife Service who had received a master's degree in zoology from Johns Hopkins University, had been writing on marine biology since publishing an article titled "Undersea" in 1937 in *The Atlantic Monthly*. She resigned from her position as chief editor for publications for the Wildlife Service in 1952 to concentrate on her writing full-time.

The four-year task of writing *Silent Spring* began with a letter from the custodian of a Massachusetts bird sanctuary that had been destroyed by aerial spraying of DDT. As a scientist of international standing, Carson contacted and received the assistance of prominent biologists, chemists, pathologists, and entomologists to assess the dangers of pesticide misuse. The final product, *Silent Spring*, caused immediate controversy. The pesticide industry challenged Carson's findings and pressured the book's publisher, Houghton Mifflin, to suppress her work. When CBS Television scheduled an hour-long interview with Carson, two corporate sponsors withdrew their advertising. Despite attacks on her scientific credentials, however, the book was a best seller. At a press conference on August 29, 1962, a journalist asked President John F. Kennedy if he had considered asking government agencies such as the Department of Agriculture or the Public Health Service to take a closer look at scientists' charges about the possible long-term effects of DDT and other pesticides. Kennedy responded, "Yes, and I know they already are. I think particularly, of course, since Miss Carson's book, but they are examining the matter."[23] Other books on pesticide abuse followed: Robert Rudd's *Pesticides and the Living Landscape* (1964); Frank Graham's *Since Silent Spring* (1970); Robert van den Bosch's *The Pesticide Conspiracy* (1978). The U.S. Congress began to review its pesticide policies and eventually banned the domestic use of DDT in 1972.

American attitudes on environmental issues had changed dramatically during the 1960s. As Hazel Erskine noted in a review of national surveys focused on pollution during that time:

> A miracle of public opinion has been the unprecedented speed and urgency with which ecological issues have burst into American consciousness. Alarm about the environment sprang from nowhere to major proportions in a few short years. When the first polls on pollution appeared in 1965, only about one in ten considered the problem very serious. Today most people have come to that realization.

The data Erskine provided demonstrate the remarkable shift. Between 1965 and 1970, those who said they were concerned about water pollution rose from 28 to 69 percent of those polled; similarly, the percentage of respondents worried about air pollution rose from 35 to 74 percent of those polled, with more than two-thirds agreeing that these problems were somewhat or very serious. These issues had even higher salience in larger urban areas, with nearly nine in ten residents expressing both awareness and worry.[24] Public concern rose concurrently with increased media coverage of environmental issues. Other researchers have marked 1970 as a turning point in raising public consciousness of these issues. The national news media devoted several special television exposés to these issues, and discussions continued in numerous popular magazines. Environment groups were forming all over the country, culminating in the first observation of "Earth Day" on April 22 of that year.

Environmental concerns soon became attached to the safety of the food made available by mainstream producers. Public opinion polls in

*Figure 5.* In 1971, the Ecological Food Society placed this advertisement in the *New York Times* attempting to capitalize on recent food scares. The concerns about DDT were widely known, but "organic food" as a viable alternative still had to be explained to the *Times*'s readers.

the late 1960s and early 1970s showed that Americans had developed a mistrust of the chemical industry in general, with more than half of survey respondents blaming it for deteriorating air and water quality. In 1968, a third of the population felt that insecticides and plant sprays were among the most important contributors to pollution. But as the 1959 cranberry scare had demonstrated, concerns about these chemicals were more immediate and stronger when they appeared to threaten personal health. A 1971 advertisement in the *New York Times* by the newly formed Ecological Food Society announced "The DDT-less apple. Yours for 9¢." Describing the society as a new, independent source for organically raised foods, vitamins, cosmetics, and household products, the ad addressed the reader in a letter format. "Dear Fellow Human," it began, "This is not a scare ad. If you can read—let alone smell, taste, and breathe—you're probably scared enough. Because you've read how poisonous chemicals can invade your family's diet. Robbing your food of its flavor and wholesomeness. Robbing you of your health, and perhaps years of life as well."

The advertisement proceeded to provide a partial list of the food horrors of which "fellow humans" should be aware, but it did so in a way that suggested these reports were common knowledge rather than isolated stories from conspiracy theorists. Truly, they *had* become a part of cultural awareness. Reviewing Ruth Mulvey Harmer's 1971 publication *Unfit for Human Consumption*, Sidney Margolius wrote in the *Washington Post*:

> Many of us are caught between two fears today. One is the specter of foods poisoned by chemical pesticides, additives, hormone threat invoked by chemical fertilizers. The other is the threat evoked by chemical manufacturers and other agricultural interests that food will cost us more—even more, that is—if these production stimulating chemicals are taken away from farmers and processors.[25]

The mistrust and apprehension concerning the nation's food growers were not limited to the counterculture. In 1972, the editorial board of the *Washington Post* confidently declared:

> It is news to no one that a high tonnage of the food eaten every day by Americans is worthless, tasteless, contrived and can occasionally be actually dangerous to health. . . . In many cases, the consumers who are rejecting are turning to what are called organic foods.[26]

Mistrust in mainstream agriculture and the institutions that supported it prompted many to look for alternatives. The organic food movement offered a vision of agricultural production, distribution, retail operations, and consumption that emphasized local and decentralized control of practices and decision-making processes. In February 1971, less than a year after the celebration of the first Earth Day brought national focus to environmental issues, Rodale Press bought a full-page advertisement in the *New York Times* stating that this "will almost certainly turn out to be the year when more people than ever 'go organic.' Growing fruits and vegetables organically. Buying more flavorful, healthful foods at local stores." In Wendell Berry's essays on the industrialization of American land and farm management, he urged readers to reconsider their connection to the earth, indicting the capitalist motivations for turning cycles of production into linear processes leading to profit and waste. In his 1971 essay "Think Little," published in *The Last Whole Earth Catalog*, he wrote:

> If we apply our minds directly and competently to the needs of the earth, then we will have begun to make fundamental and very necessary changes in our minds. We will begin to understand and to mistrust *and to change* our wasteful economy, which markets not just the produce of the earth, but also the earth's ability to produce.

Berry urged action through participation in social movement organizations as well as any small, individual changes in behavior that could make some difference:

> As odd as I am sure it will appear to some, I can think of no better form of personal involvement in the cure of the environment than that of gardening. A person who is growing a garden, if he is growing it organically, is improving a piece of the world.[27]

Early activists promoted organic food as a promising solution for social problems in three primary arenas. At the personal level, organic food was healthier because mainstream agriculture was poisoning the nation's agricultural production. For the environment, the promise of organic food rested on better land management and a reduction in the release of harmful pesticides. At the social level, an agricultural paradigm that remained true to organic ideals would lend support to smaller family farms and stronger local economies. The shared understanding of what organic actually meant, of course, was still in flux. The Ecological Food Society promoting its DDT-less apples acknowledged as much in its 1971 *New York Times* advertisement. Answering its own question "'Organic foods'—what are they?," they suggested:

> "Organic" doesn't describe the food—*but how it has been grown and prepared*. Quite simply—organic food has NOT been sprayed, stimulated, bleached, colored, fortified, emulsified and processed to within an inch of its life (and yours). Some people call it "Health Food." Others say "Natural Food." We say only this: Remember how good food used to taste? And how good it was *for* you? That's what organic food, and the ECOLOGICAL FOOD SOCIETY, is all about.

By the 1960s, rising worries about the safety of mainstream food products coupled with anxieties about environmental degradation created a "hot cause" that helped the organic food industry develop. Shared emotions of mistrust toward the governmental policies and agribusiness practices that reconstituted American agriculture had built up slowly during the twentieth century, culminating in the widespread anger and fear of the 1960s. At the same time, an emerging sense that solutions were at hand helped unite members of the counterculture to build the market structures that established the production, distribution, and sale of sustainable food items. Consumers provided the driving force behind this movement, and larger industrial players (farmers, canneries, packers, and grocery chains) eventually responded to the demonstrated demand for healthier food products grown and distributed in more sustainable ways.

The origins of organic food predated larger public concern about ecological problems, but this specific set of practices emerged as one possible solution to address some of the social, environmental, and health issues associated with industrialized agriculture. Almost simultaneously, a new wave of cooperative formation took place in the early 1970s with a particular focus on selling food products that in some way resisted the mass production and commodification that characterized the increasingly highly processed and packaged offerings in mainstream grocery stores. This parallel movement grew out of a long history of organizational experimentation that contradicted many of the assumptions behind for-profit business ventures. Though this new wave of co-ops did eventually form a strong association with eco-foods in the later 1970s, it could not have set out to sell organic foods exclusively—there simply weren't enough of these products available at the time. Instead, the cooperative movement actually began to *create* the market infrastructure that allowed the organic food industry to develop throughout the 1980s and 1990s.

# 2

---

# TWENTIETH-CENTURY
# COOPERATIVES

AS AN EMOTIONALLY LADEN SOCIAL PROBLEM, concern about the environment we live in and the food we consume captured the attention of many Americans in the late 1960s. Though environmental and organic activists certainly welcomed cooperative food stores that shared and promoted many of their ideologies, these organizations were created primarily by people interested in forming cooperatives to help empower individuals within their communities, rather than to present a major challenge to larger social and institutional structures. The process of developing and maintaining markets for the goods associated with this cause required a different type of effort, and it took longer to convince individuals to translate their passions into the practice of different behaviors.

Grocery cooperatives played a role in this larger social movement. They promoted an ethos of conscious consumerism, encouraging members to become more aware of where their food came from and the manner in which it was produced. One of the organizing principles of these stores was participatory democracy, allowing each member a say in how the stores should be run, the products they would sell, and who (if anybody) should serve as spokespeople or leaders. Politically, most of the activists who helped create and run these stores shared a critique of modern capitalism and a distrust of larger authorities, but, somewhat ironically, they also had to learn how to survive financially in a crowded, competitive economic market. While they did not have the same profit incentive as the mainstream corporations they criticized, they still had to maintain fiscal solvency if they were to continue promoting their message.

## The Rise of Cooperatives as a Parallel Movement

The environmental movement of the 1960s generated so much public concern that the federal government created the Environmental Protection Agency in December 1970. President Richard Nixon proposed this independent office to draft environmental regulations and enforce environmental laws passed by Congress. At the same time, a new wave of cooperative development began to sweep across the countercultural landscape of the United States. The stores had the express aim of selling unadulterated, "natural" foods grown by sustainable methods. Many activists believed they might also reform the larger capitalist market through the promotion of cooperative ideals.

Was this form of organization a radical departure from how Americans had conducted business during the twentieth century? Cooperatives have served as legitimate market organizations throughout the nation's history. Though these younger, politically oriented activists might have used the form in novel ways—or at least used it to promote an emerging alternative product—they adopted a retailing model that had provided decades of benefits to millions of Americans in a variety of sectors. In this chapter, after describing the basic principles embedded in cooperation, I will briefly outline the use of this economic structure in agriculture up to the 1920s, then shift to the history of consumer cooperatives between 1920 and 1950. Later, I will connect this history to the emergence of a new set of cooperative grocery stores in the late 1960s and early 1970s.

A cooperative is a form of economic organization in which a business is owned and governed by a group of voluntary members for their own benefit rather than for the profit of investors. Such organizations can range from a loose association of individuals who come together for a single purpose and then disband to a formal, self-sustaining legal entity with an ongoing mission. The members of a cooperative might be individuals, families, households, or organizations such as businesses or other cooperatives. The main difference between an incorporated cooperative and a stock-issuing corporation is that ownership is distributed equally among all the cooperative's members; it is not possible for one member to acquire the ownership stakes, privileges, and responsibilities of other owners. Cooperatives can be classified in different ways, but one of the most common is by the function that they serve in conjunction with the role of their members within an economic system. *Producer cooperatives* are primarily composed of actors who create or distribute products to be sold, while *consumer cooperatives* operate at the end of a commodity chain and enable members to obtain desired products at a discounted retail price. Within these two categories, one can further classify cooperatives according to specific activities (such as marketing or processing) or by the type of product or service they offer (such as food, gasoline, housing, or medical care).

The principles of mutual aid and concern embedded within cooperatives were found in the English system of common fields and fences and crossed the Atlantic with the earliest American colonists. All pilgrims were required to sign the "Mayflower Compact," in which they pledged to "combine ourselves together into a civil Body Politick, for our better Ordering and Preservation, and Furtherance of the Ends aforesaid." The spirit of cooperation was incorporated into the ethos of the new residents, occasionally by compulsory means, as indicated in a law passed by the Massachusetts Bay Colony in 1646:

> Because the harvest of hay, corn, flax, and hemp comes usually so near together that much loss can hardly be avoided, it is ordered and decreed by this court, that the constable of every town, upon request made to him, shall require artificers or handicraftsmen, meet to labor, to work by the day for their neighbors needing him, in mowing.

In 1752, Benjamin Franklin founded the first formal cooperative organization in the colonies, the Philadelphia Contributionship for the Insurance of Houses from Loss by Fire. Cooperative business ventures began in the early 1800s in various industries and locations, for example, dairy (Goshen, Connecticut, 1810), cheese (South Trenton, New Jersey, 1810), and hog slaughtering and marketing (Granville, Ohio, 1820).[1]

Cooperatives often form as a positive response to negative social conditions, as a tool to combat the effects of larger social forces that cannot be addressed by individual action. In England, for example, cooperatives in the early 1800s were formed to deal with the depressed economic conditions brought about by the Napoleonic wars and with the drastic changes in social conditions resulting from industrialization. Though the development of English cooperatives was peculiar to historical conditions and lack a direct counterpart in the United States, the success of these movements had a tremendous impact on the subsequent diffusion of their methods across the Atlantic. In particular, the principles of the Rochdale Pioneers established guidelines that continue to govern cooperative management today.

The Rochdale Equitable Pioneers Society, formed in England in 1844, is generally recognized as the first successful "modern" cooperative in the Western hemisphere. With an initial membership of twenty-eight individuals, the cooperative was created "to form arrangements for the pecuniary benefit, and the improvement of the social and domestic condition of its members."[2] Other consumer cooperatives, such as the Co-operative Wholesale Society in England and Wales (1863) and Scotland (1867), established wide-ranging distribution. Though it was neither the first nor even the most successful early cooperative, the Rochdale Society was notable among its peers for developing an active outreach program, encouraging and assisting others to form cooperatives. It also prepared a written list of practices and policies that seemed consistent with the success of such efforts. This list became one of the first sets of cooperative principles:

> Open membership
> One member, one vote
> Cash trading
> Membership education
> Political and religious neutrality
> No unusual risk assumption
> Limitation on the number of shares owned
> Limited interest on stock
> Goods sold at regular retail prices
> Net margins distributed according to patronage

Horace Greeley, the editor of the *New York Tribune*, introduced the Rochdale Pioneers' principles to the U.S. public in 1859 when he published the American edition of George Jacob Holyoke's *Self-Help by the People: The History of the Rochdale Pioneers*. In December 1862, the Union Cooperative Association No. 1 of Philadelphia helped popularize the organizational application of such principles, basing its constitution on those obtained from the Rochdale Society. Though the

Union Cooperative Association folded in 1868, it helped spark the formation of more than thirty similar cooperatives across the United States.[3] Many contemporary organizations continue to identify as Rochdale cooperatives.

## Agricultural Cooperatives, 1865–1930

Though cooperatives have existed in American, English, and European trades and industries for more than two centuries, their presence is most widespread in the agricultural sector. The farming economy is unique in several ways. First, though the tasks undertaken can be routinized from one year to the next, the work entails a great deal of seasonal variation. Labor requirements are very high during planting and harvesting but much lower as the plants grow. Some tasks are very time-sensitive and highly dependent on weather conditions. The phrase "make hay while the sun shines" suggests not only that a farmer needs to take advantage of favorable circumstances but also that a misstep can render previous labors worthless and create more trouble down the road. Second, the output of agricultural projects affects larger communities beyond the individual producer. Even before the advent of surplus farming undertaken specifically for trade, supplying the nutritional needs of a local community was a communal task.

Farmers began forming agricultural cooperatives in the nineteenth century to help bring their goods from the most rural areas of the country to urban centers of consumption. Several experimented with consumer cooperative retail stores as well. Many of these were not based on the Rochdale principles, and after a brief period of rapid expansion, they collapsed due to political infighting or financial insolvency. The National Grange is one example of a federated cooperative movement that rose and fell.

The National Grange, founded in 1867, is the nation's oldest agricultural organization. More formally known as the Order of Patrons of Husbandry, it was created by seven men, including William Saunders, the Superintendent of Propagating Gardens in the Department of Agriculture. The principal founder was Oliver Hudson Kelley, a native of Massachusetts and a Minnesota farmer. Following the Civil War, the restored federal government lacked information about agricultural conditions in the South, and it commissioned Kelley to survey them.

His report took special notice of sociological trends in the agricultural market, in particular the introduction of Northern "carpet-baggers" who sought to profit from the disadvantaged position of the Southern farmers.

The Grange was founded as a social and educational organization borrowing ritualistic overtones from Freemasonry, and the "General Objects" the Order adopted were twofold:

1. United by the strong and faithful tie of Agriculture, we mutually resolve to labor for the good of our Order, our country, and mankind.
2. We heartily endorse the motto: "In essentials, unity; in non-essentials, liberty; in all things, charity."

From the outset, the Grange endeavored to bring "producers and consumers, farmers and manufacturers, into the most direct and friendly relations possible. Hence we must dispense with the surplus middlemen, not that we are unfriendly to them, but we do not need them." This attitude, however "friendly" its intent, was perceived by many outside the organization as combative toward entrenched economic interests, particularly the middlemen that it sought to bypass. The targets of the Grange's efforts toward farming independence soon included the railroads that transported the harvested products and the elevator companies that stored them as they made their way to Eastern markets.

Though the Grange is popularly credited with a series of legislative actions with regard to the state regulation of railroads (often referred to at the "Granger Laws"), the organization played only an auxiliary role in removing some of the prevalent unfair trade practices after the Civil War. Several outspoken opponents of the railroad were in fact members of the Grange, but the organization (including the parent group, based in Washington, D.C., as well as the individual chapters) never formally engaged in lawsuits or the writing of legislation. In its 1874 "Declaration of Purposes," the National Grange claimed:

Unfortunately for our Order, the impression prevails to some extent that its chief mission is to fight railroads and denounce capitalists. It is a work of time to remove these erroneous impressions, and to prove that we do not wage a meaningless aggressive warfare upon any interest whatever. . . . While we aim to elevate ourselves, we avoid doing so at the expense of running down others.

Nevertheless, the National Grange gained notoriety for both the Granger Laws and a series of lawsuits challenging the monopolistic behavior of railroads and elevator operators. Its membership increased dramatically from 1873 (200,000) to 1875 (858,050), and with the influx of new members came calls for state and local chapters to adopt nonpartisan political resolutions.[4]

More members also meant more dues and increased fiscal flexibility. The Grange set out to create a number of business enterprises within existing legal and economic structures. Organization principles based on the Rochdale Pioneers were adopted during the 1875 national convention, and the Grange was responsible for the creation of hundreds of cooperative stores across the nation. The wholesaler Aaron Montgomery Ward initially provided much of the distribution support for these enterprises, and their early success compelled Grange leaders to "[rush] pell mell into all sorts of business schemes," including grain elevators, warehouses, grist mills, pork-packing plants, bag factories, brickyards, blacksmith shops, machinery and implement works, broom factories, cotton gins, and at least four banks. Poor fiscal management at the national and local levels swiftly burned through the organization's prosperity, and by 1880 membership had dropped to 124,420. By the mid-1890s, with the exception of the cooperative stores (some of which were successful for many years), not a single one of its business enterprises was still in operation.[5]

Though the federal government had enacted hostile policies toward cooperative development in the nineteenth century, attitudes began to change in the twentieth during President Theodore Roosevelt's administration. The federal government particularly recognized the need to provide a stable economic market for agricultural goods; the forces of industrialization in the agricultural economic sector were changing how farmers conducted their livelihoods, both on and off the fields. As the American frontier closed and the gross acreage of farmland began to approach its natural limit, pressure toward intensive farming emphasized a substitution of capital for labor, with an increased reliance on external equipment and inputs. Farmers became increasingly dependent on distribution agencies, and their success required greater efficiency, most easily achieved through collective behavior. Agricultural cooperatives provided farmers with some measure of control over their distribution networks,

a

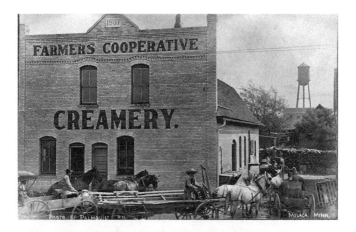

b

*Figure 6.* (*a*) The Farmers Cooperative Creamery (circa 1910) opened in 1907 to purchase raw dairy from the farmers surrounding Milaca, Minnesota, and then transport milk, cream, and butter to more populous markets; (*b*) The Franklin Cooperative Creamery Association (circa 1922) provided home deliveries of bottled milk and other dairy products in Minneapolis. Land O'Lakes is a contemporary agricultural cooperative, founded in St. Paul in 1921 as the Minnesota Cooperative Creameries Association. Courtesy of the Minnesota Historical Society; unknown photographers.

helping to ensure that perishable products would reach their consumers as quickly as possible.

The economic disarray that followed the First World War provided the strongest foothold yet for the cooperative movement. America's agricultural sector saw prices collapse. The Capper-Volstead Act (1922) gave agricultural cooperatives a federal imprimatur, a legal stamp of legitimacy in the eyes of the government. Titled "An Act to Authorize Associations of Producers of Agricultural Products," it let producers collectively process, prepare, handle, and market their goods without the threat of antitrust lawsuits. Its specific intent was to allow cooperative associations to compete against larger agribusiness concerns. Though the Clayton Act of 1914 had established the right of farmers to collectivize, it had offered no such legal protections for their business actions.

Government encouragement for agricultural cooperatives was highest during the 1920s and 1930s. Most state legislatures established agricultural cooperative acts during this time. As part of the response to adverse economic conditions, Presidents Harding, Coolidge, and Hoover all strongly endorsed the use of agricultural cooperatives. The Agricultural Marketing Act of 1929, which included the establishment of a fund for cooperative loans, helped bring about a new era of cooperative formation and development in the United States; the federal government explicitly adopted a new national policy of promoting and financing "producer-owned and producer-controlled cooperative associations."[6] Its first paragraph stated:

> It is declared to be the policy of Congress to promote the effective merchandising of agricultural commodities in interstate and foreign commerce, so that the industry of agriculture will be placed on a basis of economic equality with other industries, and to that end to protect, control, and stabilize the currents of interstate and foreign commerce in the marketing of agricultural commodities and their food products.

This act also created the Federal Farm Board, authorized to designate any appropriate product as an agricultural commodity and invite cooperative associations handling that product to report and collaborate with the board.

During this period, the federal government gradually took the sector of industrial agricultural *out* of free-market capitalism, turning it into a protected industry, a public-private partnership in which the state would subsidize the activities of farmers and allow them to manipulate their own markets within certain parameters. Together, the Clayton Act of 1914, the Capper-Volstead Act of 1922, and the Agricultural Marketing Act of 1929 not only allowed farmers cooperatives to exist without the fear of antitrust lawsuits but also created the Farm Credit Services bureau to lend money to farmers and cooperatives and to guide them in creating a profitable cooperative.

## Consumer Cooperatives, 1865–1920

Worker cooperatives, including those composed of farmers, help laborers maintain control of the businesses where they work. While the initial members of the Rochdale Pioneers were all laborers in various trades, they first banded together as a consumer cooperative to create a store that would sell food products they could not otherwise afford. Consumer cooperatives first appeared in the United States in the early nineteenth century, when two separate groups of workers opened stores in Philadelphia and in New York in 1829. Two years later, at the first annual convention of the New England Association of Farmers, Mechanics, and Other Workingmen, discussions on "cooperative trading" resulted in the formation of another forty cooperatives. During the remainder of the nineteenth century (especially after 1870), there were several different subsequent waves of cooperative formation. Many of these late nineteenth-century experiments were associated with workers' and farmers' movements, and they experienced some degree of success (measured simply by endurance) because they explicitly formed along the principles of the Rochdale Pioneers.[7]

Even so, the movement took hold very slowly, in part because most cooperatives were organized as tools to further the solidarity and economic opportunities of some homogeneous group: farmers, laborers, immigrants, artisans, or tradesmen. The goal was not necessarily to *create* a cooperative but rather to *use* a cooperative as but one means to gain power in the larger social structure. Organizations such as the Cooperative League of the U.S.A. had promoted consumer cooperation as early as the 1880s, but their political orientations placed them on the margins of society, in opposition to both competitive markets and the state. In its original 1880s prospectus for incorporation in New York State, the league declared that one of its purposes was

> to build up in the midst of present society the foundation of a new industrial system which will in the end take the place of wage slavery, when the workers in one way or another bring about the abolition of capitalism.[8]

A cooperative might be used to bolster collective bargaining positions or to fill their absence. As such, the "success" of the cooperative was in large part tied to changing labor dynamics and the vagaries of the national economy. Writing at the end of the nineteenth century, the Harvard sociologist Edward Cummings (the father of the poet e. e. cummings) wrote that statistics on the cooperative movement give "an appearance of coherence and stability which it does not possess. Indeed, these diverse, widely scattered, and disconnected remnants can scarcely be said to constitute a movement in any proper sense of the term."[9] Cooperative enterprises had failed to achieve legitimacy within the American marketplace, and they met resistance from traditional capitalist firms and the federal government. In contrast, consumer cooperatives in England had an estimated 1.7 million members by 1900.

The success of the cooperative movement for farmers in the early twentieth century provided the strongest legal and cultural support for the later resurgence of consumer cooperatives during the Great Depression. The Country Life Movement began around 1900, lamenting increasing urbanization and the perceived loss of rural values and idealizing an image of the "good farmer" who had "the ability to make a full and comfortable living from the land; to rear a family carefully and well; to be of good service to the community; to leave the farm more productive than it was when he took it."[10] Its leaders lobbied for the promotion by the federal government of rural infrastructural enhancements such as improvements to the physical condition of country roads, as well as an educational program that explicitly emphasized rural values and addressed the changing social conditions of farming communities. This movement found an interested patron in President Theodore Roosevelt, who created the Country Life Commission in 1908, charging it with enumerating the deficiencies of agricultural areas and devising methods to address them. Roosevelt's commission resulted in one of the first comprehensive attempts to explore issues of sustainability in agriculture, in both ecological and social arenas.

## Consumer Cooperatives, 1920–50

The consumer cooperative movement gained a stronger foothold on American soil following the end of World War I. Where producer cooperatives often form as a result of tensions between owners and laborers, consumer cooperatives hold the greatest appeal when individual citizens find it difficult to satisfy their needs by patronizing privately held retail operations. This might be the result of a lack of desirable choices: perhaps it is not profitable for a traditional capitalist enterprise to serve the needs of certain consumers, or perhaps a business holds a monopoly and charges higher prices because it lacks competition. Consumer cooperatives are often most appealing to residents of small communities where standard macroeconomic market theories do not apply, and they can serve to correct a deficiency of free-market capitalism.

As was the case for agricultural cooperatives, recognition by the government provided some measure of legitimacy while also guiding the practices of consumer cooperatives. Michigan was the first state to legislatively recognize cooperative associations, passing a statute in 1865 that gave consumers' societies a legal framework for organizing and conducting their business. In 1921, legal advisers of the cooperative movement drafted the so-called Standard Marketing Act, which, in the course of the next seven years, was adopted with slight variations by forty-two of the forty-eight states in existence at that time. By 1933, consumers' societies were provided for in the laws of thirty-four states, which dealt with them through agricultural cooperative laws or general corporation laws or, occasionally, as social clubs.[11]

Recognition and legitimacy from the states also prompted greater government scrutiny of cooperatives' impact on the economy. From 1920 to 1950, the Bureau of Labor Statistics (BLS) collected statistics on consumer cooperative organizations. Labor unions had advocated for the formation of the BLS from the end of the Civil War to help shed light on the working conditions of American laborers, and President Chester Arthur signed legislation creating the agency in 1884. From its beginning, the BLS provided not just statistics but interpretive analysis, and it adopted a progressive stance toward the topics it researched. W. E. B. Du Bois, for example, contributed three articles on labor issues facing black communities in the United States to its bimonthly bulletins between 1899 and 1903. At times, the agency's focus on social issues drew political fire from Congress. The 1913 reconfirmation of its second commissioner, Charles Neill, took place as Woodrow Wilson came into office and Democrats took control of Congress; the new president launched an investigation based on the commissioner's overt concern with "working conditions for women and children in the South." Neill survived this challenge, and for the next forty years the BLS maintained an emphasis on working and living conditions for the individual.[12]

The BLS began tracking statistics on consumer cooperatives in 1918. From the outset of this data series, in large part because of the advocacy stance taken by staff member Florence Parker, the bulletins produced by the BLS promoted cooperatives as a positive development in society.

> The word "cooperation" has within the past few years taken on a new significance to many of the people of the United States. Today it means more than simply "working together." Cooperation in most instances, it is true, makes it appeal to the enlightened self-interest of the individual. It is looked to as a means of lightening the burden of high prices and low wages, through the elimination of all unnecessary middlemen. But the element of idealism and altruism inherent in the movement gives it a wider significance and appeal than a strictly economic movement would have. . . .
>
> The distinguishing feature of the cooperative system is that it exists for the common good. All land or buildings acquired become the common property of all the members. Every economy in manufacture and distribution, and every advance in efficiency or improvement in machinery benefits every member, instead of going as profits to some one person or class.[13]

Parker and her associates distinguished three different forms of cooperative enterprises: cooperative credit, cooperation for production, and cooperation for consumption. The reports she generated over the next thirty years focused on the consumer cooperatives. The BLS conducted three mail surveys in the 1920s (1920, 1925, and 1929), two in the '30s (1933 and 1936), and one every year in the '40s. Parker noted in her first report:

In most of the foreign countries where the cooperative movement has attained a position of any importance, statistics of the movement are published by the central cooperative organization. In the United States statistics of the producers' cooperative movement are collected and published by the United States Bureau of Agricultural Economics and by the Bureau of the Census. No agency has yet done this for the consumers' movement. Descriptive studies have appeared from time to time, published by private or official sources, but containing few or no statistics.

The BLS studies conducted between 1920 and 1950 provide the most reliable longitudinal statistics about the national cooperative population during that period. The analysts supplemented their surveys with targeted field research on specific organizations, and they analyzed some co-ops in panel studies to track net business losses and gains during the 1920s and '30s. They also studied the birth and death rates as well as the longevity of various types of cooperatives. In the 1925 survey, for example, Parker reported that the average retail-store consumer society had been in business for just over ten years; only 22 of the 423 reporting societies had formed before 1900.

The cooperative movement existed primarily as a rural phenomenon in the 1920s, and most of the cooperative societies operating up to 1950 were in smaller cities and towns, not in the largest population centers of the United States.[14] In Minnesota, for example, sixty of eighty-one consumers' societies operated in communities with fewer than 2,500 residents. Nationwide, 80 percent of these organizations existed in towns with populations of less than 25,000; only 10 percent were in cities with more than 100,000 people. Parker suggested that the very nature of a cooperative required trust in one's fellow members, and this could be hard to foster in urban neighborhoods, where residents do not know each other well. In addition,

> Once the city cooperative society is established, it meets other unfavorable conditions largely inherent in city life, such as the well-organized and efficient chain store and the immense department store offering an almost unlimited field of selection to the buyer. Also, unless the members live in one fairly limited locality or unless the store undertakes the task of delivery, difficulties arise as to the means of getting the purchases home.

*Figure* 7. Stores organized as consumer cooperatives often filled a market void in smaller towns that could not attract or support profit-seeking enterprises. In Finland, Minnesota, Wilfred and Elina Bodie ran the Finland Cooperative Company store between 1932 and 1940. Courtesy of the Minnesota Historical Society; photographer unknown.

Though the higher population density in urban areas might seem to have been more favorable to cooperative formation, the impersonal nature of life in the city and increased competition from larger retail stores limited cooperatives' foothold there.

Even so, cooperatives had formed and had thrived in cities of all sizes, providing many communities underserved by larger business interests with an opportunity to meet their local needs. The Credjafawn Co-op Store in St. Paul, Minnesota, serves as a good example. Situated in a largely African American community in the city's Rondo neighborhood, it was located just blocks from where the current Mississippi Market does business on Selby Avenue. The Mississippi Market pays homage to Credjafawn on its website.

The Credjafawn Co-op Store was a project of the Credjafawn Social Club (1928–1980), one of the Twin Cities' earliest African-American social institutions. The Credjafawn Social Club served as a community

*Figure 8.* The Credjafawn Co-op Store at 678 Rondo Avenue served its neighborhood residents between 1946 and the mid-1950s. The name was formed from the initials of the ten founding members' names. Courtesy of the Minnesota Historical Society; photographers unknown.

building organization, sponsoring youth events, picnics, dances, concert recitals, and other public affairs in the Rondo neighborhood. During World War II, Credjafawn Social Club organized its own credit union in order to lend money to members and also bought war bonds to support the war effort. One of its immediate postwar projects was the development of the Credjafawn Co-op.

Credjafawn and many other businesses later fell victim to the construction of the interstate freeway that was plotted through the center of this neighborhood.

The BLS data demonstrate that the consumer cooperative movement showed considerable growth between 1915 and 1920, as the average age of the organizations responding to the bureau's first survey was just under five years. More than a third had been in operation for less than two years. The numbers of societies and members then steadily declined between 1920 and 1933. Throughout her reports, Parker often noted a trend she stated most succinctly in the midst of World War II: "Cooperative development in the United States has generally followed the economic curve, but in reverse order, expanding with depression times and usually receding somewhat as prosperity returned and the necessity for small savings lessened."[15] Cooperative expansions, then, lagged behind the economic cycle by two to five years; an initial economic downturn would weed out some of the weaker organizations, and new ones would gradually replace them.

The population of retail store consumer cooperatives reached its lowest point in 1933, at the height of the Great Depression. Unemployment peaked at 24.9 percent, and in that year the totals of cooperative organizations, membership, and sales were all less than a third of those reported in 1920.[16] But within three years, the movement had recovered nearly all its losses, and growth continued throughout World War II. While the total *number* of organizations began to drop after the war, membership and sales rose steadily, and cooperative sales exceeded $800 million in 1950.

The dramatic growth in the consumer cooperative movement after 1933 was a response to the inauguration of President Franklin Roosevelt and the start of his New Deal package of social reforms. These included explicit government support of the cooperative organizational form in many sectors of the economy. The federal interest in consumer

*Table 2.* **Consumer Retail Store Cooperatives in the United States, 1920–50**

| Year | Societies | Members | Members per capita[a] | Sales ($)[b] |
|------|-----------|---------|----------------------|--------------|
| 1920 | 696 | 196,352 | 18.5 | 78.2 |
| 1925 | 479 | 139,301 | 12.2 | 68.4 |
| 1929 | 407 | 123,317 | 10.2 | 53.1 |
| 1933 | 187 | 76,430 | 6.1 | 26.7 |
| 1936 | 851 | 185,860 | 14.5 | 123.4 |
| 1941 | 2,400 | 500,000 | 37.3 | 261.6 |
| 1942 | 2,500 | 540,000 | 39.7 | 288.0 |
| 1943 | 2,700 | 600,000 | 43.6 | 327.1 |
| 1944 | 2,810 | 690,000 | 49.4 | 383.2 |
| 1945 | 3,000 | 825,000 | 48.3 | 481.7 |
| 1946 | 3,000 | 1,080,000 | 75.4 | 616.6 |
| 1947 | 2,500 | 1,250,000 | 86.1 | 770.7 |
| 1948 | 2,400 | 1,356,000 | 92.3 | 827.9 |
| 1949 | 2,350 | 1,500,000 | 100.8 | 828.2 |
| 1950 | 1,800 | 1,575,000 | 104.5 | 835.0 |

*Source:* Parker (1923, 1927, 1931, 1935, 1938, 1943a, 1943b, 1944, 1945, 1946, 1948, 1949, 1951, 1952).

[a] Membership per ten thousand based on national population estimates, pro-rated between decennial Census counts.

[b] Sales in millions, adjusted for inflation, 1950s dollars.

cooperatives during the 1930s had three drivers: they provided jobs, they helped the economy (particularly credit unions), and they gave consumers a lower-cost way to obtain staples. The federal government piloted projects to create cooperative communities such as Greenbelt, Maryland, in which the majority of services were provided by cooperative organizations. It also established a variety of New Deal programs specifically aimed at helping the formation of cooperatives, just as earlier programs had promoted farm cooperatives.

Unfortunately, the BLS stopped collecting comprehensive data on the national population of consumer cooperatives after 1950. Parker retired from the agency in 1952, devoting her attentions to writing a history of the cooperative movement, *The First 125 Years: A History of Distributive and Service Cooperation in the United States, 1829–1954* (published by the Cooperative League of the U.S.A.). The BLS published

*Figure 9*. The Hanover Consumer Club Society in New Hampshire, founded in 1936, changed its name the next year to the Hanover Consumer Cooperative Society. This postcard proudly displayed the organization's new 1963 building, housing the Food Co-op Store and the Hanover Credit Union. The cooperative is still in business today, operating with more than 30,000 members.

only two more bulletins on consumer cooperatives after Parker's departure, and neither provided any statistical analysis. The first offered this note: "The BLS series on nonfarm associations has been discontinued because of the present impossibility of obtaining both a satisfactory benchmark figure for the total number of nonfarm cooperatives in a given year, and an accurate measure of year-to-year turnover." In the final BLS co-op bulletin, "Consumer Cooperatives," the authors elaborated:

> Strict adherence to the Rochdale principles is sometimes impeded by the provisions of laws under which cooperatives are organized. . . . It is also sometimes difficult to reconcile the Rochdale form (particularly difficult in housing and medical care), or with the need for attracting capital. . . . Because of these and other difficulties, there is no simple way of identifying true consumer cooperatives and this makes statistical measurement or estimates of cooperatives membership and volume of business, or volume of expenditures for such benefits as medical care, imprecise.[17]

Sociologists and statisticians, of course, always face challenges when the empirical complexities of social life don't fit into tidy analytical categories, and the decision to discontinue the study of consumer cooperatives most likely resulted from larger political and bureaucratic realities. The Hoover Commission, established by Congress in 1947 to evaluate the responsibilities of all executive branch agencies, had recommended that the BLS focus its energies on wage and labor analyses, and the current commissioner concurred. During the 1950s, the agency gradually curtailed interpretive research to focus on statistical summaries and information related to collective bargaining arrangements. For its part, the Department of Agriculture continued to support and monitor the business activities of agricultural cooperatives, but there are no reliable data on the growth (or decline) of consumer cooperatives past 1950.

In 1957, the BLS published its last report on consumer cooperatives. It was the first bulletin that included a cover illustration. The uncredited artist depicted cooperatives' many roles in American society and commerce: credit unions, telephone and electrical exchanges, and the retail store. The image of the man carrying a bag of groceries—dressed in a proper suit and tie, with cuffed pants and a fedora—away from a stand-alone storefront with big picture windows presented an image of modernity. The architecturally bold "Co-op" sign and the well-dressed women on the wide sidewalks also suggest a postwar suburban setting, away from the rural backlands where most of the cooperative activity had previously taken place. A cooperative could provide essential services, and, as the multiple "sale" and pricing signs in the store's window indicate, it could also help a consumer save money. The bureau presented the organizations and their shoppers as modern, mainstream, and normal.

## Hot Causes and Cool Mobilization

To help explain how cooperative stores selling organic food developed in the late 1960s, we must first acknowledge the tremendous challenges that face social movement activists striving to change consumer behavior. Attempts to associate specific values with particular products—such as cooperative activists' work to tie feelings of virtue to organic and natural foods—have a long history in American capitalism. What is relatively recent, however, is the trend toward instilling ethical and moral

# CONSUMER COOPERATIVES

**BULLETIN NO. 1211**
**JANUARY 1957**

**UNITED STATES DEPARTMENT OF LABOR**
**James P. Mitchell, Secretary**

**BUREAU OF LABOR STATISTICS**
**Ewan Clague, Commissioner**

*Figure 10.* The cover illustration of a 1957 Bureau of Labor Statistics bulletin focused on consumer cooperatives in many areas of economic life, but this would be the last time the BLS devoted extensive resources to the topic. Even though the second Red Scare in national politics had raised suspicions of any ideology related to socialism, the BLS treated participation in cooperative ventures as a wholesome, unthreatening, and solidly middle-class activity. Source: Flexner and Ericson (1957); Bulletin No. 1211, unknown artist.

dimensions into products. Value-based retailing emerged as a popular marketing initiative in the 1990s and 2000s. Though many researchers have explored the concept of ethical consumption, the common approach has explored the green-marketing practices of an established company that seeks to take advantage of the expressed preferences of consumers to purchase products aligned with their political, ecological, or social justice principles. Sometimes these efforts are seen as less than genuine, and they are labeled "green-washing." These newer cooperatives serve as one of a small but growing set of organizations that have embedded within their missions the promotion of products that specifically address the social and economic conditions involved in their production and sale.

As mentioned in chapter 1, the sociologist Hayagreeva Rao describes several market-based campaigns for social change in *Market Rebels: How Activists Make or Break Radical Innovations*. These include the cultural acceptance of the automobile in the United States, the push for laws to push back against the homogenizing force of chain stores, and the resistance to biotechnology in the production of pharmaceuticals. While none of these campaigns has attracted the sort of attention that would compel people to take to the streets in large-scale displays of mobilization, they have engaged topics about which individuals can hold strong, value-based opinions and that might impel them to change their behavior. Rao's analysis is thus an excellent model for describing how the "buy-cott" (as opposed to a boycott) represents a fundamental departure from more traditional social movement activities.

The challenge for those attempting to effect social change through the market, according to Rao, is "how to forge a collective identity and mobilize support by articulating a *hot cause* that arouses emotion and creates a community of members, and relying on *cool mobilization* that signals the identity of community members and sustains their commitment."[18] By defining the act of grocery shopping as a political action, cooperatives provide a perfect example of Rao's "cool mobilization." Individuals might hold strong beliefs supporting the purchase of particular food in specific market structures, but the steps they must take to act on those values take on a rather mundane character that look remarkably similar to the actions of a person who does *not* share those values: each will be found driving to a store, browsing the aisles and looking at product labels, and purchasing the items at the cashier. All of the "hot," emotional activity has taken place before the shopping excursion, and the result is to choose one destination over another—the co-op or the national grocer.

Strong ideological positions provide the foundation for the values shared by these new cooperative consumers and their chosen retailers: mistrust of mainstream agricultural companies; belief in the power of decentralized, locally based collective actions; and commitment to encouraging sustainable systems in the realms of the environment, the market, and personal health. All of these meanings get packed into the relatively mundane decision to purchase organic/natural/local foods at a member-owned retail establishment. The passions run hot, but the behavioral manifestations of these emotions take place in a peaceful, "uncharged," or cool atmosphere that neither overtly threatens traditional structural institutions nor poses any significant risk for the "activist" or consumer. Rather than making a statement by participating in a single act of defiance, adherents to the cause demonstrate their commitment by repeatedly engaging in the simple acts of purchasing and consuming.

As Rao points out, "The challenge for activists is to arouse to action individuals who are usually busy, distracted, uninvolved, or apparently powerless. Hot causes permit arousal because they frame reality."[19] In traditional social movements, these activists are often directly involved in some mobilizing project; they serve as bridges connecting a previous nonparticipant to engagement in a movement, or they attempt to motivate an individual to engage in some specific behavior. Co-ops act differently because they can feed on the hot causes created by other movements, such as those concerned about genetically modified organisms, fair trade practices, and other policies related to political, economic, and agricultural sustainability. Hot causes depend on shared emotions and framings that appeal to an individual's preexisting values. By embracing these issues and taking a firm stand on them, they are able to take advantage of the passions aroused to channel energy into the project of running a local grocery store.

Cooperatives and other venues of ethical consumption have the advantage of relying on the work of outside activists to create hot causes; the primary job of the co-op involves tying its mission to the values of the potential consumer/member. This doesn't mean that co-ops never engage in the work of creating hot causes, but, because they generally limit their activities to the physical boundaries of the storefront, they generally have access only to those who have already made the decision to walk in their doors. At that point, they can reinforce existing values, attempt to further educate, or solicit participation in a related cause, but for the most part the work of generating hot causes has already taken place.

Apart from the aspect of participatory democracy inherent in running a cooperative, most of the hot-cause activity that gave rise to these organizations long preceded their foundation. The environmental movement, for instance, grew out of the publication of Rachel Carson's *Silent Spring*, in 1962, and increased public awareness throughout the decade of the '60s culminated in the celebration of the first Earth Day, in April 1970. In July of that same year, President Richard Nixon created the Environmental Protection Agency. Similarly, the push for natural/ organic foods developed throughout the twentieth century, promoted most notably (in the United States) by J. I. Rodale, who began publishing *Organic Gardening and Farming* in 1942 and *Prevention* in 1950. By the time that new-wave co-ops starting forming in the early 1970s, public awareness of both of these issues had placed them in the mainstream consciousness—though not all individuals joined the environmental movement or sought out organic food, they were certainly aware of the issues. Cooperatives did not have to create the initial markets for natural, environmentally friendly, and sustainable products; they arose to satisfy a preexisting desire to purchase them.

The practice of value-based consumption has roots in social movement activity, particularly the practice of boycotts—consciously and publicly avoiding products or services provided by a specific vendor because of its perceived social infractions. Market (non)participation is, in a capitalist economy, an important social movement tactic. It is one of the few "weapons of the weak" oppressed groups with few resources to resist compliance can wield against larger power structures. Such boycotts often took place in social movements that challenged laws upholding and promoting exclusion, and they involved protests against companies that denied citizenship or economic rights to particular status groups. The Montgomery Bus Boycott of 1953 and the late 1960s campaign in support of César Chávez and the United Farm Workers of California that targeted grapes from that region stand out as two examples. Today, boycotts are one of the quickest "go-to" tactics when a company has offended the sensibilities of the consuming public, as when the failure of British Petroleum's Deepwater oil rig sent millions of gallons of crude into the Gulf of Mexico or when the Target corporation made financial contributions to a political action group that promoted a conservative agenda opposed (among other things) to equal rights for homosexuals. The sociologist James Jasper claims that although boycotts have become common, their effectiveness remains unclear unless coupled with another social movement tactic: "Consumer decisions can express a moral stance. But they never do so very articulately or forcefully. *A silent choice, made alone, in the aisle of a crowded supermarket, is a poor way to sustain a sense of injustice and indignation.* . . . Expressions of moral outrage are most satisfying when they are done with others, when they explicitly describe the reasons for action, and when they name the villains."[20]

Value-based consumption, in contrast, involves the active purchasing of products produced by companies that *support* a consumer's values; these resemble "buycotts" rather than boycotts. These campaigns inherently involve a different calculus of success with a much lower threshold: continued support from consumers can help ensure the continued existence of the targeted company. While co-ops do participate in boycotts, their status as retailers encourages them to instead *promote* sales by highlighting products that are aligned with consumer values. Avoiding a product to send a (negative) message to a company is different from purchasing a product to support a company. With buycotts, the trick is to validate the value-preference and get people to act on it.[21]

## New-Wave Cooperatives Selling Organic Food

The term "new wave" generally refers to post-1950s art movements that responded to and broke from modernist traditions. First associated with French cinema, it was subsequently used to describe visual art, music, and literature that was considered cutting-edge and consciously experimental, provoking re-examination of all that had come before.

Applied to cooperatives, the term "new wave" came into use in the late 1960s to describe resurgent interest—primarily among countercultural college students—in creating cooperative ventures to pursue projects of social and cultural change. As the previous chapter demonstrated, there have been several waves of cooperative development in the United

States, some predating the founding of the country. The newer activists of the '60s did not want to form co-ops to simply fill a vacuum in their current economic markets; they wanted to emphasize the principles of participatory democracy and provide a supply of products and services that promoted larger social change. The *Organizer's Handbook*, produced by the North American Students of Cooperation (founded in 1968), describes how these were "new-wave" organizations:

> Throughout the 1970s, former student activists put their ideas into action by creating food and other cooperatives based on the idea of participatory democracy and a healthy life. This activity translated into what is known as the "New Wave" cooperative movement, as opposed to the "old wave" co-ops of the 1930s. Some of these organizations existed on college campuses but most were integrated into communities and served community needs. The New Wave cooperatives, with their emphasis on healthy and organic foods, were the beginning of the contemporary health food movement.[22]

The "new" in new-wave cooperatives suggests larger political and social goals, projects of conscious consumerism, and an intentional structure that reflected the values of and relationships among the people and products that made up the co-ops. Like many movements of the late 1960s and early '70s, it also had a connotation of the Age of Aquarius. Activists were demanding a new set of relationships with mainstream institutions of the day. If they weren't dropping out altogether, they were creating roots and integrating themselves into capitalist society in order to reform it.

The activities taking place in and around the early cooperatives represented a different type of collective action. The organic/natural foods store sought to empower individuals by altering their behaviors and/or values, and it reinforced these changes by creating alternative economic options in the competitive capitalist market. These organizations focused on maintaining membership to help routinize and normalize the practice of value-based consuming. For people new to the movement, the mere act of shopping with other like-minded consumers could help provide assurances that this was an acceptable activity.

The relatively low cost of participation helped cooperatives attract members. Perhaps even more important was the fact that most of the "activism" took place in a brick-and-mortar location operating openly in the public realm. A cooperative could help foster the formation of collective identity among its patrons by providing a physical space that promoted putting beliefs into action. Individuals shopping in the storefront operation were immersed in what Rao describes as "communities of feeling" in which they encountered *social experiences in solution*, where participants actively *live* meanings and values associated with a social movement."[23] Most physical-market adventures take place in a social context; the experience of "going shopping" is inherently social, and especially in grocery stores the presence of other patrons helps validate choices, from where to shop to what to buy. Participation through buycotting both reinforces and normalizes the individual's value-orientations. Buying an organic tomato doesn't feel like a radical act when you're waiting in line with others who are doing the same.

The cooperative grocery store promotes cool mobilization of a hot cause by providing a physical space in which adherents become constituents in the company of other like-minded individuals. This results in a similar effect of large-scale mobilization activities protesting oppressive structures of society: by acting in concert, individuals realize they are not alone in their beliefs and desire for cultural and personal change. Shopping at co-ops helps promote a process of cognitive liberation and a feeling that together, individuals could make a difference.

The emergence of eco-foods as a viable social issue in the 1960s came only after painstaking work to create alternative agricultural paradigms. Where other movements resisted institutionalized power, activists promoting natural and organic foods could not point to obvious legal strictures that forced anyone to consume the products of mainstream agribusiness. Instead, their mobilization efforts took place at the level of civil society, in the marketplace. The "power" they resisted resided within the individuals who had accepted the increased industrialization of American agriculture.

Alternative food movements responded to twentieth-century modernization projects. They pointed out the social, environmental, and health consequences brought about by increasing mechanization, standardization, and consolidation of farms. Several proponents of sustainable agriculture began to explore new (or, in some cases, to rediscover old) paradigms for production, but it wasn't until the 1960s, when public awareness of environmental issues came to the fore, that a true market for these products began to emerge. Stemming ecological degradation became one of the hot causes of this decade. New-wave cooperatives, on the other hand, developed from a longer and more established tradition of creating alternative venues to help mediate some of the vagaries of capitalist markets.

Co-ops were certainly sympathetic to eco-food activism and stemmed from the same ideological critiques. Though the environmental activism of the 1960s focused on the actions and perceived moral violations

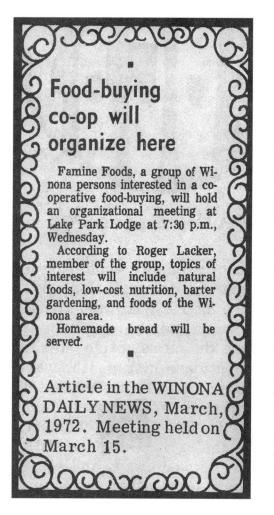

*Figure 11.* The original name of today's Bluff Country Co-op in Winona, Minnesota, was Famine Foods. This notice in the local paper has been saved as part of its origin story: a group of activists was interested in the quality of the food (emphasizing "natural"), its cost, and its acquisition through alternative forms of commerce. The emphasis on local provisioning is also noteworthy. Courtesy of Bluff Country Co-op, Winona, Minnesota.

of external actors (polluting chemical companies, mainstream agribusinesses), those who sought to create a communally run grocery relied on reciprocal emotions for solidarity and focus. They often had a wider set of goals, and we can witness the beginning of a developing market devoted to ethical consumerism.

## Running a Business and a Social Movement in One Space

A co-op will cease to exist if it continually operates at a loss. But co-ops are generally not oriented toward generating a profit. In fact, state laws often dictate that surplus revenues must be reinvested in the organization or returned to its members. The success of cooperatives can be measured both by whether they are fiscally solvent and by whether they fulfill their nonmonetary missions. Remaining true to their social values helps maintain the patronage and support of the members who consciously choose to participate, thus keeping the business viable. These organizations are mission-driven; their commitment to specific social values is a source of their persistence and strength. As such, the co-op has extra obligations that set it apart from other competitive market players. It must not only adhere to these stated values in its relations with members and purveyors; it must also pay attention to the realities of a competitive market and promote sound business practices. These practices get reinforced through regular membership meetings in which the organization explicitly discusses its current standing and future goals in both fiscal and ideological realms.

Many contemporary co-ops have an allegiance to the International Cooperative Alliance, an independent, nongovernmental association formed in 1895. In its literature, the alliance describes founding co-op values as "equality, equity and solidarity" and claims that cooperative members believe in "the ethical values of honesty, openness, social responsibility and caring for others."[24] Similar statements appear in the public presentations of Minnesota co-ops, and most make explicit references to the environment and sustainability. For example, Just Food Co-op in Northfield describes its mission in this way:

> Just Food defines its success by a triple bottom line: social, environmental, and economic sustainability. This commitment to doing business

justly is reflected in our name—Just Food. So whether you'd like to buy fair trade, want to support your local farmers, or just like the delicious soup in our deli, you're voting with your dollar for a better world just by shopping here.

The River Market cooperative in Stillwater has just two sentences on its "Our Mission" webpage:

> Be Healthy, Help the Environment, Live your Values, Build Relationships, Be Successful, Be Kind
>
> The Mission of the River Market Community Cooperative is to improve human health and the natural environment by providing the healthiest natural food and products in the St. Croix Valley.

Mission-driven endeavors like these pursue social goals and values outlined in their written charters and their rhetoric. Organizations rooted in voluntary social actions—those that support projects of social change—make decisions to engage in those actions on the basis of a distinct set of values. Economic organizations, however, are embedded in competitive markets where decisions are made on the basis of the expected behavior of others and the likelihood of successfully achieving one's desired ends. The success of a market organization is based solely on its ability to create a profit, to continually produce a higher rate on its investments. A market organization is always just one financial statement away from the abyss. Economic markets are thus rooted in a paradigm of instrumental rationality: Will this particular action lead to a higher or lower rate of return?

The grocery cooperatives examined in this book exist in *both* institutional contexts. Cooperatives, therefore, have a more complex decision-making process than do organizations that exist in only one of these two realms. Any particular course of action should be judged by two criteria: Will this promote our stated mission? Will it lead to sustainability of the organization? Or, perhaps more forgiving, will this action have a positive social effect without jeopardizing the operation? Or will it lead to greater financial stability without diminishing the chances for fulfilling its larger social mission? Note once more how the Just Food Co-op states its mission: it "defines its success by a triple bottom line: social, environmental, and economic sustainability." The presence of these two institutional logics, two separate criteria for evaluating potential actions, creates organizational strain. This strain is necessarily greater than that which exists for economic organizations that are not rooted in a social movement paradigm. To understand how co-ops might address the need to routinize decision-making processes, one must consider how they resolve tensions between their two competing and embedded goals. This is most evident when co-ops must determine what they will sell and (more important) what they *won't* sell. As we will see in the "Co-op Wars" episode in chapter 4, potentially popular products created and marketed by large corporate concerns tend to create the most heated discussions within this community.

The cooperatives' status as non-profit-seeking organizations provides the key to understanding both the challenges they face and the ways they might address those challenges. Most for-profit companies are "mission-driven" to some extent, but because co-ops do not have the same imperative to maximize profitability, they have the freedom *not* to sell a product that might enhance their bottom line if it appears to violate their social principles. The challenge always remains, however, to stay true to one's stated ideals while pursuing continued economic solvency and promoting a social mission. This can lead to lead to contradictions; actions that might promote economic goals but that contradict stated values not only open an organization to charges of hypocrisy but can also lead to dissent among its leadership and membership. Is it "ethical" to sell Heinz ketchup, even after it has created an organic line? Cooperatives are founded on the principle of participatory democracy, suggesting that all members have a potential say in decisions made for the entire group. That can force potential contradictions out into the open, with a structure that continually calls for self-examination of its multiple goals.

The cooperative model was not a radical organizational form, even for intervening in the competitive capitalist marketplace. As we have seen, the federal government had actively promoted cooperative development since the 1930s, and even into the 1960s consumer cooperatives still dotted the (mainly rural) landscape. While cooperatives per se were neither novel in American culture nor hostile rebukes to marketplace capitalism, the younger activists who "discovered" them a decade later employed this type of organization in a new emerging market. It does appear that both the organic and the cooperative movements arose in the early 1970s as market responses to perceived ills within the mainstream provisioning of food. The organic movement—composed of farmers who developed alternative methods of production—stemmed from a critique of various practices in mainstream agriculture. Its activists needed to create an outlet for their products to make their enterprises viable and profitable.

The contemporary cooperative movement that emerged in the 1970s—representing a segment of the consuming counterculture public that sought these products—wanted to create an alternative economic system that would funnel profits back to their communities rather than support mainstream corporate players. Its activists needed to create a distribution network to bring such products from rural areas into their towns and cities. In Minnesota, these two movements together successfully created a new network of cooperatives that emphasized organic and natural foods. This population of alternative markets thrives to this day. Chapter 3 takes a closer look at the spread of these storefront operations in Minnesota through the 1970s as they grew into their role as eco-food clearinghouses.

# 3

## RESISTANCE
## AND PERSISTENCE

I REMEMBER THE FIRST TIME I walked into a cooperative grocery store. It was back in the late 1980s, soon after my younger brother Andy had moved up from Nebraska (where we had both grown up) to live with me in St. Paul. He had become a member at the Mississippi Market—back when it was at its old location on St. Clair Avenue—and one afternoon I picked him up at the end of his volunteer shift.

At the time, I had little idea how a "cooperative" functioned as a business, even though I had driven past countless grain silos with the big Co-op logo when traveling the highways of Nebraska to visit my grandparents. It was easy enough to understand that a consumer cooperative was a business owned by its workers and customers: become a member, pay your dues, and get a discount. Seeing the bulk bins full of nuts and grains also made sense: less packaging was good, taking only what you needed was better, and everything was cheaper this way. When it was explained to me that "organic" simply meant that the crops were grown without pesticides and would be healthier to consume, that made sense, too: presented with a choice between an apple that had once been sprayed with a poison (however mild and however carefully washed off later) and one that had not, it seemed obvious that you'd pick the latter. Sure, the place looked a bit dingy, but it was clean enough, and I understood how it held a certain appeal for a young, anticapitalist, vegetarian punk enthusiast with a meager income.[1]

So the idea of a co-op made sense, and the notion of organic food was appealing. Beyond wondering why I had never been exposed to these things before, I was soon curious why I hadn't seen these stores or these products in every neighborhood throughout America.

Back in the late 1960s, lots of people were already asking similar questions. The increasing concern about environmental issues—coupled with a growing mistrust in corporate America and the government—helped set the stage for a major cultural shift. It would change the ways in which people paid attention to the foods they ate and the impact their behaviors had on a planet that rather suddenly seemed much smaller and more fragile than anyone had realized. Consumer desires for natural and organic foods were growing, but they were not being satisfied by larger agribusiness concerns. In this chapter, I explore how cooperative organizations in Minnesota resisted the power embedded in the larger cultural, economic, and political forces of American agricultural capitalism to satisfy the tastes of the countercultural activists who would become their members.

## Minnesota New-Wave Cooperatives in the 1970s

The remainder of this book focuses on the new-wave cooperatives that took root in Minnesota, a state with a long history of cooperative activity. At the vanguard of several national trends, Minnesota's integration of cooperatives within many diverse sectors and demographic regions provides an excellent setting in which to study the development, struggles, and survival of cooperative organizations. Minneapolis and St. Paul witnessed the introduction of several new-wave cooperatives in the early 1970s, and, though they experienced a brief period of intense ideological competition (often distinctly *un*cooperative and occasionally violent), the groups' attempts to resolve their disputes created an even stronger community of co-ops.

### A Cooperative Profile of Minnesota

Minnesota resembles most midwestern states with a pronounced urban/rural divide. In 1970, two-thirds of its population lived in urban areas; almost half lived in the Twin Cities metropolitan area. Together, Minneapolis and St. Paul create an urban core, though the Mississippi River forms a border between the southern portions of the two cities and each retains a separate identity. Each has an established downtown area and hosts sizable institutions; Minneapolis has the main campus of the University of Minnesota, for example, and its early industry concentrated on milling operations that took advantage of natural falls along the river.

In the early twentieth century, it was the flour-milling capital of the world. St. Paul is the state's capital and houses its legislative and judicial agencies. Minnesota has two additional large urban centers. Duluth is the larger, located in the northern part of the state with an active port on Lake Superior. Rochester lies eighty-five miles to the southeast of the Twin Cities. It is known principally for the Mayo Clinic, founded in 1889 and currently employing approximately 30,000 people. Of the remaining cities of Minnesota, only four had populations greater than 25,000 in 1970; more than 650 townships and villages in the more rural counties had populations of 2,500 or less. The areas outside the Twin Cities metropolitan area are often referred to as "outstate Minnesota," a term that can be use used both affectionately and derisively.[2]

Soon after the Union admitted the state of Minnesota in 1858, this region played host to a number of players in the cooperative movement. Early legislation sought to protect cooperative members. Following models for consumer cooperatives based on the New England Protective Union and farmer organizations such as the National Grange, Minnesota's rural population began experimenting with cooperative organization. In 1870, it passed one of the earliest state laws affirming the legal status of cooperative associations, providing guidelines for incorporation and ensuring that these bodies could not be taken over by a minority interest. Cooperatives formed extensively in the mining, lumber, and farming sectors, forming an unbroken legacy that many new-wave cooperative activists discovered and embraced in the 1970s.

Steven Keillor, the author of *Cooperative Commonwealth*, demonstrates how farmers used the cooperative model to "bring democracy to the marketplace," attempting to maintain both economic and political power in an age of industrialization.[3] Consumer cooperatives emerged in the early decades of the twentieth century, as evidenced by the BLS data series collected by Florence Parker. She noted that the distribution of these consumer cooperatives across the country did not occur randomly; more than a third had formed in the "West North Central" states of Minnesota, Iowa, Nebraska, Kansas, Missouri, and the Dakotas. This trend persisted through all of the surveys into 1936, the last year in which the BLS bulletins provided geographic summaries.

When the reports broke down the summary statistics by state, data indicate that Minnesota was one of the strongest regions for cooperative formation and patronage. Table 3 shows the top five states in terms of

*Table 3.* **Leading States by Cooperative Societies, 1920 and 1936**

| Rank / State | Societies | | Members | | | Sales ($)[a] | |
|---|---|---|---|---|---|---|---|
| | Count | % | Count | % | per 10,000 | Amount | % |
| 1920 | | | | | | | |
| 1. Minnesota | 79 | 11.4 | 14,552 | 7.4 | 61.0 | 9.2 | 14.1 |
| 2. Kansas | 54 | 7.8 | 9,709 | 4.9 | 54.9 | 4.2 | 6.4 |
| 3. Wisconsin | 51 | 7.3 | 31,616 | 16.1 | 120.1 | 7.9 | 12.2 |
| 4. Nebraska | 48 | 6.9 | 7,553 | 3.8 | 58.3 | 5.2 | 8.1 |
| 5. Pennsylvania | 41 | 5.9 | 8,038 | 4.1 | 9.2 | 1.5 | 2.3 |
| *All States* | *696* | *100.0* | *196,352* | *100.0* | *19.4* | *64.9* | *100.0* |
| 1936 | | | | | | | |
| 1. Minnesota | 104 | 12.2 | 23,037 | 12.4 | 89.8 | 7.3 | 10.2 |
| 2. Wisconsin | 86 | 10.1 | 17,100 | 9.2 | 58.2 | 7.9 | 11.1 |
| 3. Illinois | 72 | 8.5 | 12,754 | 6.9 | 16.7 | 5.0 | 7.1 |
| 4. Michigan | 71 | 8.4 | 13,886 | 7.5 | 28.7 | 5.2 | 7.4 |
| 5. Kansas | 57 | 6.7 | 8,291 | 4.5 | 44.1 | 2.9 | 4.1 |
| *All States* | *850* | *100.0* | *185,774* | *100.0* | *15.1* | *71.0* | *100.0* |

*Source:* Parker (1923, 1938).

[a] Sales in millions, not adjusted for inflation.

cooperative societies in 1920 and 1936. Minnesota had the highest number of societies as well as some of the highest totals for membership and sales. With only 2 percent of the nation's population in 1930, Minnesota supported about 10 percent of the consumer cooperative societies, members, and sales in each of the five BLS surveys from this period.

Minnesota's reputation as a "cooperative commonwealth," which developed in the nineteenth century, remains strong to this day. In 2003, the USDA report "Measuring the Economic Impact of Cooperatives in Minnesota" proclaimed that Minnesota led the nation, with at least 1,000 such organizations operating across a wide variety of sectors. With more than 185,000 members and at least $11 billion in annual gross business volume, cooperative ventures now form an integral part of Minnesota's economy. They contribute at least $210 million in tax revenue and employ 79,000 workers. Most of these organizations, of course, are not the new-wave cooperatives under consideration in this book. In addition to 185 credit unions, they largely represent agricultural marketing and farm supply operations. These numbers do demonstrate, however, that Minnesota has a strong history of sympathy for the principles of cooperation, making it fertile ground in which new-wave cooperatives might grow.

Minnesota, with its long history of progressive politics, has played host to both organic food and cooperative activists. Today it has the highest number of new-wave food cooperatives in the nation—more than forty. More than a dozen of these are in the greater metro area of Minneapolis and St. Paul, but the rest exist in some of the state's smallest communities, such as Bemidji (population 13,419), Blue Earth (3,158), and Hackensack (287). Many of these cooperatives have functioned continuously since the 1970s, while some have opened in recent years. Several of the co-ops in the metro area banded together to form a Twin City Natural Food Co-op alliance, while others have chosen to remain completely independent. In short, this population of organizations presents an ideal microcosm in which to investigate patterns of organizational change, continuity, and response to external stimuli.[4]

Finding the Cooperatives

I used three primary sources of data to identify and study these co-ops. The first was archival material generated by the cooperatives themselves—the organizational archives in the Minnesota History Center include board meeting notes, bookkeeping records, clippings, and flyers produced by and about the cooperatives. As minimalist organizations, many cooperatives did not place high value on maintaining a complete set of bookkeeping materials. Fortunately, Kris Olsen—a founding member of the Seward Co-op in Minneapolis and an energetic activist who spent years helping organize collectives throughout the state—donated his personal accumulations to the center's collections. Minnesota state business filings, three decades of cooperative directories, and newspaper archives supplemented this information to help me create the first complete census of these organizations from 1971 to the present.

Published articles from state and trade/industry periodicals formed my second source of data. Bulletins from the U.S. Bureau of Labor Statistics, most prepared by the cooperative enthusiast Florence Parker, helped provide a statistical overview of retail societies from 1920 to 1950. Though the government does not have more recent data, serial publications provided some assistance. Because the population of Minnesota cooperatives (especially those in the Twin Cities) quickly reached a critical

*Figure 12*. Kris Olsen (circa the early 1970s) was a tireless advocate, promoter, and organizer of cooperatives. He also archived several decades of photographs, newsletters, and financial records for cooperatives across the Upper Midwest. This book would have barely been possible without the use of his archives, donated to the Minnesota Historical Society. Courtesy of the Minnesota Historical Society; photographer unknown.

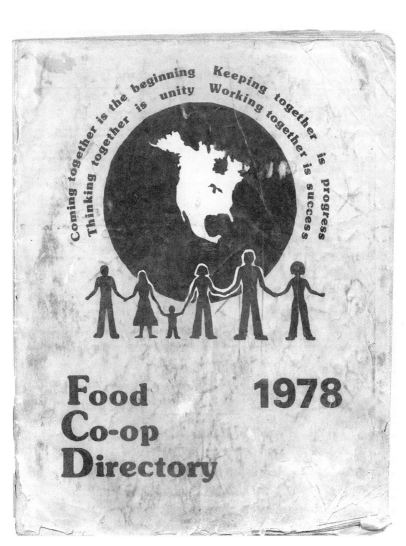

*Figure 13.* The well-worn cover of the 1978 Food Co-op Directory from
Kris Olsen's archives in the Minnesota Historical Society, published by the
Co-op Directory Association in Albuquerque, New Mexico. This was one of
several directories published during the 1970s as the cooperative community
struggled, given the many births and deaths of these organizations, to maintain
a current list of like-minded operations across the country. Each directory
adopted a different method of categorizing and defining cooperatives, often
including buying clubs and the ancillary operations of nonprofit religious,
philanthropic, or otherwise alternative enterprises. Courtesy of the Minnesota
Historical Society.

mass following the first cooperative's founding, in 1971—with fourteen such organizations in operation by the end of 1975—they created several ancillary groups to facilitate business and communication. *Scoop* was one of the early publications, published monthly starting in 1974 and continuing until 1981. This newsletter, distributed to the co-op stores by some of the grocery distributors, addressed itself to the larger "North Country" cooperative community. (As these organizations are member-owned, the community included patrons and workers.) From 1980 to 1985, the Alliance of Warehouses and Federations published its own bimonthly magazine, *Moving Food*, which it distributed to cooperatively owned distribution companies as well as to the stores themselves. In 1985, Dave Gutknecht, one of the former editors of *Moving Food*, began to publish *Cooperative Grocer*, a new bimonthly trade magazine geared toward managers of these storefront operations.[5]

Many of the articles in these publications provide invaluable insight into the challenges and concerns cooperatives faced within this network, as well as specific organizational histories. Cooperative members and consultants provided most of the material for these periodicals and undoubtedly considered how their views would affect the public reputations of their cooperatives. Nonetheless, because the main audience was other cooperators rather than the general public, these articles provide a less-varnished historical account than that found in more self-consciously produced materials meant to massage the cooperatives' public image such as articles in today's glossy magazines. Many of their stories warn others about the pitfalls of expansion and renovation and the challenges of securing financing or dealing with mainstream competitors.

My third source of data was the cooperators themselves. After contacting representatives from every contemporary new-wave cooperative in the state, I conducted personal interviews and corresponded with ten individuals who helped create the early cooperatives and/or continue to maintain them. Interestingly, they generally de-emphasized their roles in the cooperative movement. One informant urged me to make this a story of community, not of individual activists:

> I would not call myself a key figure. There may have been some (and I know for sure you will find a few individuals who'll *claim* they did it all), but this was largely a true peoples' movement. I hope you will find

a way to put some emphasis on the collective aspect of the co-ops, rather than too much attention to a few personalities.

Fortunately, I found it easy to comply with her request.

Two informants, Dave Gutknecht and Gail Graham, provided critical information about the trajectory of the cooperative movement in Minnesota and beyond. Gutknecht, mentioned earlier as the editor of *Moving Food* and *Cooperative Grocer* for a combined thirty years, also participated in the initial formation of the new-wave cooperative organizations in Minneapolis in 1971. When I asked how he first became involved with the movement, he told me:

> It grew directly out of the political protest around the Vietnam war and the draft where I was very active, and we had a very active local organization around draft resistance, draft counseling, and then of course there was a larger antiwar movement that was quite active in the Twin Cities. And as that evolved over several years of protest, as the war dragged on, people in the younger set, including myself, started looking towards ways to, I would say, deepen or broaden our response to what was going on. Broaden beyond protest.[6]

Gutknecht did not participate actively in these fledgling organizations because "in the early years of the '70s I was still sort of wrapping up my draft-resistance career and did a year and a half behind bars, so, when I got out, I resumed my activity in the co-ops." As the "Co-op Wars" heated up in the Twin Cities—an episode discussed in more detail in chapter 4—the cooperatives created the Distributing Alliance of Northcountry Cooperatives (DANCe) in 1974, one of several cooperatively organized distribution organizations that supplied the stores with their wares. Shortly after serving his time for draft-resistance offenses, Gutknecht stepped back into a community that had created its own organizational infrastructure and political tensions.

> I had very little to do with [distributor conflicts] until about 1974, when we started the *Scoop*, which was our local co-op paper or regional-bought paper. And that was actually my first involvement in a system-wide basis, and then the political struggle started the formation of a new warehouse called DANCe, and most of the co-ops shifted their business there. And I was elected to the board of DANCe warehouse

in 1975, so, from that point on, I became more of a warehouse federation networker and educator.

Gutknecht remains active in the movement, even after moving from Minneapolis to Cambridge, Massachusetts, to Athens, Georgia, and finally back to the Twin Cities. The articles he collected and the editorials he published in the *Cooperative Grocer* had a national scope, while his ties to Minnesota helped create an institutional memory of the organizations operating in this state.

A second key figure with an unrivaled résumé is the general manager of the Mississippi Market in St. Paul: Gail Graham. She first became active in the cooperative community in the late 1970s.

I grew up in this area. I moved out of state and, because of traveling around the country and different places for a number of years, and belonged to a buying club for a little bit in Chicago, but didn't really have any involvement. I was a member of the Berkeley Co-op when I lived in the Bay area, which was a large supermarket sort of cooperative, but it was a member-owned organization. And I didn't really know much about it as a co-op then.[7]

After she moved back to Minnesota in 1977, Graham became involved with the Wedge Co-op and soon ran for its board of directors.

When I first moved back here I ended up getting a job at Nutrition World, which is a regional chain health food store. More oriented towards supplements than it was towards food, although it had a little bit of food. And it really was, I got lucky and got a job there. I was shopping, and one of the people at that store told me about the food co-ops because they have really grown and developed from the time I was gone from Minnesota. And North Country was relatively close to my home, so that was the first co-op I actually stopped in and just thought it was great. It was [a] very relaxed atmosphere, high sense of community, lots of interesting food sold in bulk.

I then found the Wedge, which was actually close to where I lived, and became a volunteer at the Wedge. And I think it was in 1977, at the annual meeting . . . back in those days nobody wanted—our organizations were very loosely organized—and it was one of those meetings where somebody said, "Okay, will somebody run for the board?" so

I said, "Okay, I guess I will." And so I ran for the board and was elected, because of course there was no competition.

In the archival materials, Graham's name first appears in a 1978 *Scoop* article she authored about new cash registers installed at the Wedge. She later became a board member for DANCe and, when that organization was folded into the much larger national distributor Blooming Prairie Natural Foods (based in Iowa), became a board member there.[8]

Meanwhile, Graham served as the Wedge's first general manager when it transitioned from collective management to a three-person management team in 1980. She would later become the GM of the Seward Co-op in Minneapolis, and she took the reins at Mississippi Market in 2000. Along with Gutknecht, she helped form the Cooperative Grocers Information Network, the current publisher of *Cooperative Grocer*. Graham's presence in so many of these organizational networks provided me with a remarkable overview of the interconnected nature of this population, and she inspired me to pay much closer attention to the origins of organizational connections.

These three sources of data—organizational archives, institutional publications, and personal interviews—have helped to illuminate the levels of cooperation and collaboration that have proven integral to the success of these organizations. In many ways, all of these organizations have struggled to find the optimum balance of integration and independence. Though many of these federations have come and gone (as have many of the individual storefront operations), the continued attempts at retrospection and projection from a more global perspective evident in these data impressed me more than anything else in this research.

## Challenges Involved with Counting Cooperatives

Most researchers have a special skill of putting their audiences to sleep as they begin to discuss methodological issues underlying the collection of their data. And while transparency is an important aspect of social scientific research, these tales of toil and trouble are usually relegated to easily ignored endnotes. In some cases, however, the challenges posed by the need to identify and locate these objects of interest help illustrate their important and intrinsic qualities. Many cooperatives formed in Minnesota in the midst and wake of the countercultural movements in America consciously defied registering with or being recognized by the larger corporate and governmental structures of society. They wanted to count, but they didn't necessarily want to be counted, to be legitimated, or to be restricted according to the rules made by "the man." This is, in several ways, what made these organizations special as well as historically elusive.

There were many challenges in identifying the 1970s population of new-wave cooperatives post facto. Many were founded as "minimal organizations," and often the leaders and membership distrusted interacting with state authorities in any way. Various strategies helped identify current and former cooperatives, such as looking at state records of incorporation, combing the archives of the Minnesota Historical Society, and speaking to activists present during the early days of organizing. Identifying all of the food co-ops that formed in Minnesota during the 1970s turned out to be a more formidable proposition than I had imagined. One can create a census of the existing population of contemporary new-wave cooperatives rather easily (thanks to the Internet); tracing the histories of defunct members of this population has been more difficult.

From the outset, accurately enumerating consumer cooperatives has posed challenges. Many cooperatives in agricultural communities, for example, exist primarily to market the goods produced on the members' farms. These co-ops might also sell goods to their members (say, items required for agricultural production or those intended for personal use). Would we classify these organizations as consumer cooperatives? The BLS directories of the 1920s and '40s consumer cooperatives clearly delineate the market sector(s) of each organization, and the researchers struggled to classify agricultural cooperatives. In the early 1950s, the bureau specifically cited such taxonomic difficulties when it discontinued its data series on consumer cooperatives. The USDA continued monitoring agricultural marketing organizations.

When a new wave of member-owned consumer cooperatives emerged in the late 1960s, a similar issue of nomenclature arose, complicating the task of tracking them down. In one of the earliest studies of new-wave cooperative members, Ronald Curhan and Edward Wertheim administered questionnaires to 225 members of thirty-four cooperatives in the greater Boston area. The term "cooperative" was used rather expansively in both popular culture and in the academic realm. Instead of referring solely to formal organizations (perhaps complete with brick-and-mortar storefront organizations), it could also refer to informal buying clubs. Though Curhan and Wertheim's research agenda emphasized the organizational structures of cooperatives that resulted in their members' satisfaction, it is their research methodology that sheds the most light on the state of the cooperative movement in this early period.

> Efforts to identify all of the cooperatives in the Boston Standard Metropolitan Statistical Area (as of November 1971) were complicated by the instability of many such groups and the necessity to locate cooperatives primarily by word of mouth. Pursuit of approximately 60 "leads" resulted in a list of about 30 cooperatives. . . . Many cooperatives identified as having been active within the previous 18 months or so were found to have gone out of existence.[9]

In fact, it appears that *none* of the thirty-four cooperatives identified by Curhan and Wertheim had a storefront operation. Instead, they took orders from members and distributed the goods weekly from a central distribution point (akin to today's community supported agriculture— CSA—boxes).

The lack of a formal, consistent definition of what "counts" as a cooperative—whether based on demonstrated adherence to Rochdale principles or organizational boundaries—stymies attempts to make meaningful comparative statements about them. If two researchers confined to a single metropolitan area had difficulty identifying the scope and range of this population of organizations, attempts to do so at the national level are even more suspect. When Art Danforth, the secretary-treasurer of the Cooperative League of the U.S.A., was asked by *Business Week* in 1970 about the breadth of this movement, he could only say that "there are probably a few hundred" groups in the Chicago area. He continued, "You won't find them in the Yellow Pages. . . . They use somebody's home, garage, or a community center." After examining William Ronco's 1974 national cooperative directory, *Food Co-ops: An Alternative to Shopping in Supermarkets*, one of the earliest from this period, I discovered that only one of the supposed hundreds of co-ops operating in Chicago was actually a brick-and-mortar storefront operation; the rest were buying clubs. Similarly, the journalist Daniel Zwerdling's claim that between

# Food Cooperative Directory
## April 1, 1974

This is the second edition of the Food Co-op Directory. Many out-of-date listings have been eliminated and many new listings have been added. In the past six months we have received over 300 pieces of correspondence either requesting a copy of the Food Co-op Directory or updating a listing in some way. We have also received approximately $130 in subscriptions. This only begins to support the expenses incurred. Support us by sending in your $1.00 (one dollar) to:

FOOD COOPERATIVE DIRECTORY c/o AFSC ROOM 370 407 SOUTH DEARBORN ST. CHICAGO, IL 60605

Bulk copies of this directory as well as updated adhesive labels for the directory are available.

We are urgently seeking groups who will take responsibility for maintaining accurate information on the food cooperatives in their regions outside the midwest. This responsibility would include collecting new information on known food cooperatives, locating new groups, identifying groups which move or go out of operation, and systematically reporting this information to us on forms.

New England Contact: NEFCO Don Lubin 8 Ashford St. Allston, MA 02134

WHO IS LISTED IN THE DIRECTORY?
1. Buying clubs, food conspiracies, food cooperatives -- unless they are willing to receive information and to be contacted through another group which is listed in the directory.
2. Distribution centers -- serving many buying clubs.
3. Warehouses -- storing cases and bags for co-ops -- if they are run cooperatively or collectively, are anti-profit, and are accountable to the community.
4. Food stores and storefronts -- if they are run cooperatively or collectively, and are anti-profit.
5. Food spinoffs (bakeries, cafes, mills, ...) -- if they are run cooperatively or collectively, and are anti-profit.
6. Cooperative brokers and marketers -- if they are accountable to the community, and are anti-profit.
7. Cooperative food truckers.
8. Producer cooperatives and associations of small-scale farmers -- especially if they are interested in alternative farming, nutritious/organic growing, or selling to low-income consumers. ( Also some local farmers where no federation exists. )
9. Food information and coordinating groups and media groups relating to food cooperatives.

When sending us information -- about your group or a new group -- remember to PRINT:
1. Complete mailing address for the group. Be sure to include the ZIPCODE.
2. Days and hours of operation
3. Weekday telephone numbers and hours when useable. Include AREA CODE and extension #s.
4. Night/weekend telephone numbers and hours for calling (for cheaper 'phone rates)
5. Names, telephone numbers and addresses for 2(two) contact people.
6. Address of the group's physical distribution point, storefront, ... if it is different from mailing address
7. Name and address of a permanent group contact -- a non-mobile person to call when all other contacts fail (who can tell us if you went out of operation last March ...).
8. Names of any food warehouses or federations of coops with which your group is associated
9. What type of group yours is -- use the categories in "WHO IS LISTED ..." above. You may use codes D1 through D9

HOW TO USE THE DIRECTORY and help to improve it:
1. Locate your address -- is it complete? (see "WHAT..." above) Is it correct? If not, PRINT out the complete information and send it to us.
2. Do the same for other listings if you are absolutely sure of your corrections.
3. Add other groups which are not listed but fit one of the categories in "WHO IS LISTED..." above. Get the complete information from them or have them send it directly to us.
4. If you know that a group in the directory no longer exists, please warn us.

We want the directories to be accurate, concise, and not redundant -- please help us gather this information.

\* \* \* \* \* \* \* \* \* \* \* \* \* \* \* \* \* \* \*

FOOD COOPERATIVE DIRECTORY
c/o AFSC
Room 370
407 South Dearborn St.
Chicago, IL 60605

NON-PROFIT ORG.
U. S. POSTAGE
PAID
CHICAGO, IL
PERMIT NO. 7908

*Figure 14.* During the 1970s, several different organizations attempted to establish themselves as the clearinghouse for cooperative listings. This "Food Cooperative Directory" from April 1974 was published by the American Friends Service Committee in Chicago, an organization founded by the Religious Society of Friends. In addition to listing "buying clubs, food conspiracies, food cooperatives," it also identified ancillary or like-minded organizations so long as they were "anti-profit" and "accountable to the community." The nascent connection between organic food and cooperative stores can be seen in the characteristics of producer cooperatives and associations of small-scale farmers: "especially if they are interested in alternative farming, nutritious/organic growing, or selling to low-income consumers." Courtesy of the Minnesota Historical Society.

5,000 and 10,000 food cooperatives were created between 1969 and 1979 is highly suspect, at least in terms of formal organizations.[10]

Another hurdle is that the same political attitudes that might lead to co-op membership could also result in resisting mainstream recognition of organizational status. The purported antiestablishment attitudes of many early cooperative members led them to avoid close scrutiny; some shunned affiliation even with like-minded organizations. In Curhan and Wertheim's study, they concluded that the most important distinguishing characteristic among the membership was lifestyle. They claimed that the young members "were generally attracted to cooperative activity for ideological reasons. Members frequently were critical of society, and some profess to be radicals." (The researchers also expressed surprise that few were "cultists," a statement that begs its own questions!)

A buying club can indeed organize as a formal cooperative, and it can promote a cooperative spirit and vision in accordance with the Rochdale principles. It can also register with the state to gain legitimacy for the organization and protection for its members. Very few early buying clubs actually did any of this. To maintain a more consistent unit of analysis, then, I restricted my definition of a new-wave food cooperative to one that maintained a storefront operation. My rationale stemmed in part from methodological convenience: real estate transactions and business operations left a paper trail. In the state of Minnesota, all formal cooperative associations must register with the Secretary of State's office (and most eventually complied with this regulation); local media outlets were more likely to report store openings and closings than the creation of informal buying clubs; and cooperative directories usually listed the addresses at which the organizations conducted business. Requiring the operation of a storefront increased the likelihood that I would properly identify cooperatives, and it provided access to tools for verification.

But I did not choose this criterion solely because it would provide a more accurate accounting. I also wanted to study associations that demonstrated a commitment to creating durable organizations interacting within their local market economy. Formal organizations exist as larger secondary groups because they can fulfill tasks more efficiently than less formal ones, because they can more effectively pursue common goals, and because they can survive even after all their founding members have departed. For example, one hundred individuals can independently choose to seek out the cheapest method to obtain a similar product and decide to form a buying club. If, however, just ten of them band together to create a more formal organization for that purpose, they can have a much larger and longer impact on their community. Finally, I argue, the contemporary conception of a consumer cooperative—especially one engaged in the retail trade of groceries—has evolved culturally to assume the existence of a storefront operation, one that generally welcomes the patronage of nonmembers.

## Minimalist Organizations

For the population of Minnesota cooperatives, the definition of what constitutes a proper organization has particular significance. Most of the new-wave cooperatives formed in the 1970s fall into a category that can be characterized as "minimalist organizations," requiring the smallest possible amount of resources for founding and sustenance. Cooperatives often opened wherever they could find vacant space. The Wedge Co-op in Minneapolis first opened in the basement of an apartment building in 1974; five years later it moved to an abandoned convenience store. St. Luke's Co-op in Minnetonka began in 1972 as a buying club in a shed behind a church; it was many years before it would acquire a storefront, eventually changing its name to Lakewinds Food Co-op. And as the Spiral Food Co-op prepared to open in Hastings in 1978, it described its location as "the basement of the old armory. . . . The parking is lousy but the price was reasonable."[11]

With a smaller number of members, minimalist organizations can often operate informally. Rules and norms still abound, but they exist in a more intimate environment. Michael Doyle described how a shopper could make use of Winona's Famine Foods co-op after hours:

> For a time we actually had the key at the police department. So you would go to the police department to get the key, and then go over to the storefront, open it up, do your shopping, take the key back to the cops. We had the cash box in the salted shelled peanuts.[12]

Though minimalist organizations can easily fold and disappear with minimal loss of investment, they can also experience resurrection with a small infusion of human or financial capital. This happened at least once in this population of Minnesota new-wave cooperatives. In the same year that the Hastings cooperative prepared to open with 240 sold shares, *Scoop* reported that, in nearby Faribault, the Hearthstone Food Co-op had undergone a reorganization.

> [The co-op] reopened December 1 after ceasing operations for two months. The co-op, which was formed by a small group of people without extensive community support, suffered from a lull in interest during late summer and was forced to close its doors in October.[13]

Minimalist organizations are also unlikely to suffer a "liability of newness." That is, they do not tend to fail at the same rate as other businesses because their continued existence demands far fewer inputs. As pointed out in one study examining the remarkably low mortality rate of church congregations, "Minimalist organizations are relatively easy to start . . . but they also are more likely to continue to survive even after they become shadows of their former selves." In her report on the 1936 BLS survey of national consumer cooperatives, Florence Parker provided one description, apparently in the "bad examples to not follow" category, that helps illustrate the minimalist organization's approach to standard business practices.

> One of the Bureau's investigators found that in a small miners' association visited in Pennsylvania no records of the transactions had ever been kept; he found also that there had never been any net earnings. This association was started in 1929; it had always been operated entirely with volunteer help. In 1936 it had 29 members and its business in that year amounted to approximately $10,000 (as nearly as the secretary could estimate). The wonder is that it had lasted for 7 years.

Some of the 1970s new-wave co-ops remain minimalist. In response to a request for archival documents, one cooperative's director sent an email describing his store's current condition:

> We wrote by-laws etc. in the beginning . . . i believe in the late 70's. we are rural and never were able to reach a critical mass to keep a formal co-op going. the store still operates but only due to the persistence over the years of my 2 former wives and myself. since the demise of my 2nd marriage 4 years ago i keep the store going with volunteer help, very informal, shoe-string operation. the only records

*Figure 15.* Steven Schwen operated Oak Center General Store as a formal cooperative in the 1970s until he realized that he was doing all of the work—an extreme example of the free-rider issue experienced by many of these organizations. He later formed the Full-Circle Cooperative of like-minded organic farmers in the mid-1980s to share production and marketing costs as they sold their products to Twin Cities markets. The store still sells mostly nonperishable organic and local food, and it hosts musical groups and other community events in its second-floor performance space on the weekends. Photographs by the author.

left are sales slips and yearly taxes, and those are somewhat guest-imates as people help themselves in the store and leave money on the counter.

Peace and love, Steven[14]

Though this minimalist organization might have always appeared to be on the brink of dissolution and destruction, it had remained open, operating continuously for more than forty years.

Even those cooperatives that enjoyed a more robust collective with regular sales were barely making a financial mark in comparison to their established for-profit colleagues in the grocery sector. Financial records in the 1970s archives often indicate total inventories of just a few thousand dollars and monthly sales of less than $10,000. Even by 1978—as many of the Minnesota new-wave cooperatives were fairly well established and becoming fixtures within their communities—a store such as Mill City Co-op (founded 1972) reported its inventory stock value as $4,500, listing its primary assets as "2 scales, one freezer, cash register, adding machine and a van estimated at $1900."[15]

The new-wave cooperatives illustrate two more properties of minimalist organizations described by Terrance Halliday and his colleagues: niche definition and norms of competition. Minimalist organizations form most readily when they can fulfill tasks other organizations have neglected. This does not mean that a minimalist organization is best suited to fulfill this task, nor is it the only model a group might choose. Rather, the market setting most conducive to the minimalist organization might involve "well-defined niches and segmented competitive environments that require minimal defense."[16] Such niches can actually accommodate multiple minimalist organizations, and their common standing helps establish anticompetitive norms, allowing each organization to survive without violating the turf of its market brethren. Trade unions and professional associations offer the best examples of this principle: while they fiercely guard their principal domain, they often operate in "segmented competitive environments" and encourage the rise of other groups, more comrades in arms than competitors. Within the Minnesota cooperative community, most organizations explicitly adopted this ethos of noncompetition, inspired by the Rochdale principles and stated as "cooperation among cooperatives." Although the infamous Twin Cities

*Figure 16.* In the days before spreadsheets were created, disseminated, and presented electronically as computer files, the books were kept by hand. Next to the scale and a working cooler, the adding machine was probably one of the most valuable assets a cooperative could own. This mid-1970s balance sheet was written on the chalkboard for a board meeting at the North Country Co-op. One of the original Twin Cities cooperative organizations on the University of Minnesota's "West Bank" (of the Mississippi River), and nestled among many like-minded businesses, this was considered by many to be the heart and soul of the "North Country" cooperative scene. Courtesy of the Minnesota Historical Society; photographer unknown.

Co-op Wars, described in chapter 4, are an intriguing counterexample to this ideal, even in that case the strong reaction against the revolutionaries who sought to forcibly take over neighboring cooperatives, as well as the renewed anticompetitive spirit that followed, actually reinforced this property of the minimalist organization in the long run.

New-wave cooperatives initially formed as minimalist organizations in part because they could but also because they often had no alternative. Some failed, leaving few archival records of their brief existence. The vast majority of those that survived beyond the 1970s eventually adopted nonminimalist structures. Within the largest urban areas, the tremendous expansion of the organic and natural foods market—primarily in the conventional grocery sector but exacerbated by the entrance of Whole Foods—obviated the "niche definition," making the minimalist organizational structure a liability and offsetting any advantages it might bring.

Some of the organizations that remain today formed as buying clubs. Often operating from an individual's home, distributing orders taken beforehand, the informal arrangements developed into more formal business ventures. Such origin stories often figure heavily in a cooperative's lore, repeated in the brief histories found on their websites. For example, the Lakewinds Food co-op in Minnetonka traces its emergence to the basement of a founder's home and an outbuilding of a local church.

> In the beginning, there was a small buying club called the Minnetonka Buying Club, started in 1972 by Edith Stodola and Helen Davis. In the basement of the Davis' (long since demolished) Glen Lake home, a handful of volunteers stocked as many natural food items as they could find. The Davis' garden provided organic produce and the little hen house provided fresh eggs. The members loved buying food for their families from "people they could trust." The club moved to a couple of other houses before settling into the famous "Red Shack" behind St. Luke church in 1975. A progressive church with an enlightened worldview concerned with poverty, health, fairness and cooperation, St. Luke was the perfect environment for the co-op's growth.
>
> By 1983, the little red shack was overwhelmed, and the co-op moved to a small building at Minnetonka Blvd.[17]

The Lakewinds cooperative now boasts three major outlets in the western suburbs with more than 10,000 members.

## Statutory Requirements for Minnesota Cooperatives

After exhaustively consulting cooperative directories and listing services from the 1970s, I created an initial set of possible members within the population of Minnesota new-wave cooperatives. I employed one organizational feature that helps to distinguish formal cooperatives from their buying club counterparts and that provides guidance for founding dates: larger institutional recognition. As an example, I would place the founding year for Lakewinds at 1975, when the buying club established a storefront operation and registered as a cooperative association with the state.

The regulatory environment of Minnesota actually provides an excellent setting to study cooperatives. Two chapters of the state statutes cover these organizations, and the law distinguishes between "cooperatives" (308A) and "cooperative associations" (308B). By law, no organization can use the term "cooperative" in its business name unless it has complied with the regulations in chapter 308A of the Minnesota Statutes, the Minnesota Cooperative Law (1989). (State statutes 308A and 308B specify which organizations can include "cooperative" in their name but

*Figure* 17. The Seward Community "Cooop" attempted to operate as a cooperative without being formally classified as such in state business records. Though founded in 1971, it didn't register with the Minnesota Secretary of State's office until 1976. It has maintained its business listing every year since and has grown into one of the larger Twin Cities area cooperatives, with multiple locations and operations. Courtesy of the Minnesota Historical Society; photographer unknown.

do not mention restrictions on the term "co-op.") These groups conduct business in areas such as agriculture, dairy, marketing, and trucking and include areas of commerce subject to strict regulation: mining, telephone service, manufacturing, electrical service, and water distribution. This excludes all consumer cooperatives, which are governed by the separate chapter 308B, the Minnesota Cooperative *Associations* Act. The organizations covered by this statute include those that market or process agricultural products or that provide products, supplies, and services to their members. Many of the older (pre-new-wave) consumer cooperatives, such as the Finland Cooperative, came into existence prior to the passage of this statue, though few of them have survived into the twenty-first century. For this reason, most of the forty-two grocery cooperatives in the state include the term "co-op" in their name (thirty-two stores), with others referencing the genre of products sold. Several include phrases like "Natural Foods," "Natural Market," or "Healthfood Market" in their name. For many years, the Kandi Cupboard in Willmar was the only store whose name gave no indication of either its organizational form or its product line; today it calls itself the Kandi Cupboard Food Co-op. In the early 1970s, the Seward Co-op went so far as to initially misspell its name with an extra "o" (as in the "Seward Cooop") to purposefully avoid falling under the auspices of either statute.[18]

All cooperatives (and cooperative associations) operating within Minnesota must register with the Secretary of State's office, providing a principal address and designating a registered agent of the organization. Following the initial filing of these articles, they must re-register with the state every two years. When a cooperative registers with the state, it declares the total number and types of shares available, a statement that each shareholder is entitled to only one vote in the organization (one of the original Rochdale principles), and a list of the officers on the board of directors. By law, each cooperative must have at least five board members. The statutes also describe the procedure by which cooperatives may alter their articles of incorporation, specifying how to distribute notices to members, and how they may vote to change their bylaws. Minnesota defines a quorum for all cooperatives: fifty members or 10 percent of the membership, whichever is smaller. Each cooperative must, by law, meet at least once annually, at which time the board members must provide business reports and discuss the current fiscal condition of the organization.

All cooperatives must distribute at least 50 percent of net profit as dividends to their memberships annually.

Just as a newborn child might not receive a social security number for several years, further investigations revealed that several of the earliest co-ops did not register with the state before conducting business. Several did not understand the requirement, or they ignored it. (Though government agencies rarely penalize an organization for not filing, a recognized legal status can actually protect a cooperative in the event of an ownership dispute.) In some cases, the co-ops delayed incorporating and registering because organizational minimalism suggests that they should adhere to regulations only after receiving some threat of enforcement. For others, registering with the state represented a form of subjugation; perhaps it seemed to acknowledge authority they wished to deny. Still, I chose to use this registration status to help establish the boundaries for inclusion. The dates provided an upper limit to the time of formal organization though they cannot serve as a definitive starting period.

Particularly in the first wave of cooperative formation, complying with local- or state-level regulations did not rank high on the list of priorities. Between 1971 and 1975, only ten cooperatives registered with the Secretary of State, though more than twenty had been formed. Winona's Famine Foods co-op, for example, registered in October 1977, but had been in operation since 1972. In the *Scoop*, reporters stated that Mill City Cooperative Foods (one of the more politically strident worker cooperatives, founded in 1972) had announced in its spring 1976 newsletter that it had "incorporated itself as a legal cooperative. Membership is defined as ownership of one share of Mill City stock, now on sale in the store for $3 each." In the same column, *Scoop* reported that the Seward Co-op—also founded in 1972—had announced that it was "discussing becoming legally incorporated as a co-op." By 1978, all existing cooperatives had completed their registration paperwork.[19] As the cooperative community progressed through the 1980s, it began to produce pamphlets giving advice for administering and managing this form of organization within the state—a sort of Minnesota cooperative how-to guide.

Investigating the institutional recognition of the cooperatives provided an inadvertent benefit: identifying a potential actor's true organizational form. For example, the Pomme de Terre Food Co-op formed on the Morris campus of the University of Minnesota (which wryly proclaims the motto "Going out of business since 1971!"), was originally named the Prairie Dog Store. It operated as a standard buying club, serving both students and faculty, and used various dormitory facilities as its headquarters. Though it includes the term "Food Co-op" in its name, it actually registered with the state in 1975 as a nonprofit corporation. At the Pomme de Terre, "members" pay an annual five-dollar fee and each member has one vote at its annual meetings, but the organization pays no dividends to its members and its board of directors holds all legal responsibility for the corporation. Does this qualify as a new-wave cooperative? I chose to include it here as a special case, noting that the distinction has been lost on all cooperative listing services. Even more important, however, the organization has attempted to replicate the organizational form of a true Rochdale-style cooperative in every possible way (including its nomenclature).

In the end, I have chosen to use Secretary of State registrations as a guide for inclusion, but this is not a hard and fast rule. The department's database proved most useful guide for identifying potential actors, especially those early organizations that have since disappeared.

## The 1970s Census of Minnesota New-Wave Cooperatives

After identifying the population of new-wave co-ops in Minnesota from 1971 to 2010, I created an organizational profile for each. I accounted for founding and possible closing dates and found relocations and renovations in industry publications and newspapers of public record. I contacted extant organizations to confirm the information and inquired about their current status: members, annual sales, and square footage. I wanted to determine how this organizational form spread across the state and to find patterns to help explain why it took hold in some areas rather than others. After combing through the Kris Olsen archives in the Minnesota History Center to supplement this database, I conducted interviews with current and former organizers from cooperatives across the state to better understand how these storefront operations helped create the market infrastructure for retailing natural foods during the 1970s.[20]

Three-quarters of the seventy-five Minnesota cooperatives I identified that opened for business as storefront operations did so in the 1970s.

As Figure 18 indicates, the peak years for the total number of cooperatives operating in the state were 1980 and 1981, when fifty-eight storefronts were in business. This population declined over the next decade, stabilizing in 1996 and remaining fairly constant into the 2010s. Beyond the Twin Cities, where residents have had a choice of at least eight different co-ops for the past thirty-five years, the only city with multiple organizations was Duluth—and the two cooperative organizations there merged in 1982. Of the twenty-three that disbanded throughout the state, fifteen were in the Twin Cities, but only eight of the forty-four that formed in smaller communities have folded—a remarkable 72 percent survival rate in the highly competitive grocery sector.[21]

The first period of cooperative formation took place between 1971 and 1975, when eighteen cooperatives opened their doors (all but three in the Twin Cities metropolitan area). The cities of Duluth (Whole Foods Co-op, 1971), Winona (Famine Foods, 1972), and St. Cloud (Good Earth Food Co-op, 1973) represent the lone "outstate" communities where cooperatives began operations in this period, and each was home to a regional four-year university that both attracted and retained youth from the surrounding rural areas.

In the second phase, from 1976 through 1980, an additional forty-four cooperatives formed, thirty-one in cities well beyond the urban

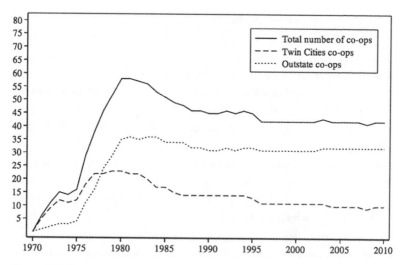

*Figure 18.* Minnesota new-wave cooperative grocery stores, 1970–2010.

cores. The cities in which these new organizations took root did not necessarily have anchoring educational institutions, nor were they particularly large: seventeen cooperatives formed in cities with populations less than 10,000, three in villages of fewer than 1,000. These outstate cooperatives proved remarkably resilient; as of 2010 thirty-two were still in business, from a high of thirty-six in 1981. The majority of the observed decline can be attributed to the Twin Cities cooperatives; there were ten as of 2010, but the number of organizations reached a high of twenty-three in 1981.

The data represented in Figure 18 raise three interesting questions to be explored in the next two chapters. First, what precipitated this process of organizational diffusion from the Twin Cities metropolitan region to more rural areas? Second, how did this population stabilize following the period of decline during the 1980s? Finally, why did the subset of organizations beyond the Twin Cities maintain a higher post-1980 survival rate than the Twin Cities co-ops?

## Connecting the Organic and Cooperative Movements

Before we examine the history of this cooperative community, it is important to step back and revisit the rationales for their formation. Cooperatives obviously present a clear organizational example of collective behavior, and the members who devoted their time, energy, and resources to these ventures often did so with hopes of enacting larger social change. In interviews, co-op members have repeated the mantra that "food is power," suggesting that it is the products, not merely the stores, that provided greater agency to the collective and its consumers. Though these early activists faced many obstacles in keeping their businesses running, they did not present a direct challenge to authority figures or attempt to fundamentally alter larger social structures. Much like the intentional communities of the late eighteenth century (often replicated in communal living structures in the 1960s), they more generally led by example, providing an alternative structure they hoped others would join.

During the new-wave cooperatives' initial formation, most members focused much more on changing individual lives and decisions than on asking the larger culture to adopt a new set of values and orientations. As Michael Doyle of Winona's Famine Foods co-op suggested,

We didn't necessarily intend to change the world, we wanted to make room in that world for people who were looking to change your diet and looking for these other principles, like eating locally and supporting small-scale agriculture. Keeping the money circulating in the local economy. And who knows, maybe someday it will become the mainstream.

If by provisioning local, healthy, and possibly organic food cooperatives could provide an individual with power, toward what end would that power be used? In terms of political science, power is traditionally conceived of as the ability of person *A* to get person *B* to behave in a way that is against *B*'s true desires. When cooperative activists speak of food as power, however, they are actually referring to acts of *resistance*, to a renewed ability to pursue one's own interest unfettered by larger social or institutional forces. In these cases, the consumer (or member-owner) of the cooperative is person *B*, liberated from pursuing an agenda established by somebody else. Very simply, consumers need to be empowered to buy food that serves their interests rather than those of larger corporate agricultural concerns.

In this particular narrative of the early 1970s, the diets of American consumers had become heavily dependent on homogenized, purified, fortified, and institutionalized food products that were not healthy for individuals, producers, or the environment. Through cooperatives, consumers could make a decision in their own best interest that was also a benefit to larger society. Counter-cuisines could channel individual and family purchasing abilities into worthy projects of social change. As Warren Belasco puts it, "the counter-cuisine represented a serious and largely unprecedented attempt to reverse the direction of dietary modernization and thereby align personal consumption with perceived global needs."[22] These principles of organic food were both simple and appealing—and a tremendous challenge to the status quo.

But why did so many choose to form *cooperatives* as they pursued social goals? Henry Hansmann, a prominent scholar of these organizations, suggests that cooperatives form primarily as the result of market failure—they arise to combat monopolistic pricing and give individuals a measure of control in specific areas of commerce. Alan Ware suggests a different *form* of market failure: the absence of desired goods and services from existing, for-profit companies.[23] In other words, cooperatives form either to do things that nobody else *can* do or things nobody else *wants* to do. In the 1960s, a new consumer market began to develop for natural and organic foods. Larger agribusiness companies were dismissive of this demand, and for several years members of federal agencies and the scientific community derided the very concept of organic food.

### "Market Failure"

The U.S. Department of Agriculture never took a formal regulatory stand on organic food until Congress directed it to develop a national standards program in 1990. Prior to this legislative act, however, the USDA had attempted to dispel positive claims made about organic or natural foods for several decades. The department published an annual *Yearbook of Agriculture* from 1894 to 1992. The subject of its 1959 volume was simply "Food," and it contained more than sixty essays on such topics as health, nutrients, quality, and trends. In "Don't Be Fooled by Fads," the author warned:

> Food faddists are apt to recommend so-called "natural" foods along with raw or unprocessed foods. . . . Except for price, there is no objection to these foods, but neither is there anything detrimental about the processed food that is condemned.

The 1965 yearbook's theme was "Consumers All," and in its entry "Nutrition Nonsense" the author suggested that natural and organic foods "are frequently a very expensive source of nutritional factors that are readily available in ordinary foods that cost much less." A separate article in the same volume included a section on "Food Quackery" that questioned what "organic" meant:

> Organic and natural are terms that have been used by some groups to refer to foods grown in soil fertilized with only compost or manure. However, no sound scientific evidence demonstrates that such foods have nutritive values or health factors superior to foods produced with an appropriate combination of fertilizers.

Government dismissal of organic food continued into the 1970s. Earl Butz, President Richard Nixon's Secretary of Agriculture, offered the veneer of statistical analysis in his 1972 disregard:

> We could go back to an organic agriculture in this country if we had to. We know how to do it. We did it when I was a kid. We didn't use any chemicals then. But before we go back to organic agriculture somebody is going to have to decide what 50 million people we are going to let starve. . . . You simply could not feed 206 million Americans even at subsistence levels with the kind of agriculture we had 50 years ago. It would be impossible.

Government officials were not going to lend their endorsement to organic farming anytime soon; their agencies both influenced and reflected the views of mainstream agricultural corporations.[24]

Officials at the USDA were not the only institutional actors who sought to limit the production or consumption of organic food. Scientists and journalists also weighed in, frequently deriding those who desired organics. In 1971, the *New York Times*, having run several stories on the rising popularity of organic foods, felt obliged to remind its readers, in an article titled "The 'Organic' Craze," that:

> Organic gardening is a "philosophy" of horticulture that includes strict use of organic sources for plant nutrition (manures, cottonseed meal, composts, etc.) to grow what is believed to be nutritionally superior foods. Soil science research shows, however, that the source of plant nutrition, chemical or fertilizer, makes little difference to the plants.[25]

The newspaper then reprinted a 1965 USDA bulletin that refuted claims that organic produce was the most nutritious.

Henry J. Heinz II, the chairman of the condiment company founded by his father, wrote a 1972 commentary, "Nutritional Illiteracy," in which he charged:

> Food faddism is becoming a national problem. Advocates of everything from dandelion coffee, unpasteurized milk and organic gardening to the Zen macrobiotic diet are persuading thousands to adopt foolish and costly eating habits. . . . Unfortunately, in their choice of natural or so-called organic foods, they often display alarming and self-damaging ignorance of nutrition.[26]

(Despite Heinz's contention that the appeal of organic foods was primarily spurred by consumer ignorance about modern food science and technology, the Heinz company introduced its line of organic ketchup in 2002. A 2016 article in the Pittsburgh *Tribune-Review* newspaper claimed that the Kraft Heinz Co. was "introducing products that emphasize natural and organic ingredients, adjusting some items with an upscale look and expanding into new categories . . . and removed all artificial flavors, colors and preservatives from its mainstay Kraft Mac & Cheese dinners."[27])

Experts also derided organic enthusiasts as woefully misinformed about plant biology. A 1972 *Science* magazine editorial, written by a professor in the Department of Soils and Plant Nutrition at the University of California, Davis, claimed:

> We have witnessed in recent years an amazing recrudescence of a quaint lore about "organic" gardening and food production that reveals an almost total ignorance among many people, including a sizable fraction of our college population, of the most basic facts concerning the nutrient elements of plants and their absorption.

A professor of chemistry at the University of California, Berkeley, agreed: "The rise of the cult of 'organically' grown food is one more example of the fact that some minds are more open to superstition than to knowledge."[28] Placing the term "organic" in quotation marks or preceding it with qualifiers such as "so-called" underscored these writers' disdain and their reluctance to grant legitimacy to this agricultural production process.

Dr. Jean Mayer, a respected nutritionist and regular columnist for the *Washington Post* who later became president of Tufts University, repeatedly lambasted the purported health claims and criticized the higher market costs of organics. One reader wrote in response: "I was really pleased to read your comments about the meaningless [*sic*] of the term 'organic foods.' I admit I was taken in!" In 1974, Mayer again criticized the lack of regulatory rigor behind the term "organic" and continued to cast doubt on any purported health claims in 1977:

> Not only is there no evidence that these foods are additive and pesticide-free, but there is absolutely no evidence that plants grown with organic fertilizers and meats from animals raised on organically-grown feed are in any way superior to foods raised in the usual way.

Other scientists blasted what they considered simplistic (and factually incorrect) ideas about plant biology circulating among the public. At the 1974 annual meeting of the American Association for the Advancement of Science, one panel session explored "The Food Supply and the Organic Food Myth." During the presentations, a biochemist from the University of California, Berkeley, stated, "Reading the literature of the organic food movement, one is astounded by their ignorance of chemistry and their wishful thinking." Another scientist confessed to a journalist that although he was a firm believer in the advantages of scientific agriculture, he *had* been experimenting with organic farming in his home garden: "I'm an advocate of commercial agriculture and the use of synthetic fertilizers," he said, "but at home I like going the organic way."[29]

In short, "the establishment" of the 1970s was hostile to organic food and certainly wasn't about to step up to satisfy the growing consumer desires for organic foods. This market failure created an opportunity for cooperatives.

## "Food Is Power"

In the 1960s, the new wave of consumer cooperatives appeared in response to the needs of a new constituency. Composed primarily of young people associated with the counterculture, interested in ecology and nutrition, and with few ties to the established consumer mainstream, consumer cooperatives supporting liberal or progressive political agendas concerned with participatory democracy, consumer health, and environmental protection arose. When I asked long-time members of this movement to describe the ideals of the cooperatives, I often heard variations of the slogan "Food for people, not for profit!"[30]

New-wave cooperatives also served as an outlet for energies directed toward political change. Literature described their ideology as "a marriage between the political values of participatory democracy and the economic realities of shoestring operations."[31] The early relationship between the cooperatives and organic food lay in shared sets of political orientations among their respective advocates. At their core, however, new-wave co-ops were committed to *food politics*, a constellation of attitudes and practices centered around the production, processing, and distribution of food. Food was seen as a reflection of the social and political order and an important determinant of personal and communal health.

A 1970 *Business Week* article stated the food cooperatives were "shooting up like mushrooms after a rain all over the country."[32] In 1974, William Ronco published one of the first national listings in *Food Co-ops: An Alternative to Shopping in Supermarkets*. He listed 1,000 organizations and claimed that more than 95 percent had been founded within the previous five years. Most writers attribute the meteoric rise in the number of food co-ops during this period to increased consciousness about diet and nutrition, and many of the stores were developed to provide an alternative to the high prices charged by private health food stores. Others began as a first source of bulk natural food in a given area—a welcome outpost for working- and middle-class neighborhoods when food prices increased almost 24 percent between 1972 and 1976.[33]

This "new wave," as it came to be called, also reflected a growing disenchantment with the commercial food marketing system on ecological grounds (e.g., wasteful use of resources, excessive packaging, reliance on long-distance transportation and fossil fuels), on political grounds (consolidation trends within the food industry, association with multinational corporations allied to repressive governments, and economic exploitation of farmers, employees, and consumers), on social grounds (dehumanization of the marketplace brought about by impersonal supermarket merchandizing, increased distance between producer and consumer, and the elimination of local producers and suppliers), and on nutritional grounds (promotion of food with a low nutrient-to-dollar ratio, overprocessing, and excessive use of additives).

Doyle, the early organizer of Winona's Famine Foods who later became a professor of history at Ball State University, explained that the politicization of his generation (or at least certain segments within it) led many of its members to consider alternative institutions:

> So we were looking at every aspect. Car repair; bicycles; "Durable Goods," which was the department store in the West Bank run along cooperative lines; cooperative bakery. Of course the food co-ops, restaurants, you know, pretty much you name it, we had somebody that was working along these lines. So those people who considered themselves

within the counterculture—within the alternative community—went out of their way to patronize those collectives, those businesses. And whenever possible we wanted to keep our money circulating within the alternative economic system. So it was a real world view.

The focus on what food to sell, purchase, and consume followed from the same analysis, Doyle said:

> To change the material system in order to affect the changing consciousness, you affect the changing consciousness by getting at the underlying culture of values and norms. . . . Going to first principles. What do I put in my body? Where does this stuff come from? You open up the cupboards or the refrigerator in any American home, '50s and '60s is when they started introducing processed food in a big way. And you know, you can't pronounce half of the chemicals that are in some of this stuff, you have no idea why it's in there in the first place. And you know you're wondering, why are we doing this? Why do we want a food product that can stay on the shelf for years on end without getting stale?

In the early 1970s, organic food was not only considered tasty, nutritious, and cost-effective for bulk buyers; it was also a manifestation of an antiestablishment rebellion against mainstream agriculture and the institutions that supported it.

### Whither the Organic Food?

There's no a priori reason to have expected eco-food activists to settle on the organizational form of the cooperative. Given increasing interest in healthier, safer, and more sustainable food products, one would expect to see traditional market organizations step in to satisfy those desires. Of course, the first big problem presented itself rather quickly: although increased ecological awareness started to create consumer demand, there was no ready set of marketable goods for mainstream grocers to offer. Organic food didn't really exist as market commodity. Thus, if the traditional grocery store chains were not going to, the co-ops had to begin with encouraging organic production to satisfy consumer demands. The lack of a reliable supply chain actually set the stage not just for cooperative development but also (at least in the short term) for their continued existence. Interviews with early cooperative activists help show that these organizations formed as a movement parallel to those centered on environmental concerns and gradually adopted their status as standard bearers for organic food and purveyors of eco-food products.

Although J. I. Rodale had been describing different production methods since he began publishing *Organic Gardening and Farming* in the 1940s, there was no widespread agreement (or official guidelines) regarding what this term meant for the purposes of commercial sales. Organic food was perhaps understood as everything that conventional food was not. Dave Gutknecht, the early Twin Cities cooperative organizer, describes the relationship between organic food and cooperative movements as based on a shared sense of mistrust:

> People were in [the new-wave cooperative movement] because they wanted better food, and they didn't trust the mainstream food system to provide some of what they wanted. So it was in reaction to a lot of over-packaged, over-processed grocery items that were in the mainstream and were primarily available . . . a lot of this activity simply started with a bag of rice and a bag of beans. Some people had a little more trust that they knew what they were getting in that bag of rice and bag of beans. Of course it got much more sophisticated as time went on, and there were a lot more choices, and they got organic raisins from California.

All of the organizers and activists I spoke with testified to the importance of organic food in the operation of Minnesota's early cooperatives, even though the term centered on a shared understanding rather than regulatory definition. Tori Reynolds, who helped start the North County Co-op in Minneapolis and later helped found the Minnesota-based Organic Growers and Buyers Association (OGBA), explained:

> For me, organic food was always an important consideration in the co-op movement. Our motto was "Food for People, not for Profit" and that included people's health. I was married from 1965–67 to a brilliant scientist who was recruited just out of college to become a food research chemist for General Mills. He confessed to me that he knew many of the ingredients he was putting in foods were carcinogenic, but that they were approved by the FDA, so he had every intention of doing his

*Figure 19.* In the days before scales were connected to cash registers and scanning wands, customers like these at Winona's Famine Foods in the mid-1970s had to weigh their own bulk-item purchases before checking out. They quickly learned what "tare" meant in order to not get charged for the weight of their containers. Courtesy of the Bluff Country Co-op, Winona, Minnesota; photographer unknown.

employer's bidding. I found his complacency and complicity horrifying, and realized the truth: that Betty Crocker really didn't care about the public health. Many of us at this time were beginning to connect the dots. My father died a horrible death from lymph cancer in 1969, I became a mother in 1970, and I became sincerely motivated to work to take the toxins out of the environment.[34]

As I mentioned earlier, throughout this book I have tended to use the phrases "natural," "organic foods," and "eco-foods" to refer to the category of food products favored by most of the cooperatives. I have done so in part because until 2002, no single national definition of "organic" existed in the United States; each state chose whether to adopt its own production standards to earn the label. Thus we must keep in mind that in any archival document—especially from the early 1970s, before *any* state had statutes or guidelines regulating the term—references to organic food had a cultural rather than a legal meaning. When I asked Gutknecht about the importance of organic food to the early cooperatives, he said these products

> scarcely existed then . . . at least in the form that we use it now. Of course there was no certification until years later, so it was the growers as well as the sellers that eventually developed some standards that became known as "organic" but in those early years it was a lot more of a generic kind of term. We sort of knew what it meant but not really, because there weren't any clearly articulated standards. Basically had to do with avoiding unnecessary additives, pesticides, herbicides in the production stage and added ingredients in the processing and packaging stage were generally looked on with skepticism if not dogmatic rejection. And so the emphasis at least in the beginning was unprocessed or minimally processed, minimal additives or no additives, and that was kind of the notion of "organic." Not that it was inaccurate, it's just that it wasn't as well defined as later years.

For this reason, and because so many of the cooperatives have continued to explicitly promote themselves as purveyors of "natural" food, I continue to use these terms somewhat loosely and synonymously.[35]

Even if the co-ops did not solely stock organic foods—due to limited availability, none of them *could*—this did not mean they weren't in sympathy with the goals of alternative agriculture. During the rhetorical build-up to "the Co-op Wars," described in chapter 4, and in response to a provocative 1975 manifesto known as "the Beanery Paper," two authors signed "Jeb Cabbage" and "Emma Evechild" suggested that the organic foods and the cooperative movements were independent but sympathetic to each other. Their analysis best describes how the co-ops could promote but not stock organic food.

> And has there ever been a "coop policy" to "eat organic?" (and is such a policy bourgeois? It certainly appears to be a goal worth striving for.) In fact, coop history is full of examples where the clear decision was made in favor of the "best food at the cheapest price." The first rice carried by the Warehouse was medium grain commercial rice at the pre-depression price of 12¢/lb. (!) The more expensive organic short grain was stocked only after much demand by coop shoppers in all the stores. A conscious policy was agreed upon to not seek "organic" food because the coops' large demand would only drive up the prices of an already limited supply on the capitalist market. Instead, we would encourage local growers to engage in farming without chemical fertilizers, pesticides and herbacides [sic] by paying the market price or more for their crops.[36]

This was a time before established distribution circuits made the acquisition of organic food items a simple matter of placing an order. Cooperatives worked with local suppliers to support their efforts to grow food sustainably and sought to make connections to those involved in organic agriculture. The members of Red Star Herbs, a small cooperative distributor, described in 1976 how the group "had hoped to contract with some farmers at the OGBA conference, but had no success." Cooperative organizers, then, spoke of the close associations among natural, wholesome, and organic foods. Reporting that same year from the Northfield Co-op (operated out of a church basement), a correspondent simply named "Bonnie" explained that "we sell only whole foods, mostly organic, plus cheese."

Organic growers, for their part, eagerly attempted to make connections with those in the cooperative community. They believed in their methods and products, but they also needed markets. In a 1975 letter to *Scoop*, a new monthly magazine distributed to cooperatives, Ray Hubbuch made a plea from his farm in Wisconsin.

Dear Co-op People,

I'd like to find out if there are any people around the coop scene who would like to spend some time on an organic farm this summer. I was at the warehouse last year, talked with some folks and got on the mailing list for the *Scoop*. At that time I noticed a sign-up sheet for city folks who would like to get their hands in the soil for a while. . . .

This is our second year of operation and we have over 400 acres under cultivation, haven't been able to sell anything to the co-ops yet (except a load of squash and pumpkins) because of problems of storage, cleaning and bagging, and transportation. Hopefully we'll get more organized soon.

An announcement in the March 1975 issue of *Scoop* provides evidence of another attempt to link organic farmers and cooperative members:

The 4th Annual Spring Farmers Meeting, sponsored by Organic Growers and Buyers Association and North Country Eco-Agriculture Center, has been scheduled for . . .

And, of course, the meeting is great opportunity for everyone involved in organics to get together. Basic money charge is the $5.00 membership; if you can't scrape that up, come anyway. Organic meals this year will be catered and will be paid for separately. . . .

By the way, all this isn't happening overnight, so if you have spare energy to throw our way, Call Monica or Barb as soon as possible.

Those interested in organic farming and organic consumption found a natural affinity with the actors and principles associated with the budding new-wave cooperative movement. That bond would grow stronger throughout the decade.[37]

As the organic food industry began to mature in the late 1970s and early 1980s—and as the term started to acquire regulatory legitimacy in conjunction with cultural meanings—the products' prominent presence in the new-wave cooperatives was unquestioned, so much so that Andy Ferguson, a partner in the social action–oriented Catalyst Group working with the Organic Food Producers Association of North America, explicitly acknowledged the important role the new-wave cooperatives had played in the promotion of organic food over the previous two decades. Gutknecht, who helped create an early cooperative trade magazine titled *Moving Food* and later become the editor of *Cooperative*

*Grocer*, recounted Ferguson's comments from a meeting of the International Federation of Organic Agriculture Movements (IFOAM) in Brussels in 1990:

> FERGUSON: This is an area where co-ops need to get back to providing leadership. *I don't think there has been a more effective marketing vehicle for organics than the co-ops.* And co-ops understand it, they understand it's not just a safe food issue but a matter of developing a holistic approach to food and agriculture. . . .
>
> GUTKNECHT: Well, organics is their lifeblood.[38]

At least one analysis much closer to this time period helps confirm how consumer co-ops and organic food were mutually reliant in their early years. In 1981, an economist at the University of Missouri's Cooperative Extension Service, John Noller, provided this summary in one of the last issues of *Moving Food*:

> I want to emphasize two particular approaches which the '70s cooperatives have taken to creating a differential advantage in the market. First, in product selection, most have specialized in offering "natural foods." . . . During the late 1960s and into the 1970s, selling natural foods afforded an effective entry strategy for groups of cooperators with commitment to cooperative principles but little capital or experience in the grocery business. . . . Finally, many of the members of the new cooperatives associated natural foods with cooperative principles and were willing to contribute underpriced management or labor to the cooperative.[39]

In the United States, the organic and cooperative movements shared common underlying aspirations: the economic well-being of local foodsheds, personal health and safety through the consumption of unadulterated food, and a stronger social (if not spiritual) connection to their members' communities. The link between organic food and cooperative stores helped influence how this industry formed. Similar to the work of Heather Haveman and Hayagreeva Rao on the early development of the thrift industry in the United States, we might characterize these organizations as "embodiments of particular institutional logics," what Haveman and Rao call "theories of moral sentiment."[40] The early organizations of the organic food industry involved in production, distribution, and retail were in large part organized cooperatively; their logics and sentiments had a profound influence on the development of the industry over the next two decades.

In many ways, that relationship between new-wave cooperatives and organic food looked like the free-love commitments of the late 1960s and early 1970s. While the histories of both the cooperative and the organic movements extend to the early twentieth century—these weren't just two teenagers hooking up after a good psychedelic concert—they seemed to find each other at a critical juncture, when a large segment of younger Americans was maturing and looking to turn what it perceived as its revolutionary ideals into practical organizational ventures.

Organics were not easily obtained in the mainstream market, so organic activists, including farmers and distributors, found cooperatives to be eager vendors even as larger institutions not only ignored but actively campaigned against this new paradigm of agricultural production. In effect, organics were the co-ops' most visible market differentiator. As interviews with early organizers indicate, both movements shared a distrust of larger agribusiness concerns and the government bodies that supported and regulated them; both challenged the conventions shared by the larger culture surrounding not only food but nearly all consumer goods. In short, if you were an organic farmer looking to sell your wares, you would find the co-ops to be willing takers. If you were a co-op organizer trying to decide what to stock on your limited shelf space, you would see organic food as one of the most ideologically compatible products to sell.

Cooperatives emerged at a propitious moment in the development of organic (or sustainable or ecological) agriculture, for they could serve as a direct contact point with their members/consumers and help negotiate the ambiguity of the larger market. As Michael Haedicke has suggested in his cogent analysis of how the organic food industry took shape,

> the co-op experience is one that involves the management of ambivalence in an effort to create compromises between market growth and systemic change. These compromises appear in hybrid organizational arrangements within and between co-op stores, and they reflect negotiations about the identity and purpose of co-ops as much as they do strategic thinking about the stores' economic position in a changing market.[41]

Co-ops were ideally situated to help negotiate and exploit the uncertainty that existed within the emerging organic food market, whether they realized it or not, whether they did so intentionally or unconsciously.

The renewed interest in cooperatives during the 1970s took place during a period of heightened political, cultural, and economic unrest, and these organizations generally adopted an explicit anticapitalist stance. They sought to provide goods and services to advance their ideological goals. During this resurgence, various communities in the Upper Midwest (particularly in Minnesota) created more than forty cooperative grocery stores. Many new-wave cooperative members in the 1970s would point to Minnesota's long tradition of cooperative retailing to help explain why their movement took off so quickly—this organizational form seemed "natural" to them. The Twin Cities–based All Cooperating Assembly produced a booklet, *Origins and Legacies: The History of the Cooperative Movement*, that tied the contemporary movement to earlier ones. The first page of a co-op–produced history of Minneapolis's North Country Co-op states:

> Economic "cooperation" in this area of the country didn't begin in 1971. There was a booming cooperative movement throughout the Upper Midwest (including Minnesota, Wisconsin, Upper Michigan, Iowa, Nebraska, the Dakotas and beyond) in the 1920s. The movement grew out of a strong wave of populism and farmer discontent in this region. The ideals and strategies of cooperation were borrowed from Europe—particularly England, Finland, and other Scandinavian countries.[42]

New-wave cooperators were aware of their past even as they attempted to chart a new future.

While the product (natural/organic food) and the retail venue (cooperatives) did not *have* to come together in the 1970s, they shared common cultural and ideological principles. Each helped cover deficiencies in the other: co-ops provided a welcoming and forgiving outlet, while organic food helped cement a market identity for the cooperative stores. From their inception, cooperatives promoted themselves along two fronts. First, they emphasized their organizational structure—the fact that they both represented local ownership and provided local control of the operation of their stores. Second, they chose to sell natural and organic food products not readily available on the shelves of mainstream grocers. The success of these organizations relied on selling (in an ideological sense) both concepts and scarce products to potential consumers, although landing individual members required that they bite on only one of the two proffered hooks.

Cooperatives certainly drew many consumers who simply sought cheaper groceries, but the co-ops could accurately point out that this incentive existed only because of their organizational structure; when price-conscious consumers ended up purchasing bulk beans and grains instead of highly processed and packaged foods, their consumption patterns naturally changed to more closely resemble those of people who based their decisions to purchase these products primarily on ideological rather than economic reasons. In fact, the broader incorporation of organic food into the mainstream grocery industry today has coincided with a larger emphasis on issues of environmental sustainability in both business practices and popular discourse. (Note that when President Obama and his wife chose to create an organic garden on the White House lawn, no one in the mainstream press cited this as proof that our first family was a bunch of radical hippies. It seemed like a completely suburban, yuppie, yet natural thing to do.)

Just as all cooperative members have their own unique stories about how they first encountered this strange type of store, each cooperative has an idiosyncratic story of its own to tell. These generally involve narratives of hope, heartache, community involvement, financial distress, and (one hopes) eventual success in overcoming tremendous obstacles to survival and success. Many co-ops underwent tremendous transformations as they progressed from renting tiny storefronts to financing the construction of buildings that more closely resembled full-service supermarkets. Many began relying on a volunteer-member staff stocking the shelves; later they boasted fully paid and often professional staffs alongside memberships in the thousands.

What sets this population apart, however, is that none of these organizations operated in isolation, even if the closest neighboring cooperative was a hundred miles away. Market-based retailing organizations, the co-ops did not even see themselves as competing with one another. Almost all claimed adherence to one of the founding principles of the Rochdale Pioneers: cooperation among cooperatives.

The two phases I have identified in cooperative formation in Minnesota did not occur independently. From 1971 to 1975, as I will demonstrate in chapter 4, the activities of the co-ops based primarily in the Twin Cities created an organizational infrastructure that promoted the distribution and sale of natural and organic food. This propelled the expansion of the outstate segment of this population in the second half of the decade. In the winter of 1975–76, this community experienced a brief period in which discord reigned—an episode that became known as the Co-op Wars. It was the *response* to this episode, however, that helped spread the organizational form. Because these organizations chose to create a loose federating body named the All Cooperating Assembly, they set the stage for sharing organizational resources beyond the urban core. This, in turn, helped to solidify distribution networks and promote fiscal prudence, while still allowing the population to retain a decentralized structure. Each organization maintained independence; together they institutionalized the use of networks, providing a more solid foundation for all. The following chapter focuses on the Co-op Wars as a watershed moment in which Minnesota's cooperative organizations collectively debated their ideological focus, ultimately separating the promotion of pure food from the cause of social change in larger economic and political structures.

# 4

## DISSENT AMONG THE DISSENTERS

### The 1975–76 Co-op Wars

WITH TODAY'S PROFUSION OF SPECIALTY FOOD OUTLETS—from classical French restaurants to fusion bistros, from smaller ethnic cafés operated by families of recent immigrants to larger fine-dining experiences operated by the descendants of the best-known scions in Minnesota retailing, and with food trucks roaming the streets of Minneapolis and St. Paul offering Banh mi, Italian water ice, beer-battered walleye sandwiches, and manoomin salad—going to "the co-op" generally means going to a store that offers organic, natural food with an emphasis on food from local farmers and a certain disdain for products with too much packaging or processing.

New-wave food cooperatives have always been free to carry whatever products their members desire, and most currently operating in Minnesota associate themselves with organic, local, and/or sustainability movements. Those with websites proclaim their missions on their front page. For example, the Good Food Store in Rochester (established 1974) states:

> We are a consumer-owned and operated store providing quality whole foods to support diverse lifestyles. We base the quality of our products on freshness, flavor, nutritional value, and respect for the environment. In recognition of the interrelatedness of every part of the world, we support positive efforts relating to the environment, nutritional education, and human and animal rights, especially as they relate to food issues.

The Pomme de Terre Food Co-op in Morris (founded 1975) describes its purpose similarly:

To provide our community with quality natural foods and local products, promoting care for the environment in a spirit of cooperation and volunteerism.

Brainerd's Crow Wing County Food Co-op (founded 1979) offers itself as *your* source for various products in this genre, including:

Organic Produce
Local & Naturally Raised Meats, Eggs
Bulk Grains, Herbs & Spices
Medicinal Herbs
Gluten Free Products
Organic Snacks
Organic, Natural & Fair Trade Coffees and Teas
Natural Health & Beauty Products
Eco-Friendly Cleaning Supplies

Indeed, it is the rare co-op that does not situate itself as a purveyor of food that is fresh, natural, or sustainable; most co-ops emphasize local sourcing as well.

It might not have turned out this way.

Minnesota's new-wave cooperatives formed in the 1970s with the express purpose of promoting social change. But exactly what sort of change they desired varied among the activists who ran these stores, along with the strategies and tactics they were interested in taking. Some were fervently devoted to reforming the larger structures of society, especially what they perceived as the oppressive postwar political and economic institutions that had privileged corporations over individuals. Others were focused on the cultural and personal value systems that, in their view, discouraged ethical consumerism. In these early years, however, the specific motivations mattered less than a desire to make society better in some way; cooperatives served as a vehicle for social change, even if the destination wasn't entirely clear.

A cooperative is an economic form of organization that suggests a particular ownership structure and a system of governance, but it doesn't inherently imply a particular political ideology, and it certainly doesn't dictate what products or services the co-op will offer. It was not a given that the activists in both the cooperative and the organic movements would become as strongly linked as they did. During the 1970s, food was defined as "organic" largely through a system of shared understandings among producers, retailers, and consumers; organic certification processes were in their infancy, especially regarding state oversight and regulation of the label. The organic food that was being sold was not available exclusively through new-wave cooperatives, and many organic producers operated as independent farmers rather than in a communal or cooperative fashion. How do we explain the affinity that developed between cooperative grocery stores and organic food? This chapter explores how the sale of natural/organic foods emerged as the primary retailing domain for new-wave cooperatives in the state of Minnesota, a process that was propelled by discord rather than harmony.

During the 1970s—when cooperative formation was at its peak in the state—we can identify two distinct periods of cooperative formation, separated by a contentious period in which cooperators were forced openly to define their raison d'être. In the first phase, cooperatives formed primarily as oppositional structures in the urban confines of Minneapolis and St. Paul. In the second, they more actively promoted the production and consumption of "pure food" as their primary goal, firmly linking cooperative grocery stores to the sale of natural and organic foods.

Between 1971 and 1975, co-ops promoted ideologies of opposition to larger capitalist structures. Particularly in the Twin Cities, new-wave co-ops opened primarily in areas characterized by institutions of higher learning and strong leftist political leanings. They formed as part of a larger rejection of mainstream economic policies, attempting to place more power in the hands of lower-income consumers; the array of foods they sold reflected a liberal cultural and political agenda, balanced by the need to sell enough product of any kind to stay in business. Toward the end of this period, these organizations themselves became objects of desire, representing strategic resources to a more militant branch of the cooperative movement that sought to further radicalize, liberate, and remove the "false consciousness" of the consumer base. This group, known as the Co-op Organization, explicitly challenged the sale of natural foods, proclaiming that the product was born of bourgeois capitalism, and instead supported the sale of packaged and processed goods perceived as staples of the working class.

Minnesota's first period of new-wave organizing culminated in what was quickly named The Co-op Wars, in which members of the Co-op

Organization attempted hostile takeovers of several storefront operations, as well as their primary distribution center. Their defeat marked
the beginning of the second phase of cooperative development in Minnesota, from 1976 to 1980. An increase in the number of nonurban
cooperatives throughout the state coincided with a greater emphasis
on distribution networks, mostly serviced by cooperatively run warehouses and delivery services. The maturation of this organizational field
resulted in a form of retail isomorphism: the stores began to resemble
one another more and more, mimicking one another's successful features. They helped fill a natural-foods vacuum in the retail grocery market at a time when organic food was starting to become more accepted
in mainstream culture.

In short, the early formation of cooperative stores favored the sale of
natural foods because of shared oppositional political orientations, while
their continued survival depended on their ability to establish a competitive edge within a capitalist market. Though the first period was marked
by organizational innovators who promoted anti-imperialist ideologies,
the second reflects a continuing legitimation of both form and product.

## The Initial New-Wave Cooperative Community, 1971–75

The first period of Minnesota cooperative formation took place primarily in the Twin Cities metropolitan region. The cooperatives represented attempts by community activists in the early 1970s to put their
political principles and countercultural ideologies into practice. They
challenged the dominant corporate retailing paradigm that separated
buyers from sellers with a system based on democratic management
and labor-based ownership. The most successful of these market-based
endeavors focused on the sale of food products and emphasized less packaging and processing; they were tied to the concurrent hot causes of
sustainable food production and ethical consumption. Explicit discussions about which motivating feature was more important—the type of
product or the form of the purveyor—would eventually reach a public
forum, but the retailing community had to become established before
any such conflict would be meaningful.

In February 1971, the Selby Food Co-op in St. Paul opened as the
first formal new-wave storefront cooperative in Minnesota. It was housed

in a small storefront in an older neighborhood experiencing economic decline. Several informal precursors had already experimented with the purchase, storage, and distribution of bulk "natural" food items in the Twin Cities. For instance, in May 1970, the People's Pantry had begun on the back porch of a home in a Minneapolis neighborhood near the University of Minnesota known as the West Bank, and two months later it started sharing quarters with the Cedar Riverside People's Cooperative Center. It continued operations for half a year before the Minneapolis Health Department shut it down.[1]

Just two months after the Selby Co-op opened, the North Country Co-op formed and leased a West Bank storefront owned by Augsburg College. North Country not only outlasted the Selby Co-op by several decades but also serves in the collective memory as the start of the new-wave cooperative movement in Minnesota. It earned a special standing in large part by spawning a cooperative organizational fervor in Minneapolis. This particular collective formed in a community that had already begun to experiment with the cooperative form of running a business, and community support for North Country helped encourage the rapid formation of the Whole Foods Co-op, several blocks away in the Cedar-Riverside neighborhood. (There is no relation between the Whole Foods Co-op and the mega-chain Whole Foods that was founded in 1980 in Austin, Texas.) By September 1971, North Country had spun off its wholesale arm, informally organized as the People's Warehouse, a distributor that began operating rent-free in an unused building owned by the University of Minnesota. In October, the cooperatively run People's Bakery and the New Riverside Café both opened in the West Bank as well.

Speaking of the 1972 formation of the Seward Co-op, Gail Graham described how customers suggested that North Country Co-op open a new branch. "'You can come start a co-op in our neighborhood,' and [the workers] said, 'No, you go start your own co-op, and we will help you.'" By the summer of 1972, the Twin Cities had seven functioning co-ops scattered across several neighborhoods. With the exception of the Selby Co-op in St. Paul, all laid roots within a three-mile radius centered on North Country and the Whole Foods Co-op on the West Bank: West Bank Co-op Supermarket (adjacent to the university campus on the West Bank of the Mississippi), the Seward Co-op just south of the university, Mill City Co-op in the Phillips neighborhood, and the Beanery in South Minneapolis. Within a year, six more had joined their ranks: St. Anthony Park and Green Grass Grocery, both in St. Paul, and four Minneapolis outposts named for their respective neighborhoods: Bryant Central Co-op, East Calhoun Co-op, Northeast Whole Foods Co-op, and Powderhorn Co-op. The Northside Food Community and Wedge Community Co-op opened in 1974, bringing the total urban core of new-wave cooperatives to fifteen, five of which continued operations for at least the next twenty-five years. Three new-wave food cooperatives formed outside the Twin Cities during the same period, in Winona, Duluth, and Morris, which all had sizable college populations.[2] Table 4 provides a list of all eighteen organizations that formed between 1971 and 1975, in their order of formation.

Many of these Twin Cities food cooperatives seemed to gravitate toward corner storefronts. While this probably didn't reflect any particular architectural preference, in many cases it provided clues about

*Table 4.* **Minnesota New-Wave Co-Ops Formed 1971–75**

| Cooperative name | City | Year founded |
| --- | --- | --- |
| Selby Community Food Store | St. Paul | 1971 |
| North Country Co-op Grocery | Minneapolis | 1971 |
| Whole Foods Co-op | Duluth | 1971 |
| Whole Foods | Minneapolis | 1971 |
| West Bank Co-op Supermarket | Minneapolis | 1972 |
| Beanery | Minneapolis | 1972 |
| Mill City Co-op | Minneapolis | 1972 |
| Seward Co-op Grocery & Deli | Minneapolis | 1972 |
| Famine Foods | Winona | 1972 |
| Northeast Whole Foods Co-op | Minneapolis | 1973 |
| Bryant Central Co-op | Minneapolis | 1973 |
| East Calhoun | Minneapolis | 1973 |
| Powderhorn Co-op | Minneapolis | 1973 |
| St. Anthony Park Grocery | St. Paul | 1973 |
| Green Grass Grocery | St. Paul | 1973 |
| Northside Food Community | Minneapolis | 1974 |
| Wedge Community Co-op | Minneapolis | 1974 |
| Pomme de Terre Food Co-op | Morris | 1975 |

the geography of the communities in which they were located. In the 1970s, most of these collectives formed in distinct neighborhoods, many of which were well established prior to the widespread use of personal automobiles. These neighborhoods, often composed of mid- to low-priced housing stock, often had one- or two-story commercial buildings on the corner lots to house businesses that served basic early twentieth-century mercantile needs: hardware, laundry, pharmaceutical, or grocery businesses took up residence in these corner buildings. With the rise of first-tier suburban shopping malls during this period (referred to as "the Dales"—Rosedale, Southdale, and so on) and the emergence of larger grocery supermarkets with oversized parking lots, many of these neighborhoods were experiencing some economic decline, characterized by fewer small-scale grocery stores and several "for rent" signs in the corner buildings.

The early relationship between new-wave cooperatives and natural/organic food lay in a shared set of principles among their respective advocates. As we've already seen, organic food in the early 1970s was associated with an antiestablishment rebellion against both mainstream agriculture and the institutions that supported it. The active dismissal of organic food by leading scientific and political authorities during this time certainly contributed to this antagonistic stance. Mainstream agricultural interests felt threatened by the suggestion that organic food was superior to conventional products on nutritional, health, and ecological grounds, and if "the man" was against it, that meant there was probably something good about organic food that should be pursued.

The countercultural appeal of cooperatives selling organic food was based on values and ideological orientations that extended beyond the provisioning of groceries. When adherents of the new-wave cooperative and the organic movements began to form a critical mass in the 1970s, many other activists saw themselves as members of a larger liberal/progressive vanguard challenging a dominant (conservative) culture. Michael Doyle, an early participant in Winona's Famine Foods co-op, says that the members explicitly discussed the relationships among food, culture, and politics:

> Our critique as culture radicals was sort of the reverse of Marx. Material conditions produce politics and culture kind of rests at the apex of

*Figure 20.* From top left and moving clockwise, a small collection of early new-wave corner store cooperatives: Seward Cooop, North End, West Side, and East Calhoun. Photographs courtesy of the Minnesota Historical Society; unknown photographers.

the pyramid. It's not relevant to the base, and I think our perspective was, culture was the base. It produced the consciousness out of what you decided were your social arrangements. Who's going to be on top; who's going to be deprived of power and wealth? So if you wanted to change consciousness in the material relationships between people, you really had to change the culture. So that's where we put our emphasis. And the alternative economic system that cooperation represented was our expression of that. At least here I'm speaking [about] specifically Upper Midwest types that were active in the food co-op movement.

Several of the early leaders in the Twin Cities cooperative community had cut their organizing teeth in the antiwar movement, protesting America's participation in the Vietnam War. Gutknecht, who served time for draft resistance and who would later publish the *Cooperative Grocer* newsletter, emphasized this connection between political activism and his involvement with the cooperative movement.

What I noticed very clearly and can still remember is that in the early co-op meetings I saw a lot of the same faces that had just been at the antiwar or draft resistance meetings. . . . it grew out of the antiwar movement and a desire to have something more lasting or sustainable or grounded, if you will, than simply protesting.

Though most of the new-wave cooperatives formed in Minnesota during the 1970s began operations after the Vietnam War had ended, the genesis of this movement—particularly in Minnesota—cannot be separated from the countercultural attitudes of the late 1960s and early 1970s. The connection between antiwar protests and 1970s cooperative activism not only predates the conflict in Vietnam but has roots extending back to World War II.

Chester Bruvold's activist biography provides an example. Bruvold had participated in the peace movement in the 1930s while attending law school at the University of Minnesota. He registered as a conscientious objector in 1940, following passage of the Selective Service Act. When his agricultural deferment expired in 1945, he spent the next fourteen months working at a conservation camp, a common fate for conscientious objectors in World War II. After passing the state bar in 1947, he began to provide legal services to other conscientious objectors and antiwar protesters. He had served on committees of the Socialist Party of Minnesota during the war and later became active in the cooperative movement by lending legal expertise, helping organizations file articles of incorporation, complete real estate transactions, and distribute shares. His archives at the Minnesota Historical Society include documents for the fuel cooperative Co-operative Services, Inc. (1954–59), the Gung-Ho Cooperative in Minneapolis (1951–52), and the Rochdale Agency (1959–66), which provided insurance for the Twin City Co-ops Credit Union. (Bruvold was a trustee and president of the agency.)

Bruvold would later serve as legal counsel for the "Minnesota Eight," a group that broke into a St. Paul post office in January 1970 and stole completed draft cards and 1,200 draft stamps that indicated completion of service. One of the defendants was Don Olson, with whom Gutknecht would later become a principal cooperative activist. Bruvold continued his cooperative activism as well, helping to file papers for the Great River Warehouse Co-op in Winona and the Common Health Warehouse Co-op Association in Duluth. He lobbied extensively for the creation of the National Consumer Cooperative Bank in 1978.

## Examining the Origins of Minnesota New-Wave Cooperatives, 1971–75

The majority of the first food co-ops formed in Minneapolis and St. Paul, the two largest cities in the state. With another organization in Duluth, the second-largest metropolitan area, it is tempting to consider the cooperatives primarily an urban phenomenon. Perhaps the two outstate co-ops—in Winona (1970 population 48,018) and Morris (3,309)—were simply outliers. But that wouldn't explain why co-ops *didn't* form in several of the other major cities in the state with populations of 30,000 or more: Rochester, St. Cloud, or Mankato. The Twin Cities are also surrounded by several populous suburbs, including Bloomington, St. Louis Park, and Richfield, each with more that 45,000 residents. An additional seven cities with populations above 25,000 ring the urban core, yet none of these played host to a cooperative in the early years. All of the first stores opened in a city with a four-year college, but Minnesota had more than a dozen cities with such schools across the state in the early 1970s, and most of those did *not* become home to a co-op.

Residents in the cities and neighborhoods where cooperatives formed shared a different connection: shared political orientations. In particular, cooperatives began to emerge in communities with liberal, anti–Vietnam War sentiments and a desire to help the oppressed. (Many of the co-op newsletters they produced in the early 1970s mention political activities and boycotts of products like California grapes or Florida citrus, all in solidarity for the migrant farm workers. And, yes, they also included the occasional picture of Che Guevara.) Allan Malkis, an early volunteer at the Southeast Co-op, moved to Minneapolis after graduating from Hamilton College in New York in 1973. He was attracted to the community he found.

> I'd been active in college in a small way in a small college, in anti–Vietnam War activities. I had become very interested in a lot of radical politics that were going on and ideas about participatory democracy in alternative to the capitalist economic system, and I found at [the Southeast Co-op] particularly, people who shared a lot of those same ideas and I saw the co-op as a model of potential new economy. And not just of the new economy, but of the new way of people relating to each other and doing things cooperatively, collectively, with more of a volunteer basis, etc. That seemed to be the worldview of a lot of people at the co-op.[3]

There is a lot of anecdotal evidence that cooperatives formed in "leftist" neighborhoods, and it can be difficult to identify such places beyond recollections forty years after the fact. This is especially true for cities in outstate Minnesota. By examining Minnesota's 1972 general election returns from each ward and precinct, however, I discovered patterns of organizational development that go beyond an urban/rural explanation for the initial placement of new-wave cooperatives.

The 1972 presidential election pitted Senator George McGovern of South Dakota against the incumbent, Richard Nixon. McGovern, a decorated veteran of World War II, had first questioned the U.S. involvement in the impending Vietnam conflict in a 1963 Senate floor speech. His opposition to the war grew dramatically following the 1968 election of President Nixon, and, as an outspoken Senate "dove," he called for an immediate ceasefire and the withdrawal of troops in December 1969. As the Democratic nominee for president in 1972, he was without doubt the antiwar candidate. He ran an ineffective campaign, however, and suffered one of the worst defeats in history, losing the popular vote 61 to 37 percent. His only electoral votes came from Massachusetts and Washington, D.C.

In Minnesota, McGovern fared better: he received 46.1 percent of the ballots cast, while 51.6 percent went to Nixon. (In his native South Dakota, he received 45.5 percent.) In any election, one can identify pockets of support for a particular candidate in specific counties and cities, and this was certainly true in the 1972 contest. More important, given the candidates' stark contrast on the most important issue in that election, the percentage of votes received by McGovern in a specific locale can provide an indication of relative antiwar sentiment, a rough gauge of liberal/progressive attitudes for a given community.

So I began mapping. In 1972, Minnesota had eight congressional districts, with the Fourth contained wholly within Hennepin County (Minneapolis) and the Fifth in Ramsey County (St. Paul). Each had more than fifteen wards, each further divided into at least a dozen precincts ranging from a few blocks to half a mile wide. All of the remaining congressional districts shared a border with one of these metro areas, extending from the suburbs of the Twin Cities to the more rural edges of the state. Not surprisingly, some of McGovern's strongest support came from the urban Fourth (54.4 percent) and Fifth (50.9 percent) Congressional Districts.

These percentages are a simple measure of McGovern's overall political support in a particular locale. A more sophisticated and illuminating barometer involves identifying liberal outposts, taking into account how the returns there differed from those in the larger surrounding geographic area. This metric captures how well the candidate "outperformed" or exceeded expectations in smaller neighborhoods of cities across Minnesota. For example, how did the backing Senator McGovern received from the West Bank neighborhood, where the North Country Co-op formed in 1972, compare to the overall Minneapolis results? I created a smaller boundary surrounding each cooperative's location, then identified the wards and precincts associated with this perimeter. After tallying the results for each co-op neighborhood—most containing between 1,500 and 3,000 ballots cast—I then compared the returns within each boundary to the results for the entire city.

As Table 5 demonstrates, residents in these locales turned out for McGovern in much higher numbers than did those in the cities as a whole. Near the Selby Co-op in St. Paul, for example, the four surrounding precincts supported McGovern with 68.5 percent of the vote, a positive 17.5 percent differential over the rest of the city. In one of these precincts, Nixon received only 37 out of 384 ballots cast. The residents living closest to the North Country Co-op also supported McGovern with one of the highest margins in Minneapolis, 75.2 percent (20.8 percent higher than he received in the city as a whole). McGovern outperformed in fourteen of the fifteen Twin Cities neighborhoods containing an early new-wave cooperative—and even in the four precincts surrounding the Powderhorn Park Co-op, he received 54.4 percent of the vote.[4]

*Table 5.* **Relative 1972 McGovern Support Surrounding Co-Ops Formed 1971–75**

| Cooperative name | City | Votes (%) | Ward/city differential (%) |
|---|---|---|---|
| Selby Community Food Store | St. Paul | 68.5 | 17.5 |
| North Country Co-op Grocery | Minneapolis | 75.2 | 20.8 |
| Whole Foods Co-op | Duluth | 54.7 | -2.7 |
| Whole Foods | Minneapolis | 64.3 | 9.9 |
| West Bank Co-op Supermarket | Minneapolis | 70.6 | 16.2 |
| Beanery | Minneapolis | 58.1 | 3.8 |
| Mill City Co-op | Minneapolis | 65.4 | 11.0 |
| Seward Co-op Grocery & Deli | Minneapolis | 70.4 | 16.0 |
| Famine Foods | Winona | 57.3 | 15.9 |
| Northeast Whole Foods Co-op | Minneapolis | 60.6 | 6.2 |
| Bryant Central Co-op | Minneapolis | 69.5 | 15.1 |
| East Calhoun | Minneapolis | 56.4 | 2.0 |
| Powderhorn Co-op | Minneapolis | 54.3 | -.1 |
| St. Anthony Park Grocery | St. Paul | 62.3 | 10.4 |
| Green Grass Grocery | St. Paul | 61.2 | 10.3 |
| Northside Food Community | Minneapolis | 60.6 | 6.2 |
| Wedge Community Co-op | Minneapolis | 63.6 | 9.2 |
| Pomme De Terre Food Co-op | Morris | 51.6 | 3.2 |
| *Average McGovern support* | | *62.2* | *9.4* |

*Note:* "Ward/city differential" represents the difference between the percentage of votes received by McGovern in the wards/precincts surrounding the co-ops and the percentage he received in the entire city. A positive differential indicates the strength of a "liberal oasis" in the region.

Only three of the early cooperatives in this first wave formed out-side the Twin Cities urban core: Whole Foods Co-op in Duluth, Famine Foods in Winona, and Pomme de Terre Food Co-op in Morris, and two of the three precincts in which they were located followed the same vot-ing pattern as their larger urban cousins. Though the Duluth precinct did not outperform the larger county, it still offered McGovern 54.7 percent of its votes. (Its surrounding St. Louis County has long been a Democratic bastion, and it provided McGovern his strongest sup-port of any county in the state, with 57.4 percent.) The ward surround-ing the co-op in Winona represents one of the largest differentials with the surrounding community, with 57.3 percent voting for McGovern, as opposed to 41.4 percent in the county.

After considering other possible predictors of these formations—a city's population density, its income levels or poverty ratios, its average educational attainment, and its previous history with cooperative organi-zations—it turns out that this measure of the political attitudes expressed in the 1972 presidential election is also by far the most reliable indicator of where future cooperatives would arise. All of the early cooperatives formed in cities where at least one precinct area demonstrated high sup-port for McGovern, and communities containing a liberal oasis—a sin-gle precinct area where McGovern's proportion was 50 points higher than Nixon's advantage in the surrounding community—became home to a cooperative before the winter of 1975.[5]

From 1971 to 1975, then, politics mattered for Minnesota's co-op development. Resistance to mainstream capitalist structures had become a hot cause, and the formation of a cooperative in which any potential profit was returned to the workers and consumers who made it possible represented a tangible, physical act that went beyond a simple expression of ideology. The activists were devoted to social change. As the organi-zations began to mature, the exact nature of those ideological underpin-nings received much closer scrutiny, requiring further examination of the goals and aims of the cooperators.

## The 1976 Twin Cities Co-op Wars

Between 1971 and 1975, the Minnesota new-wave cooperative move-ment flourished largely in the Twin Cities, with thirteen stores opening in neighborhoods characterized by strong political support for McGovern in 1972, frequently within walking distance of one another. Most of the activists knew each other by name and reputation. As Allan Malkis, the New York transplant who became the coordinator for the Southeast Co-op, stated,

> One of the things about the co-op movement I found was I ran into the same people all over. Not just at the co-ops but at the dances and the bands we followed, like at political rallies for other causes like Central America or anti-war or whatever. I kept running into people from the co-ops. It was a very . . . I want to say incestuous, but it was a very small, tight-knit people who were very likely to be found at many of the same kinds of alternative culture events.

Despite some shared ideologies, however, the cooperatives began to develop distinct personalities. A small number of worker-owner-members could easily dominate any one organization, and these early 1970s countercultural activists were attempting to address several issues at the same time: local control of economic structures, independence from mainstream corporations, lifestyles that embraced antiwar sentiments, and the lack of readily available healthy food produced by ecologically sound practices. Many participants wanted to create a better society for themselves and others, and the new-wave food co-op could inspire their active involvement from several different fronts. As you might guess, however, any organization can pursue a variety of goals, but multiple aims in diverging areas can inhibit its ability to achieve any of them particularly well.

A rift developed across the Twin Cities cooperative community during the winter of 1975–76 that forced these activists to explicitly define the collective purpose of their organizations. Did they want to pursue a project of national political and economic reformation across the United States, or were they more interested in promoting the production and consumption of "pure" food? With which hot cause did their primary allegiance lie?

Most of the new-wave co-ops now organize themselves as consumer cooperatives, and very few continue to follow the model characterized earlier by Philadelphia's Mariposa Co-op, where all members contributed a set number of labor-hours to maintain storefront operations; such stores are not just "member-owned" but also worker-owned. (At most contemporary consumer cooperatives, membership requires the payment of annual dues without further obligations.) In the early 1970s, though, the organizations generally formed as worker cooperatives, expecting a higher degree of member commitment. This arrangement provided much more control over the business operations, and it allowed the co-ops to more fully implement their ideals of participatory democracy. It also left them vulnerable to higher levels of contention and dissent. As minimalist organizations, they could function with a smaller core of active members, but this also meant that only a handful of members could radically alter the mission and practices.[6]

The ideological fragility of this community became apparent in 1975 with "the Co-op Wars." Though the manifest fault lines revealed themselves and led to a resolution by the summer of 1976, they had developed over the previous two years. They came to a head when one Twin Cities faction, calling itself the Co-op Organization, attempted to "correct" the course of cooperative development in the metro area. Chronicled eighteen years later by Craig Cox, an active participant in the movement, the Co-op Wars described in his 1994 work *Storefront Revolution: Food Co-ops and the Counterculture* represented the most public demonstration of internal conflicts regarding the aims of the cooperative movement at this time.[7]

The roots of the conflict formed in a debate over organizational structure. Soon after the North Country Co-op opened, in April 1971, it created a wholesale division to help serve the needs of other co-ops and buying clubs. (Sales at North Country in that first summer had climbed to nearly $50,000 a month, and during one Saturday afternoon of brisk sales, a working member put up a sign reading, "If the line is too long, start a co-op in your own neighborhood.") The North Country wholesaling operation soon spun off as its own organization, the People's Warehouse, with no corporate or formal business standing; instead, it was run by volunteers from the various cooperatives that benefited from the distribution service.

> Like the Pantry and a number of the early co-ops, the warehouse wasn't "owned" by anyone. There were no incorporation papers, by-laws, or structure. Somebody paid the bills, and others made sure the various tasks were accomplished, but there was no ultimate authority,

no accountability beyond whatever individuals routinely placed on their brothers and sisters in the community.[8]

This model served the needs of its client cooperatives for several years, but in September 1973, when it had to vacate its original rent-free space donated by the University of Minnesota, it had to create a more formal structure to lease or purchase a new location. In spring 1974, its members incorporated as the People's Warehouse, Inc., registering with the state as a nonprofit corporation. The fact that the group had not chosen to incorporate as a cooperative—a pragmatic decision reached in the absence of legal advice but saving the group time and financial resources—later left it open to conflict and contention.

The Co-op Organization members considered themselves to be reformers within the cooperative community, questioning the aims of this fledgling movement. A major source of conflict centered on what to stock (and sell) on their shelves, and canned goods were a focal point. Seen as a necessary staple for poorer consumers, canned goods contradicted many of the original activists' visions of wholesome food. The Selby Co-op struggled internally to resolve this dilemma, in large part because of its location. In the late 1960s, the construction of I-94 had ripped apart St. Paul's Rondo neighborhood, the oldest established African American community in the city, destroying a two-block-wide swath of older housing stock and established businesses. Property values plummeted as "white flight" transformed the once mixed-race neighborhood. Selby Avenue (just four blocks south of the freeway) served as a dividing line between the newly formed low-income, largely black community and the wealthier "Summit Hill" community of upper-class Victorian homes and white residents.

The organizers of the Selby Food Co-op, most of them white counterculturalists, attempted to reconcile the needs of both the northern and southern neighborhoods. Their limited ability to acquire canned goods without buying them at retail from the nearby conventional Red Owl grocery store added logistical problems to the ideological challenge. In a 1973 work journal entry of the Selby Co-op, an anonymous worker wrote: "Carrying canned goods has always been an issue in the coop . . . and been resolved by *not* carrying them. For many this issue has been linked to the question—why don't co-ops serve more poor people/working class?" The writer then outlined a "concrete analysis of conditions" laying out several tensions that cooperatives continue to struggle with to this very day. Should co-ops cater to the needs of the members, who largely want healthy, natural foods, or try to appeal to the tastes of the surrounding neighborhoods to increase membership? Is it better to attract patrons by "looking like" a normal grocery store and then attempt to educate customers later, or does this represent a sacrifice of founding principles? How does a cooperative define a successful operation—do increased sale volumes justify a dilution of the larger goals that center on providing a true alternative to mainstream agribusiness?

One of the central issues raised by this Selby Co-op activist revolved around how conflicts should actually be resolved: "Where does democracy fit in with this decision for co-ops? Should all shoppers decide? Or should only workers decide?" The class issues described in these

*Figure 21.* The short-lived East 7th Co-op in St. Paul was firmly sympathetic to the views of the Co-op Organization, with stacks of canned goods proudly displayed inside the store. As they pitched themselves as "a working class co-op," they also advertised in their windows the sale of cigarettes and beer. Courtesy of the Minnesota Historical Society; unknown photographer.

anonymous notes lay at the heart of the conflict that would escalate into the Co-op Wars. Because many of the cooperatives had fewer than two dozen active members experimenting with participatory democracy, it was relatively easy for a small cadre of politically charged volunteers to assume leadership. In the year leading up to the most contentious actions in the Co-op Wars, that is exactly what happened.

In Minneapolis, the Beanery was a focal point. In March 1975, Rebecca Comeau and Bob Haugen, two former People's Warehouse workers, took control of the Beanery co-op in Minneapolis to reorient it toward a decidedly Marxist agenda. In a six-page manifesto titled "The Beanery Policy," they outlined the Co-op Organization (CO) agenda, which sought to use the cooperatives to achieve political ends. Copied on a mimeograph machine and distributed by the storefront, what was soon referred to as "the Beanery Paper" provoked a strong reaction across the entire cooperative community. The CO's interpretation of how the new-wave co-op movement started—and, more specifically, how it had failed ideologically despite apparent organizational success—brings the issues into much sharper relief:

> We want to take time out to run down a very brief history of the co-op because it is imperative for you, the customer, to know some of the reasons behind our policy and why we are asking you for your support.
>
> The co-op stores emerged from the latter days of the anti-war movement and the beginning of the anti-imperialist movement. What is the difference? The anti-war movement was at its heart a peace movement which saw the war as threatening people's lives which other-wise were quite secure, peaceful and happy. The essence of the anti-imperialist movement is that it is the struggle of oppressed people under the heavy weight of a privileged people of which the struggle against the Vietnam war was part and parcel.[9]

They explained that the original cooperative organizers did not fully take the step from being antiwar to anti-imperialist because they "were grounded in the colleges and universities" and could not overcome their white, middle-class backgrounds and orientations.

The authors of the Beanery Paper asked, "Does the co-op stores' politics respond to its political context?" and emphatically stated "The answer is NO!!" They accused the founders of replicating the larger class structures of American society, characterized by "upper class snobbishness, elitism, and upper class domination of the lower class," and suggested that the co-op movement had not just turned its back to the communities it purported to serve but had also alienated them. Through their contempt for the working poor, the COs wrote, these co-ops reified the capitalist system they were to have opposed. Only by explicitly catering to the working class could a cooperative truly fulfill its mission. This required a renunciation of the focus on healthier foods, which had become associated with bourgeois consumerism. The Beanery workers claimed they had "made an all out effort to destroy upper class attitudes on food" in an attempt "to ascertain, for one thing, once and for all, if there is any such thing as organically grown food in modern times."

> And if so, who is it available for—for those with lots of money in their pockets, etc., or is it available for everyone? Because of the high infla-
> tion rate, recession and the gathering depression, we are optomistic [sic] that the hard core working class will continue to bring us their mandate—away with class snobbishness, cultism, food purists and on with stocking the type of food which is nutritional and cheap.

This organization had a completely different vision of how a co-op should fit into a neighborhood.

Though Comeau and Haugen might have seized control of the co-op, they had certainly not completely won over other members and workers in the community of cooperatives. Within weeks, two members of the Mill City Co-op wrote and distributed their own four-page, single-spaced, mimeographed declaration, "A Response to the Beanery Paper," in which they refuted and dismissed many of the allegations related to class issues across the cooperative community. Chuck Phenix and Nancy Evechild (using the pen names "Jeb Cabbage" and "Emma Evechild") characterized the original manifesto as "a pseudo-marxist revision full of generalizations and accusations delivered in a divisive and vindictive tone," and they provided their own explanation of how the cooperatives originated and why they continued to respond to the needs of their members.

Phenix and Evechild did not dispute that the cooperative movement arose from political ideologies. But they suggested that these organizations had also attempted to proactively create a greater sense of community in their neighborhoods.

> What an alternative food distribution system represents for many people is a turning away from the university (the seat of protest) and *protest* in general, to a rooting in community—a commitment to a neighborhood, to settling down. The coops were born of the spirit of all liberation movements—to hell with the rich and the bosses—people working together can do it and do it better. The coops met a need that was not being met for a lot of people. Those people came together and said, let's distribute good food in bulk cooperatively, to all living in our neighborhood.

The missive also addressed the continuing issue of canned food in the cooperatives.

> And who are the "food purists." Are we to be more revolutionary if we would just eat the junk food currently so popular? Or is it "elitist" to say *NO* to the deluge of cans, plastic, chemicals, preservatives, and the heavy use of grain-fed, adulterated meat? Is that the same elitist "escapism" that said *NO* to participation in the imperial destruction of Vietnam?[10]

Perhaps not surprisingly, a third volley was lobbed, signed by three members of the People's Warehouse, the distribution center coming under the control of the CO. Possibly more inflammatory than the first two missives, it began by dismissing the credibility of the previous writers.

> What Jeb [Phenix] and Emma [Evechild] did in responding to the Beanery paper was in effect to throw a nasty bourgeois-intellectual stone from the unsanitary cesspool of anti-communism. . . . Anyone who is acquainted with political revolutionary history cannot stand by and let someone like Jeb—who is a pseudo-intellectual anarchist—molest socialist history and its authors and contributors.

It refuted much of the second's pro-food analysis, in the end suggesting that anyone who did not explicitly support a revolution was complicit with the ruling class.

> Any time an organization or a person feels that strongly held principles must be compromised to reach the masses of workers, then there is no doubt that the organization or person is counter-revolutionary

and the strongly held principles are anti-working class. After all we are not making a revolution for a class clique.[11]

Looking back on these rhetorical battles, preserved in the archives of the Minnesota Historical Society, a double-sided sentiment becomes clear: many who interacted with the cooperative community felt the organizations had established themselves as viable and stable and that they had themselves become resources for achieving other ends.

The CO sought to reform the storefront operations by emphasizing cheaper rather than "natural" food. By appealing to a broader working-class base, it would then mobilize to destroy the larger capitalist economic structures. And though the CO could not directly dictate what the co-ops would sell, once it had control of the primary distribution organ, the People's Warehouse, it could absolutely influence what the co-ops were able to *buy*.

That is, the CO sought the support of co-op members and workers, but it also recognized the importance of the People's Warehouse (PW) in its efforts to transform the ideological orientations of the cooperative community. The PW was the largest and most important distributor to the storefront operations, as well as the most loosely organized. It had no articles of incorporation, and its ownership was unspecified. Recognizing this fragility, the cooperatives in the North Country organized an All Co-op Meeting in the spring of 1974 to form a Policy Review Board (PRB) composed of two members from each cooperative the PW served. The PRB failed to effectively direct its goals and orientations. In April 1975, following yet another fruitless meeting, members of the CO effectively seized control of the PW by walking into its offices and taking the checkbook and financial records. The CO had seized physical control of the People's Warehouse by May.

As mentioned earlier, Craig Cox's book *Storefront Revolution* describes the events of the Co-op Wars in much greater detail, and it is not my intent to duplicate his work here. Some of his accounts of this time period are riveting. Talking about the night the Co-op Organization took over the PW, Phil Baker said, "I was there Sunday night when the iron pipes were swung and the phones were ripped out and the doors were blocked. I was one of the ten who had been asked to stay at the Peoples' Warehouse overnight. 'Just in case,' it was said, 'they'd come in

*Figure 22.* When the Co-op Organization attempted to march on the Mill City Co-op—yet another corner store cooperative—on January 17, 1976, residents of the neighborhood (and certainly other area cooperators not sympathetic to their goals) converged to counter them. With the local news outlets showing up with cameras, and as the confrontations began to get more personal and physical, somebody called the law to help maintain order—a decision that was discussed and debated a great deal afterwards. Photographs by Pete Hohn for the *Minneapolis Tribune*; courtesy of the Minnesota Historical Society.

the middle of the night.' They did come, and they came with a military plan of action and with weapons."[12]

In the fall of 1975, those co-ops opposed to CO's views created a new distributing organization, the Distributing Alliance of Northcountry Cooperatives, whose working business name was DANCe. The warring distributors spent the next several months courting Twin Cities co-ops and West Coast suppliers, fighting their ideological war on an ironic battlefield: the capitalist marketplace. Both employed the powers of persuasion to convince individual storefronts to choose one over the other as its main supplier, but in January 1976 the tensions spilled into physical conflict. One cooperative leader claimed he was physically assaulted for resisting the entreaties of CO reformers and later found his truck destroyed by fire outside his apartment. When CO organizers attempted to physically take over the Mill City and Seward storefronts by seizing records and cash registers—in a strong-arm effort to convince the co-ops to use the People's Warehouse as their primary distributor—the conflict attracted the attentions of law enforcement and the media. After the police arrived and shut down the stores, the CO decried the turn to state authorities to resolve the conflict and refused to disavow its tactics to convince the co-ops to shut down DANCe.

Writing for the *Minneapolis Tribune*, reporter Linda Sanderson summarized the most recent events. For those unfamiliar with the cooperative community, a philosophical dispute centered on selling canned goods in a grocery and resulting in physical violence must have sounded very obtuse, perhaps confirming their worst fears of the counterculture:

> A philosophical split over how to govern people's food cooperatives culminated in confrontations between rival co-op factions last week in Minneapolis. A "stocking policy" difference has turned into a major political feud between the Co-op Organization (CO), a group favoring "cheap food for the working class," and several Minneapolis co-op members who contend that the organization is dictating co-op policy for political ends.
>
> Coordinators at Mill City Foods, 2552 Bloomington Av. S., and Seward Co-op, 2291 E. Franklin Av., plan to file charges today against several people whom they identified from two groups that allegedly entered and seized control of the two co-ops Friday. Pete Simmons, a coordinator at Mill City Foods, also has plans to sign a burglary

complaint against four Co-op Organization members who allegedly reentered Mill City Foods Friday night, violating police orders. Police arrested the four Friday night but have not yet charged them.

The weekend turmoil followed nine months of controversy between the two groups. Last May, organization members seized control of the People's Warehouse, formerly the main supplier for the co-ops, claiming that the food distributors were not serving the needs of the poor people. In September, an alternative warehouse was formed by co-op members who opposed the organization's "violent" tactics.

. . .

Both Seward and Mill City Foods hold monthly community meetings to decide objectives and what foods to sell. Organization members say this method of decision-making excludes many customers who cannot make monthly meetings and does not represent a true measurement of community needs.

"The CO believes that those working in the People's Warehouse can best decide what the community shoppers want while we say, 'Let the community decide,'" said Ellen Wersan, a Seward Co-op coordinator. Ms. Wersan said the People's Warehouse decided to order canned goods for the co-ops last fall and subsequently began "pushing" canned good without consulting the co-ops and the community.

Annie Young, an alliance coordinator, said the canned goods issue instigated by the People's Warehouse and the Co-op Organization, a group that has called itself Marxist-Leninist, represents the organization's attempt to "use the food co-ops as a vehicle for the revolution." The Alliance has not carried canned goods because it has "tried to steer clear of unhealthy foods," Ms. Young said. But, she added, the food distributer plans to begin ordering canned goods and sugar within the week.

"The poor people in the community want foods they can get elsewhere but at cheaper prices. If a co-op is truly to serve the community, it'd look like a 7–11 store with cheaper prices," said one organization member. "What happened Friday was necessary to get some co-op coordinators to listen to us. If violence occurred, it was necessary and it will be used again if needed," said Ms. Janssen.[13]

Only a few days later, after DANCe decided to formally incorporate with the state as a cooperative, unidentified assailants threw two Molotov cocktails through the front windows of the Bryant Central Co-op, and coordinators at Selby Community Foods in St. Paul found the storefront sprayed with the words "shit foods" and "commies." The word "Community" was obliterated by paint. As Craig Cox later reported,

> That evening, members of SAP Foods reversed an earlier decision to buy primarily from Peoples' Warehouse, voting 13 to 3 to buy wholesale items from the cheapest source available but giving preference to DANCe when the prices were the same. The switch in policy was attributed to the attacks at Seward and Mill City.[14]

The conflict played out over several more months, marked by nonviolent marches on various co-ops organized by CO and several heated meetings

'YOU CAN MOVE OUT, YOU ANTI-WORKING CLASS ELITIST HIPPIE! ME AND JERRY AND BOB ARE TAKING OVER!'

*Figure 23.* The celebrated editorial cartoonist Pete Wagner was working at the university's *Minnesota Daily* during the Co-op Wars. His cartoon (along with numerous newspaper articles) demonstrates how knowledge of "the Co-op Wars" extended beyond the cooperative community. Wagner was ironically pointing out how hippies were being cast as elitist and antiworking class as they were attempting to create an alternative consumer option resisting mainstream forces. Wagner later won the national Society of Professional Journalists award that year for his work at the *Daily.* Reprinted with the permission of the artist.

to discuss the issues, but by March 1976 the People's Warehouse had essentially bankrupted itself. In a second ironic twist, the questionable state of the People's Warehouse's legally constituted organizational form, which led to the uprising in the first place, was a major factor in its downfall. One of the final blows came when a restraining order kept CO leaders out of the warehouse until a Hennepin County court could decide who actually owned the business.

In April 1976, as the dispute over the legal ownership of the People's Warehouse started to make its way through the court system, the Policy Review Board obtained a restraining order barring the CO members from the distribution center. It was shut down by the end of the year.

## Challenging Power

Throughout this book, I have considered the activists involved in the 1970s cooperatives as members of a social movement. They wanted to use their smaller grocery stores as vehicles for social change. I am suggesting that they initially started with multiple missions and ideologies. As they became more established within the social fabric and the economic market, however, it became untenable to pursue all of these goals within the same organization. At the heart of the dispute between the Co-op Organization reformers and those who wanted to promote organic food—in the heated debates about stocking canned beans on their shelves—was a disagreement about what form of power the consumer cooperatives needed to challenge.

Building on the historical critiques of previous activists, these cooperators wanted to reform several aspects of contemporary society. By tapping into several concerns at the same time, they were (using Hayagreeva Rao's conceptual framework) capitalizing on "hot causes" to embark on "cool mobilization" projects to further their goals. The multiplicity of grievances, as is often the case with any social movement, focused on what was wrong with the status quo. These concerns centered on the ways capitalist enterprises received support from the state to create a food production and distribution system that did not serve the interests of the people.

After this network of cooperatives had been established, however, decisions about future tactics and strategies required a sharper focus on their primary objectives. In addition to pursuing social change, they also needed to establish a sound business model for the organizations to remain fiscally solvent. To better understand the underlying disputes among the different factions of these cooperative activists—to help explain why the Co-op Wars had to take place in order for these groups to solidify their standing as long-term social movement organizations—we can consider how they positioned their larger challenge to power in society. If we identify more clearly what types of power they resisted, it becomes much easier to see why they favored one course of action over another.

This perspective recognizes that social movements present challenges to power and authority. Power, however, can take many different forms. To properly understand how and why the cooperatives developed over time, it is important to first understand the different ways power can be exerted. In *Power: A Radical View*, the political scientist Steven Lukes describes three methods by which authority figures can coerce populations to comply with their values, orientations, and demands.

## First Dimension of Power

Lukes's first dimension of power embodies a familiar definition: the ability to force individuals to engage in actions against their desires, wills, or interests. This coercion might take the form of threatening or actually inflicting physical harm or imposing bodily restraint. As the state is the sole modern institution with the legal authority to engage in acts of violence, it naturally becomes the focus of attention in this view of power. For most of the twentieth century, social movements centered on citizenship rights—directly challenging the state, which has the sole discretion to grant them—or securing protections from the state against unfair treatment from institutions and organizations in civil society.

Resistance to this form of power formed the basis for early studies of populist collective behavior. The sociologist Charles Tilly suggested we recognize social movements by their explicit and public activities agitating against established governments and by the participants' attempts to gain standing and recognition in order to participate fully in civil and political life. He characterized social movements as "a distinctive form of contentious politics—contentious in the sense that social movements involve collective making of claims that, if realized, would conflict with someone else's interests, politics in the sense that governments of one sort or another figure somehow in the claim making." The "classic" social movements that attracted the attention of Tilly and his predecessors focused primarily on either disenfranchisement or the working conditions of laborers, the two principle causes of major political upheavals in modern societies. Indeed, these dual concerns—full citizenship and economic justice—dominated much of the activist landscape up to and continuing through the 1960s, forming what we might consider the core of social movement collective actions in the civil rights era.[15]

Lukes associated his first dimension of power with situations in which attempts to win advantages were explicit and overt. He summarized this as "a focus on *behavior* in the making of *decisions* on *issues* in which there is an observable *conflict* of (subjective) *interests*." In this way, he provides a useful description of the type of power wielded by the state when it denies basic rights of citizenship or participation in labor markets. This distinction becomes even more apparent (and illuminating) when we consider his second dimension of power: setting the agenda for making critical decisions that will affect others.[16]

## Second Dimension of Power

This second dimension addresses the power to control the topics discussed by authority figures or to raise issues in the political process. The ability to determine what topics will be discussed and which options will be considered to resolve a problem (as well as which topics will not be discussed and which options will not be considered) can essentially stack the deck so that any chosen course of action will benefit an aristocracy over the interests of the underprivileged. Observers of any congressional session in the past dozen years or so can certainly attest to the majority parties' power to determine which bills to bring to the chamber floor for debate, effectively shutting out those issues they prefer to leave untouched.

Introducing this conception of power to the study of social movements allows us to interpret the changing focus of activist groups in the aftermath of the civil rights era. Most social movement activities in the late twentieth century shifted from campaigns to secure rights and privileges for marginalized status groups—LGBTQ+ and immigrants remain two major exceptions—to raising specific issues and pursuing specific policies. Few would argue, of course, that African Americans or women (to name just two prominent social categories) have truly secured equality in our society, but the major remaining areas of contention do not challenge the state so much as attempt to force it to live up to its ideals. The problem isn't so much a lack of laws banning discrimination as it is ensuring that stated rights are realities in practice. As marginalized groups consistently and successfully removed state-supported institutional barriers to fair employment and housing, the focus of collective actions has turned toward the *enforcement* of legislation regarding newly won rights and toward continued efforts to change the cultural values that had given rise to structural inequalities in the first place (that is, to secure the legitimacy of the now politically established rights). Most contemporary social movements pursue one of two goals. First, they might struggle to maintain the gains won in previous campaigns and expand them to more areas of state and civil society—as seen with the activities protesting proposed policy changes with periodic power shifts in partisan politics. Movements might also attempt to establish themselves as moral arbiters, addressing perceived social problems that go beyond a collection of personal grievances and speak to a higher set of social values and ideologies.

These projects include promoting policies that emphasize environmental protections, decrease or eliminate nuclear arsenals, end participation in armed conflicts abroad, or promote social and economic justice for citizens in underdeveloped nations. In each case, the pool of potential beneficiaries extends well beyond the individual activists pushing for these issues to be considered by their state authorities. In some cases, the actions would not provide any *direct* benefit to the activists at all. So their grievances stem not from personal deprivations or limitations but from personal moral codes and values ignored by the powerful. It is their very *lack* of personal grievances that gives such activists the ability to devote their time and energy to such causes: the general rise of living standards throughout the twentieth century helped shift social movement activity away from citizenship and economic issues and toward ideological causes.

## Third Dimension of Power

Lukes's first and second dimensions of power speak to the ability of authorities either to enforce compliance with their dictates against an individual's self-interest or to refuse to allow consideration of wants and needs expressed by an individual. In both of these conceptions of power, cultural change takes place in a structural context. Therefore, Lukes suggests a third dimension of power: the ability to instill values in individuals even when those values might contradict their self-interest. He asks rhetorically, "Indeed, is it not the supreme exercise of power to get another or others to have the desires you want them to have— that is, to secure their compliance by controlling their thoughts and desires?" This points to a very different type of social movement activity, one that focuses on cultural values. Certainly, many movements in the late twentieth century focused on issues of empowerment and raising collective consciousness.[17]

I contend that collective movements that resist this third dimension of power—those that seek to uncover and counter the internalized values of an individual against his or her self-interest—constitute a fundamentally different type of social movement activity. Because they seek to provide a counterforce to socialized values imbued by the larger culture, they do not directly challenge larger institutional structures; there is no true antagonist that can serve to deny (or grant) legitimacy to stated grievances. This third type of power represents, then, the most deeply embedded form of institutional power. Groups that challenge it must address cultural issues rather than structural ones, ideology more than a specific set of power arrangements. They aim to reform the individual, rather than the state or elements of civil society.

Empowering individuals, however, is fundamentally different from resisting power that constricts one's behavior in more overt and identifiable ways. Individuals might resist their socialization in an area as fundamental as the preference structures that dictate their food choices, but the refusal to accept these norms and values differs significantly from the demand to have access to adequate food supplies from social structures that have systematically denied that access. Rejecting internalized preference structures does directly involve posing a threat to authority or taking a personal risk in resistance by putting oneself in harm's way. A movement challenging this third dimension of power does not attempt to change the institutions of state or civil society so much as to shake off their effects and point individuals toward a new path.

As market organizations promoting a social movement, what types of power did cooperatives resist? Their primary hurdle involved convincing the larger public to abandon its reliance on large, faceless corporations that made, processed, distributed, and sold food to an unquestioning consumer body. The conveniences offered in the modern grocery market were, activists believed, causing hidden damage to both agricultural lands and human bodies. To resist these products would mean adopting a different perspective and value system, to actively oppose the larger culture that had already been internalized. "Question Authority" can be interpreted as "question what you have implicitly accepted as normal and good." As a distinct category of social movement activity, we can perhaps help to explain cooperatives' resilience even when the "movement" makes but incremental steps toward its larger goals. Rather than evaluate co-ops on their effectiveness at transforming societies, we might look instead at how well they challenge individuals to become intentional consumers.

This not only helps us conceptualize cooperatives within the larger realm of social movement activists; it allows us to better understand the conflicts that resulted in the Co-op Wars. To review: as social movement organizations, they might rally individuals to challenge larger institutions and pursue a particular project of social change, but this would appear to conflict with their desire to coexist alongside other retailers in a competitive capitalist market. They might also have developed during an important era of social movement activity and adopted some of the trappings of protest campaigns, but fundamental differences can help explain why they have survived more than four decades when most of their activist organizational brethren have long disappeared. As Rao might explain, they rely on the attraction of hot causes that can build ideological passions, but they survive through the tactic of cool mobilization. The act of buying groceries might be political but need not be accompanied by bombast.

As market retailers, cooperatives must emphasize the purchase of particular products they support rather than simply boycott those they do not. Their physical location is intimately tied to their community, and they aim to establish themselves as certifiers of value-added products. Most important, they eschew the motive of profit maximization, lending legitimacy to their claims as arbiters of ethical consumption. Because they participate in multiple institutional realms, cooperatives must abide by different and competing rationalities. While they must operate their business soundly in order to generate internal sustainability, they must also explicitly remain true to the values they uphold and demonstrate a commitment to the external sustainability that underlies their mission.

## Addressing Power, Hot Causes, and Cool Mobilization

The CO faction advocating for the cooperatives to challenge larger institutions of society failed to take hold because it was attempting to challenge the first dimension of power, characterized by raw oppression or the denial of basic human rights to specific groups through institutional domination. Most of the countercultural activists didn't see evidence of that in the mainstream grocery market, as individuals had the freedom to grow or purchase food products in any way they pleased. (While there was a lot of talk about anti-imperialist ideologies, those suggesting that the co-ops should be in the vanguard of the coming revolution rarely spoke in specific terms about who was being systematically excluded or what forms their oppression took. For most, it appears that the cooperative was simply a convenient tool for helping instigate and possibly supply the coming revolution.)

I contend that the Co-op Wars took place because many of these activists saw their greatest mission in challenging the third form of power: internalized preferences that derived from culture rather than structure. These early co-ops formed in order to sell a product that threatened existing social orders, and they could survive only if they convinced enough people to become conscious consumers, if they could address the larger cultural values that manifested themselves in people's purchasing decisions. It was going to be a difficult proposition to sell.

Since the end of World War II, when the technological prowess of American engineering was coupled with agricultural production and distribution, every advance has been characterized as progress, an improvement in both convenience and efficiency. Large supermarkets promised fewer shopping trips (one could now visit the baker and a butcher at the same time). Food preservation technology—an essential component of feeding millions of soldiers stationed abroad for several years—was now available to all through frozen and canned products. The conversion of these wartime technologies made all of these foods appear to be advances in modern living, luxuries available to the common family. While they

are often derided now, at the time they were seen as conveniences leading to a higher quality of life. Why purchase fresh, perishable vegetables
when you could buy them weeks in advance and pull them out of the
freezer as needed? Why soak beans overnight when you could have them
in an instant with a can opener? All of this was made possible through
packaging and processing, and as discrete food products became homogenized commodities grown, distributed, marketed, and sold on larger and
larger scales, Americans were induced to sacrifice taste, health, and even
safety in their daily consumption.

It has become clearer that the first period of cooperative formation fed off of the antiestablishment fervor best characterized by the
anti-Vietnam protests of the era. Proposing an economic structure that
defied one of the basic principles of the capitalist marketplace—the
maximization of profit—the early new-wave cooperators in Minnesota
succeeded quite well in creating a nascent organizational infrastructure
that supported the daily maintenance of storefront operations in a highly
competitive market. The hot cause, however, was actually a constellation
of grievances defined more by what their holders *opposed* than by what
they promoted. The activists of this period were not only against the
war and the increasing industrialization of agriculture; they also decried
a culture that denigrated the working class, promoted the homogeniza-
tion of both values and food products, and ostracized those who did not
conform to prevailing norms.

Organic food provided an opportunity to change all of that. The
cooperative had the ability to challenge the power of this mercantile and
culinary culture, but it was going to require a long-term commitment
to convince others to forgo some of the conveniences of modern society
in order to lead what the activists believed was a richer, healthier life.
Organic food, as ill defined as the concept may have been in the early
years, cost more and was more difficult to procure and prepare. Still, it
represented a hot cause that one could promote rather than oppose.

In the end, the attempts to challenge two different types of power—
the agendas of mainstream society and the internalized culture of its
members—became too difficult to pursue within the same movement
organization. The Co-op Wars forced many activists to state more
clearly what they were actually *for*—to make a decision, for instance,
about whether the prevailing guidelines of the cooperative grocery store

should be to work toward greater social change at a higher level of social structure or to promote the communal pursuit of healthier lifestyles among individual workers and patrons. In this case, a can of Campbell's soup was an appropriate though conflicting icon: did it represent simple, cheap food for the masses or a hermetically sealed distillation of preservatives designed to further remove individuals from a stronger connection to their bodies and the land? Was it a tool of the revolution or a symbol of its suppression?

The Co-op Wars didn't destroy the cooperative movement in the Twin Cities or stop its advancement in greater Minnesota. One could argue that by bringing underlying tensions out in the open, the bitter conflict exposed organizational fault lines and allowed activists to address them to maintain the storefront operations once the initial period of entrepreneurial enthusiasm had passed. In large part, the Co-op Wars episode involved a further clarification of what running a cooperative entailed. Although the CO reformers failed to turn Minnesota's cooperatives into a stronger political force able to destroy the larger capitalistic economic system, the organizations did not lose their ideological focus. In fact, the resolution represented a sort of return to form. From its outset, the movement sought to create an alternative framework within the current market system, to channel the resources of potential members toward the project of healthier food consumption and more sustainable agricultural production. For a period, that mission was contested, but it prevailed.

The power perspective, focusing on how activists challenged the internalized culture of society and encouraged people to be more conscious about their food consumption, helps to explain the longevity of the cooperative grocery store selling organic food. Changing culture takes a long time, and you're never really sure when you're done. If people continue to shop at these stores, buying their alternative products, perhaps some values have fundamentally shifted.

While many took some time to develop that sense of cool mobilization described by Rao—and had to walk through fire a few times to get there—they eventually came to consistently brand and market themselves as "natural foods co-ops." After establishing the sale of "pure" food as its primary aim, Minnesota consumer cooperatives continued to develop both market infrastructures and organizational identities that would help them survive into the twenty-first century. The ultimate resolution in favor of the "food faction" stabilized this community by providing its members with a clearer focus that enabled a coherent mobilization of their resources in the following years and decades. By the end of the 1970s, the state had more new-wave co-ops than any in the nation, and it retains this status. Even though the Marxist faction (the Cooperative Organization) introduced a contentious and occasionally violent dispute, by forcing a choice they ultimately gave those who remained a clearer roadmap toward survival and expansion.

# 5

---

# DEVELOPING ORGANIC MARKET
# INFRASTRUCTURES

THE COOPERATIVES THAT FORMED in the early 1970s had a strong political orientation, opened in neighborhoods characterized by strong opposition to the Vietnam War, and adopted an antiestablishment stance. They were confident in their mission and their ideology, but they had yet to establish a secure footing in the retail landscape.

The cooperatives' new distribution center, DANCe, was able to lighten the loss of the People's Warehouse, but the Co-op Wars clearly demonstrated how fragile their distribution network was. Thus, perhaps the most important result of this conflict was the creation of the All Cooperating Assembly (ACA), a quasi-federation of co-ops that sought to increase coordination, education, and outreach beyond those in food retailing. Created in the spring of 1975 at the early stages of the People's Warehouse and Co-op Organizations crisis, ACA sought to divorce political issues from the distributing warehouses and to address a division of labor across members of the organizational field. The ACA was rife with its own conflicts and perennially underfunded during its eight-year tenure, but it helped expand the field and promote continued interactions across the membership.

## New-Wave Cooperative Growth after 1975

Even prior to the 1970s, Minnesota was no stranger to the cooperative model of organization. Soon after the Union admitted the state in 1858, this region played host to a number of players in the cooperative movement. Early in its history, Minnesota's rural population began experimenting with cooperative organization models, from consumer cooperatives based on the New England Protective Union to farmer organizations such as the National Grange. In 1870 Minnesota passed one of the earliest state laws affirming the legal status of cooperative associations, providing guidelines for incorporation and ensuring that these bodies could not be taken over by a minority interest. As the data from Florence Parker's extensive Bureau of Labor Statistics bulletins demonstrate, Minnesota had some of the highest levels of cooperative formation in the early and mid-twentieth century.

The first phase of new-wave cooperative development—connecting this type of organization to natural/organic food products—witnessed a rapid rise in the number of these stores, primarily in urban areas with strong liberal politics. This network of organizations did not disappear following the Co-op Wars; in fact, it was supplemented by the emergence of many new ones. The primary feature evident in Figure 18, demonstrating the rise of cooperatives in the state from 1970 to 2010, is the apparent stability of this population of organizations. A closer examination of the founding years, however, shows that cooperatives did not crop up uniformly throughout the state. Instead, the pattern of formation evolved during these two distinct phases of the 1970s. In the second half of the decade, most of the growth took place in much

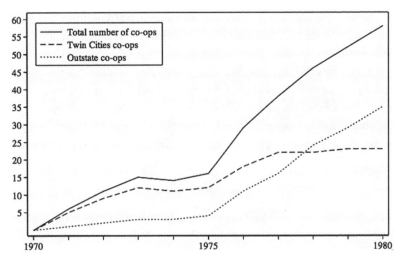

*Figure 24.* Minnesota new-wave cooperative grocery stores, 1970–1980.

smaller cities in the "outstate" areas; by 1978, this subset of organizations outnumbered those in the Twin Cities.

Most of the principle battles in the Co-op Wars took place in the Twin Cities, where, until 1975, most of the new-wave grocery cooperatives were located. The People's Warehouse primarily served those stores. Following the tentative resolution of these conflicts in 1976—with the new distributing organization DANCe and the creation of the All Cooperating Assembly—thirty-six new grocery cooperatives opened in Minnesota. All but seven formed in communities much smaller than the Twin Cities.

The cooperative form had never been restricted to this one metropolitan area. Recall that, in the north of the state, Duluth's Whole Foods Co-op had opened its doors in August 1971, and in the south, along the banks of the Mississippi River, Famine Foods had started operations in Winona in 1972. Still, most of the outstate cooperatives open by the end of the decade did not take form until after the Co-op Wars in the

*Figure 25.* In 1979, after operating for five years in a garden apartment, the Wedge Co-op prepared to open its first true storefront operation on Lyndale Avenue in Minneapolis. The Wedge would eventually become one of the larger cooperatives in the Twin Cities, consolidating with Linden Hills Co-op and creating its own wholesaling distributor to serve other co-ops in the state. Courtesy of the Minnesota Historical Society; unknown photographer.

Twin Cities and the Vietnam War abroad had come to a close. As each new storefront opened, it expanded the state's cooperative population in numeric and geographic terms, both making use of the existing distribution networks and helping to expand their reach.

One might have expected this next wave to take hold in the remaining pockets of liberal communities surrounded by conservative neighbors, as had been the case earlier in the decade. The majority, though, did not display the same political orientations as their early Twin Cities progenitors. Shared political orientations do not help explain why these new cooperatives formed in some cities but not others.

The political environments of cooperatives formed between 1976 and 1980 are presented in Table 6. These cooperatives did not exist in areas demonstrating the same pattern of partisanship as the earlier ones in the Twin Cities. They often were located in areas that showed *less* support for George McGovern's candidacy than the larger county. For example, the Rainbow Food Co-op opened in October 1979 in the town of Blue Earth, 135 miles southwest of the Twin Cities. Though McGovern had received only 26.2 percent of the 2,190 ballots cast in Blue Earth, in the greater Faribault County results he had received 33 percent of 10,447 votes. Blue Earth certainly did not represent a liberal bastion near the southern border of the state. Of the thirty-six new cooperative organizations that opened after January 1976, twenty-one were in communities that had given *less* support to McGovern than the surrounding county.

It is much more difficult to craft a compelling narrative tying a liberal-leaning community to cooperative formations in this second half of the decade. Is it possible to explain why this organizational form spread to some areas of Minnesota rather than others? The first period of cooperative development, from 1971 to 1975, was infused with anti-imperialist sentiment, and creators were innovating (even improvising) the organizational form. The co-op structure represented an alternative to mainstream capitalist enterprises, and their founders and members openly debated what roles these organizations could and should play in raising class-consciousness. The three principal centers of activity—the Twin Cities, Duluth, and Winona—all had four-year colleges, and many of the activists participated in anti–Vietnam War demonstrations. Though the Co-op Wars did not expel political activists from the ranks of the cooperative memberships, those who remained expressed concerns with maintaining the organizations for their own sakes, rather than hoping to use them for more explicitly political/revolutionary ends.

During the second wave of cooperative formation, beginning in 1976, individuals who were more pragmatic and dedicated to issues of food production and consumption took the initiative. The preexisting cooperative community provided organizational models that allowed the newly formed food co-ops to be less affected by local circumstances; the diffusion across the state must be attributed at least in part to the legitimization of that form.

To analyze Minnesota cooperatives' spread, then, we must examine local circumstances beyond political leanings. What were the structural and demographic features of the communities that did and did not witness the formation of cooperatives? In addition to population and density of residents per square mile, this analysis should also consider educational attainment, income/wealth differentials, and poverty levels. The presence of institutions of higher learning—more precisely, the residency patterns of current and former students drawn to them—was strongly associated with the formation of co-ops in the earlier period, so we will take those into account as well. Finally, proximity to the earlier established cooperative centers of the Twin Cities, Duluth, and Winona should be considered as possible explanatory variables, since they offered the possibility of organizational assistance, access to a distribution infrastructure, and constituencies accustomed to cooperatives who might be likely to support them.

It turns out that this last factor—measured by the presence of any type of consumer cooperative in the 1940s—is the best predictor of the formation of a cooperative grocery store after 1975. Many rural cities developed cooperative organizations between the 1920s and the 1940s. The fact that many of these areas were settled by Scandinavians (who were very familiar with this economic model from their native lands) was undoubtedly one factor that contributed to this phenomenon. And the prior presence of these earlier co-ops had a strong impact on the likelihood that a new-wave version would develop decades later. If some form of a consumers' society had formed previously in a city—even if it had long since disbanded—the city was nineteen times more likely than a community without such a history to play host to a new-wave cooperative in the mid- to late 1970s. It is possible that prior experience with

**Table 6.** Relative 1972 McGovern Support Surrounding Co-Ops Formed 1976–80

| Year formed/cooperative name | City | Votes (%) | Ward/county differential (%) |
|---|---|---|---|
| **1976** | | | |
| Bryant Central | Minneapolis | 69.5 | 15.1 |
| Community Food Store | Mankato | 47.3 | 3.3 |
| Cook County Whole Foods Co-op | Grand Marais | 35.3 | -4.4 |
| Cove Whole Food Co-op | Grand Rapids | 40.1 | -10.9 |
| Good Earth Food Co-op | St. Cloud | 52.2 | 6.4 |
| Heartland Foods | Little Falls | 46.5 | -1 |
| Merri-Grove Co-op | St. Paul | 57.3 | 6.4 |
| Wintergreen Food Co-op | Albert Lea | 42.2 | 1.1 |
| *Average McGovern support* | | *48.8* | *2.0* |
| **1977** | | | |
| Anoka Food Co-op | Anoka | 38.1 | -7.3 |
| Family Food Co-op | Marshall | 46.3 | -0.4 |
| Harmony Food Co-op | Bemidji | 45.6 | 0.9 |
| Mille Lacs Area Food Co-op | Isle | 36.5 | -4.5 |
| Valley Foods Co-op | Stillwater | 40.2 | -3.9 |
| Valley Natural Foods Co-op | Burnsville | 32 | -3.8 |
| *Average McGovern support* | | *39.8* | *-3.2* |
| **1978** | | | |
| Countryside Co-op | Hackensack | 38.1 | -0.5 |
| Everybody's Healthfood Market | Long Prairie | 36.2 | -4.9 |
| Good Foods Store | Lengby | 46 | 0.9 |
| Great River Co-op | Big Lake | 47 | 0.8 |
| Kettle River Trading Post Co-op | Sandstone | 37.9 | -8.1 |
| Spiral Food Co-op | Hastings | 49.7 | 1.6 |
| St. Luke Community Co-op | Wayzata | 30.7 | -6.4 |
| Whole Valley Food Co-op | Red Wing | 37.3 | 3.2 |
| *Average McGovern support* | | *40.4* | *-1.7* |
| **1979** | | | |
| City Center Market | Cambridge | 53.5 | 6.5 |
| Crow Wing Food Co-op | Brainerd | 42.1 | -1.3 |
| Harvest Food Co-op | Owatonna | 30.9 | -2.1 |
| Natural Harvest Food Co-op | Virginia | 56.7 | -0.7 |

| | | | |
|---|---|---|---|
| Rainbow Food Co-op | Blue Earth | 26.2 | -7.5 |
| Southeast Co-op | Minneapolis | 75.5 | 21.1 |
| St. Peter Food Co-op & Deli | St. Peter | 43.9 | 2.5 |
| Wholesome Harvest | Park Rapids | 37.6 | 0.1 |
| *Average McGovern support* | | *45.8* | *2.3* |
| **1980** | | | |
| Buffalo Family Foods | Buffalo | 38.7 | -5.3 |
| Good Food Buyers | Montevideo | 45.5 | -1.5 |
| Kandi Cupboard | Willmar | 43.9 | -5.2 |
| Natural Foods Co-op / Market | Litchfield | 35.4 | -3.9 |
| Plum Creek Food Co-op | Windom | 42.1 | 5 |
| Prairie Foods | Northfield | 48.3 | 3 |
| *Average McGovern support* | | *42.3* | *-1.3* |

*Note:* "Ward/county differential" represents the difference between the percentage of votes received by McGovern in the co-op's city and the percentage he received in the entire county.

this organizational form helped legitimate it. Perhaps that "cooperative spirit" referred to by Florence Parker in her BLS bulletins still lingered in the municipality's ethos.[1]

These patterns suggest three conclusions. First, the formation of cooperatives after 1976 did not depend on prevailing community political attitudes to the same extent as in the earlier period. This might be true because most of the areas characterized by politically active liberal ideologies had been exhausted during the first phase, but the cultural dynamics surrounding cooperatives had also changed. Given that cooperative organizations had been present in the state throughout the twentieth century and had actually been a primarily *rural* phenomenon prior to the 1970s, this suggests that the organizational model of the new-wave cooperative had already achieved some legitimacy independent of its earlier countercultural associations.

Second, the new-wave cooperative never did represent a wholly urban phenomenon. Cooperative storefronts did not seem to require cities with higher populations or areas of population density; the cooperative still had relevance to those in smaller communities. Because agricultural cooperatives remained strong throughout the twentieth century, a new-wave cooperative might not have seemed as novel an idea in a rural area in the 1920s as it did in Minneapolis even in the 1960s. During the 1970s, cooperative organizations formed in every region of Minnesota. From 1970 to 2010, they opened storefronts in forty-two of Minnesota's eighty-seven counties, and as early as 1980 a hiker could start from the southern border with Iowa and find a co-op in every county until she reached Canada. Starting in Wisconsin, she could make it nearly to South Dakota, so long as she stocked up in Kandiyohi County's Kandi Cupboard before the sixty-two-mile trek through co-op-free Chippewa County, finally reaching the Western Prairie Food Co-op in Lac Qui Parle County, on the state's western border.

Finally, the diffusion of cooperatives did not take place randomly throughout the state; rather, most new members entered this field near the earlier organizations that had already begun to create organizational infrastructures that facilitated their daily maintenance. In addition to the distribution networks, the cooperatives collectively sought to increase their presence in the state with an outreach program. In particular, the newly formed All Cooperating Assembly, created in the aftermath of the Co-op Wars, recruited individuals to act as regional advisers, providing them with meager resources, including some funds for travel expenses. As Gutknecht explained, the ACA continued the push for a large number of independently run cooperatives that had been present from the beginning of the 1970s. The fights were fierce, but the impetus for creating more co-ops won the day:

> Beginning in 1975, there was an All Cooperating Assembly which had a more [of an] education function, which again drew people to the city but also went out to a lot of places to help people organize co-ops. . . . Kris Olsen [the first head of the ACA], among other people, did a lot of traveling throughout the region to help overcome isolation and to help people start new co-ops. It got more active, more busy as the '70s went on. The North Country Development Fund was launched as well to help with the financing and development of new co-ops.

Many of these post–Co-op War organizations emphasized the local desire for and the unavailability of natural foods as their primary raison d'être, such as the St. Peter Co-op. Located in one of the several towns outside the Twin Cities that hosted a small higher education institution (in this case, the Lutheran Gustavus Adolphus College), this cooperative formed in 1979. Ross Gersten, a volunteer coordinator, explained in a 1987 *Cooperative Grocer* profile, "Initially, people came together in this co-op out of their interest in nutritional foods and to find a way to provide the community with an alternative to pre-packaged, chemically-laced products commonly found in mainstream stores." Though the cooperative movement focused on the politics of food, it now made a concerted attempt to avoid alienating anyone in smaller towns that, like so many others, had displayed more support for Nixon than McGovern in the 1972 election:

> We do everything possible to bring as many people as we can into the store and do nothing to turn people away. The co-op makes a concerted effort to keep its prices competitive; to maintain a clean store and friendly environment; *to refrain from endorsing political stands or candidates of any kind*; and to maintaining a commitment to whole and nutritious foods, while not automatically excluding products like white sugar, white flour and chocolate from an ever-growing and everchanging inventory. The co-op has also chosen to maintain a high visibility within the community, participating in many civic functions and Chamber of Commerce-sponsored events.[2]

The St. Peter Co-op's members and leaders worked to create an image as an inclusive, supportive business member of the community rather than a challenge to existing economic and social structures.

Cooperatives in these smaller towns generally operated in local environments vastly different from those of their urban counterparts. The small community of Hackensack (1970 population 285) is in the heart of Minnesota's "lake country," an area with a long-standing tourist economy, with 127 lakes within a ten-mile radius of the town. Countryside Co-op had started as a buying club in nearby Walker, Minnesota, and moved to its own storefront after merchants pressured the Army Reserve center that had been lending the group space for its operations. "Affordability and availability were the keys to making the decision to start the new venture in an old grocery store in Hackensack," according to the retail representative of the co-op's major supplier.

A 1985 profile in *Cooperative Grocer* reported that Countryside had acquired 743 members and averaged more than $1,000 in daily sales. A description of its offerings indicates how far removed it was from the food-issue disputes that had consumed its neighbors to the south:

The selection of products at Countryside reminds one of the "staples" for sale in an old-fashioned country store: juices, canned goods, nuts, fruits, grains, baking supplies, honey, cheeses, sweeteners, condiments, spices, beans and prepackaged items. Because the store is only open on Wednesdays and Saturdays, it can't carry highly perishable products such as produce, baked goods and milk. Their main supplier is Common Health Warehouse Cooperative in Superior, Wisconsin. Local honey and wild rice come from the only two other suppliers.

Though the profile made no mention of natural or organic products, these were certainly one major focus of the primary distributor. We can also note the continued emphasis on local provisioning, a recurring theme across many of these new-wave cooperatives.

Several of these newer outstate stores gave direct credit to the community of cooperatives and the outreach/extension resources they had created. When this population reached a critical mass, a process of institutional isomorphism began to settle in. It had become easier to open a co-op because there were many existing models for what one could look like and how it should behave. As the Spiral Food Co-op in Hastings prepared to open thirty miles south of the Twin Cities, its leaders claimed:

> Organizing the co-op has gone much more smoothly than any of us anticipated. This may be due to the diligence of the board and the guidance received from ACA. In fact, we recognize that all of the co-ops before us have made it easier to put this one together. The Stillwater Co-op was a big help to us in the beginning, and our by-laws have an uncanny resemblance to those of Seward Co-op, and we have called all over to find out details about equipment, food, scheduling and laws.[3]

When these cooperatives mention the role that the ACA played in helping them get off the ground, they generally mean the efforts of Kris Olsen, its only paid member. Olsen devoted himself to outreach and to spreading the gospel of cooperatives across the region. He helped many groups make the transformation from pre-order buying clubs to full-scale storefront operations between 1976 and 1979, until the board of the ACA directed him to spend more effort on education among the existing organizations.

This second wave of cooperative organization came to an end in 1981. The Good Food Co-op in Rochester became the last new storefront to open in that decade. For the next twelve years, most of the cooperatives just struggled to stay alive in a rapidly changing political and cultural climate.

The resolution of the Co-op Wars in favor of those promoting food purity and sustainable agricultural practices came at a propitious time. Associating new-wave cooperatives with natural and organic food helped provide a unique, consistent identity. Perhaps more important, it helped establish these stores as the *arbiters* of natural and organic during a period of regulatory and cultural uncertainty.

Throughout this book, I have focused on the population of new-wave cooperatives rather than on individual organizations. Though each particular collective has its own idiosyncratic history of challenges and triumphs, heartaches, and resolutions, none of them operated in isolation, ignorant of its larger institutional environment. Most social-scientific analyses of new-wave cooperatives took place in the 1980s. Those tended to consider co-ops as singular organizations, autonomous actors struggling imperfectly to implement principles of participatory democracy. Explanations of their rise (and, very often, their fall) looked inward, to the characteristics of the bounded group and to the motivations of individuals to join or contribute resources for its maintenance.

I have demonstrated, instead, that from their earliest days, new-wave cooperatives have acted collectively as a community of organizations to further their individual and collective goals. This best explains how so many have survived to the present as well as how they more effectively pursued larger projects of social change. In particular, I point to how cooperatives put into practice one of the founding principles of the Rochdale Pioneers: cooperation among cooperatives.

The remainder of this chapter explores how new-wave cooperatives established themselves as the recognized leading purveyors of organic food in the 1970s. It first describes the environment of regulatory uncertainty in this period, then looks at the distribution networks created to help form the structural infrastructure of the organic food industry, and finally considers how cooperatives moved beyond their initial status as minimalist organizations.

## Filling a Market Void in the Organic Food Industry

From the 1950s through the 1970s, claims and counterclaims about food safety related to food additives and pesticide use helped propel the rise of organic food sales. As late as 1974, the USDA's annual *Yearbook of Agriculture* explained, "Different people have different reasons for choosing to eat organic, natural, and health food." It did not, however, seem to give these reasons much credence:

> Still others are bored or dissatisfied with their way of life and go to extremes in focusing on their food as a means to a new and better life style. A number of young people, especially, have focused on different food ways as one means of revolting against established patterns of culture, the capitalist system, waste of natural resources, and contamination of the environment.[4]

Neither the larger agricultural business community nor the federal government was very interested in granting this new market niche of organic food any legitimacy. Together, they helped create a void in the market—in terms of production, distribution, marketing, sales, and oversight—into which creative entrepreneurs would step to satisfy consumers' desires. Enter the new-wave cooperative store.

Throughout the Co-op Wars, few of the issues being debated actually affected the goods offered by the distributing warehouses. As one cooperator opposed to the CO wrote during the 1975 exchange of typewritten and mimeographed manifestos,

> The contradiction in the co-op struggle has been described as a struggle between canned foods and brown rice. Perhaps this description more than any other goes to the heart of the matter. Here at last we have a material basis for discussion. *Rhetoric and accusations aside, the only concrete changes in the People's Warehouse has been their change in stocking canned goods.*[5]

Though the writer then somewhat hyperbolically referenced the work of Mao Zedong, in describing "canned food and ketchup as the rising force defeating brown rice, anarchists and community-control," he captured the essence of the dispute rather well. The methods by which the reformers attempted to raise their concerns had everything to do with the limited nodes of supply within the natural and organic food industry.

In 1971, a *Washington Post* article by Hank Burchard, "The Search for the Great Puny Potato," described the challenges of finding reputable organic food:

> There are growing numbers of suspicious shoppers in the Washington area who are on the lookout for spotty oranges, wormy apples, dirty carrots and puny potatoes. When they find such items they buy them, at premium prices, and take them home. These shoppers range from longhaired self-styled "freaks" to close-cropped conservatives. What they have in common is the belief that most of the food sold in this country is unfit for human consumption. So they pass up the more luscious-looking food sold at supermarkets and buy from stores in the city and suburbs that advertise organic foods. The term is supposed to mean food that is grown, processed and packed without the use of artificial fertilizers, pesticides, preservatives or other additives.
>
> . . .
>
> Not only do organic food buyers pay more, their only assurance that the products are genuinely organic is the word of the store owner, who in turn must rely on a chain of trust that extends back to the original producer. All but one of the three dozen local organic merchants interviewed by *The Washington Post* said they could not be certain all their merchandise is truly organic, and most said they favor adoption of federal standards and regulations governing production and sale. Shoppers in organic stores will find labels that range from a simple, unsupported statement that the product is organic to exhaustively detailed accounts of where, when, how and by whom the product was produced—along with an invitation to drop in for a tour of the farm.[6]

The scenes and the uncertainties described by Burchard aptly characterize the chaotic yet impassioned organic landscape of the 1970s. The Minnesota cooperatives were uniquely positioned to take advantage of this market disarray because they were willing to work collectively in order to create a sense of order in the procurement and distribution of this emerging commodity.

In this book I have made several references to Hayagreeva Rao's 2009 work, *Market Rebels: How Activists Make or Break Radical Innovations*, in particular his concepts of "hot causes" and "cool mobilization." By this point, the hot causes that began to coalesce in the late '60s and early '70s should seem quite obvious: healthier food, environmental and agricultural sustainability, and freedom from control of corporate business structures all provided motivations for countercultural activists to get involved in consumer cooperatives. Rao's concept of "cool mobilization," first described in chapter 2, makes more sense in light of the accounts provided by these activists as they struggled to implement their ideologies and visions through concrete organizations. Rao writes:

> The key in cool mobilization is to engage audiences through collective experiences that generate *communities of feeling*, in which audience members don't just have their emotions aroused but encounter what literary critic Raymond Williams has called *social experiences in solution*, where participants actively *live* meanings and values associated with a social movement.[7]

The key terms here include "communities" and "experiences." When cooperative activists describe their work, they tend to refer repeatedly to shared values and collective action, both of which extend well beyond the boundaries of their individual operation.

This came across most vividly during interviews in which respondents were asked to describe their relationships with other businesses. Allan Malkis, who spent several years at the Southeast Co-op, provided a typical response:

> We'd say, "Hey, our freezer broke, who do we call? Who's a good maintenance person?" So there was a guy that all the co-ops used to do that type of work. I think his name is John O. So information like that would get passed around. There were times when we'd approach other co-ops for loans when we were at Southeast when we were running out of money. There were times when we'd ask our distributors to carry us for a while so we could put ourselves back on our feet. . . . There was a sense that nobody wanted to see any of the co-ops go under.

In Winona, Michael Doyle described how this spirit went beyond helping other cooperatives:

> MD: I have a poster in my collection of a farmers' market we started in 1976, because we were aware of the fact that we wanted to find ways to have more locally produced food sold. This was not a co-op situation. It was people in the co-op wanting to find another way to reach out to the wider community. A half a block away

urban renewal had come in and knocked down a 19th-century business block—it was an empty lot—basically we got permission from the city to start a farmers' market there.

CU: And when you are saying "we," can you be more specific?

MD: Well, naturally, people from the co-ops, and from the back-to-the-land movement. And those are largely the same people, but not always.

CU: Members of the co-op were basically supporting creating an alternative competitive market within their same town. A traditional economist would take a look at the farmers' market as being competition for the co-op.

MD: Right, and it's so strange to say it that way, because I never remember the conversation coming up that we were competing. I mean, that's just how thoroughly we were steeped in cooperative ideology. Even the co-ops realized that they were competing against capitalist enterprises that were for-profit oriented, privately owned, but I guess we assumed what we were trying to do was change awareness and having people think about food and offer them more opportunities to get fresh food.

These organizations addressed challenges by seeking help and providing assistance to one another. As individual cooperatives, they marshaled resources from within their membership, but, as a collective of collectives, they also worked together to solve shared problems.

One of the biggest issues involved procuring the food they wanted to sell and their customers wanted to buy. Regardless of the appeal of the cooperative *form*, it was the product line that helped the cooperatives stand out in a crowded retail environment. Lori Zuidema, an early member of the Seward Co-op in Minneapolis who later worked for the cooperatively owned Cheese Rustlers, tried to keep the challenge of those early stores in perspective:

Well, I think, I would agree . . . that food was probably the central motivating force behind the retail co-ops in the beginning, and one thing I think that is somewhat lost when you go in today's retails or even in the last ten or fifteen years, is that in those days you couldn't get food that you bought in co-ops elsewhere. I mean now you can, you can go into any mainstream supermarket and you can get organic milk, and you can get, you know, brown rice . . . you can get tofu and wheat germ, and you can get things that you could not get at that time. And so that was a lot of the emphasis, . . . just so people could get brown rice—you couldn't get brown rice in a supermarket in the '70s.[8]

Southeast Co-op's Malkis was one of those activists first attracted by the organizational model of the co-op, but he agreed that the food played a central role in their success:

> I wasn't motivated by the purity of the food originally, but I absorbed that sensibility when I got to work in the co-ops. But I really was a lot more motivated by the type of organization and the alternative to the existing economic structure. I think that was a minority point of view. I think originally people joined the co-op because they wanted to buy . . . foods that were raised in a certain way that they could not get commercially. Nobody else was carrying them. Nobody else was carrying anything. People who wanted organics had to develop their own institutions, and I think that was a primary motivation for many people involved in the co-ops.

Organic food was in relatively short supply during the early 1970s. And it was unlikely that this fledgling commodity would garner much support from the larger agricultural market or governmental regulators. The federal government was naturally reluctant to sanction farming processes that questioned its own motives and rationales for approving the very processes activists fought. Federal regulators were concerned about whether organic food products were actually safe to consume, but they were not interested in sanctifying the methods used to create them.[9]

Back in the 1970s, only the Federal Trade Commission ventured into this arena at the national level. Its regulations had no effect on product labeling (then the jurisdiction of the Food and Drug Administration or, more broadly, of the Department of Agriculture). The FTC was simply concerned about nonverifiable claims made in advertising using the terms "natural" or "organic." Calls for production and labeling standards at the federal level, however, met stiff resistance. The USDA and the FDA were not just reluctant to offend their corporate farming constituents; certifying organic food would require complex, multifaceted inspection of processes rather than products, and federal officials had tended to focus on the safety of the food being offered for sale rather than the means by which it was created.

Mississippi Market's Gail Graham, who spent four decades in cooperative management, reflected on her early years in the movement when organic food was a difficult product to procure:

> When I was first involved with the Wedge Co-op, all of the food that we sold, almost exclusively was bulk food or fresh produce. We had a small amount of frozen foods. The only canned foods we had were like a handful of things from Universal Cooperatives, the co-op private label at the time. Canned tomato products, apple sauce, mustard, orange juice. So mainly we were just buying from warehouses. Buying from growers in fifty-pound bags of stuff. And we started developing relationships with some of those growers. . . . You had a high level of trust with your growers, you knew them. But as the industry really grew it was apparent we needed to have regulations in place to protect everybody up and down the line.

All of these market transactions were based on trust—between the grower and the vendor and between the vender and the consumer—but that created a tentative and potentially fragile arrangement. All parties recognized the need to augment these handshake deals with standards and enforcement. Quite early in the formation of the organic food industry, several actors recognized the need for a consistent set of organic standards to preserve the market integrity of the label. Consumers might be attracted to alternative food products, but they also wanted to know they were purchasing something authentic and authentically different.

In California, J. I. Rodale tried to create a certification regime that evolved into the California Certified Organic Farmers in 1973. Composed of fifty-four growers, the association began devising its own set of organic standards and offered certification to others. Growers in other regional areas created an additional eleven certifying organizations by the end of 1974. These nongovernmental, primarily nonprofit organizations sought to codify and protect the meaning of the organic label and to encourage organic farming by providing information to those who might be interested in entering the market. Some organic distributors and marketers, on the other hand, lobbied state and federal legislatures for clearer standards to protect their positions within the organic food industry.[10]

In Minnesota, some of the cooperative activists also actively supported the production of organic products. Tori Reynolds, an early member of the North Country Co-op in Minneapolis, helped form the Organic Growers and Buyers Association (OGBA) after she moved to Winona in the early 1970s.

> The founding and sustaining meetings of Famine Foods, for example, would usually consist of about thirty people with our chairs arranged in a big circle, exchanging ideas and reaching consensus, with frequent kid interruptions. Organic vs. Local was a frequent topic. Organic certification for locals was a big issue, hence the eventual founding of the OGBA.

Efforts were under way to create organic certification regimes, but these processes were going to take a long time to resolve. In the meantime, cooperatives formed with no preestablished production or distribution systems to stock their shelves with natural foods. Under normal circumstances, the enterprises should have been doomed.

A growing consumer public wanted organic food, but it did not have the time to verify the status of the individual growers. The cooperatives established themselves as trusted purveyors of these products. This trust that consumers granted to the cooperatives would last only if vendors made sincere attempts to ensure the integrity of the organic label, even as these certification processes were being established. One solution involved creating a market infrastructure for organic food, effectively developing the supply lines that these businesses needed to survive. Of all the members of the new-wave cooperative business community, those involved in the distribution network helped most to solidify the storefront's standing in the larger competitive grocery market. This helps explain why the conflict involving the People's Warehouse had such tremendous implications even beyond the Twin Cities.

## Additional Organizations Supporting the Cooperatives

Throughout this period, individual storefront operations further refined their market niche and their organizational acumen. Ancillary actors like Chester Bruvold helped them establish stronger legal and financial structures. The major changes that took place over the next twenty

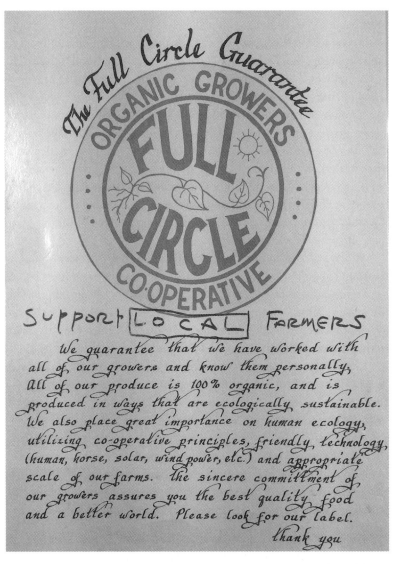

The Full Circle Guarantee

ORGANIC GROWERS

FULL CIRCLE

CO-OPERATIVE

Support LOCAL Farmers

We guarantee that we have worked with all of our growers and know them personally. All of our produce is 100% organic, and is produced in ways that are ecologically sustainable. We also place great importance on human ecology, utilizing co-operative principles, friendly technology (human, horse, solar, wind power, etc.) and appropriate scale of our farms. The sincere committment of our growers assures you the best quality food and a better world. Please look for our label.

thank you

*Figure 26.* Even in the 1980s, after organic standards were being adopted by various states, issues of trust remained in the absence of a well-established certified market. The Organic Grower's Cooperative formed in the 1980s to help promote local farmers; this undated "Full Circle" label states that the markets had met with the farmers and "know them personally," providing a guarantee based upon social relationships in the absence of regulatory standards.

years occurred at the level of individual co-ops rather than for the population as a whole. Even so, one can see the continued development of the cooperative and organic food markets by looking beyond the activities of individual storefront operations to consider the larger organizational environment in which they did business.

Though co-ops might be competitive retailers with regard to mainstream grocers (be they large chains or smaller independent merchants), they do not exist as isolated retail islands in the sea of the agricultural market. Rather, they form a sort of archipelago: existing independently but freely accessible to one another, operating as separate units but willing to lend neighborly assistance. At the risk of overextending the metaphor, the other groups in this ocean of organizations provided communication lines and seaworthy transports.

When I asked Dave Gutknecht which of the intermediary organizations contributed most to the success of the cooperative stores, he did not hesitate: distributors "are absolutely, I would say, *the* most important thing that enabled co-ops to start and to grow a little bit." He said the distributors recognized the need for the storefront operations to thrive so that their organizations would do so as well.

Gutknecht, who had contributed his time and energy to DANCe (the Distributing Alliance of the Northcountry Cooperatives) and the *Scoop*, a local co-op newsletter, in the '70s also spent spent six years as editor of the trade journal *Moving Food*. His true passion was cooperative distribution. To that end, in the 1980s, he began publishing and editing the *Cooperative Grocer*, a national bimonthly trade magazine disseminating news and commentary about business practices, expansions, closings, and resources available to the larger cooperative community. Gutknecht explained why he felt the magazine would find success:

> Well, it was launched in 1985, and this is the period in which our distributors were continuing to go down. They were consolidating, merging, and their numbers were being reduced, and there was a recognition that our retails were our greatest strength, in terms of food cooperatives, as opposed to manufacturers or distributors or buying clubs . . . at least myself and the co-op distributors and a few other leading national and regional players supported the publication with the feeling that the retails needed improved professionalism, needed to learn from each other, and that was probably our most important focus.

In 1998, a group of Twin Cities co-op leaders, including Gutknecht, Dan Foley, Bill Gessner, Gail Graham, and Alan Mathewson, created a new organization, the Cooperative Grocers Information Network (CGIN), which eventually took over publication of the *Cooperative Grocer* magazine. The CGIN formed to exchange information across organizations; its mission is "to strengthen all retail food cooperatives by creating community and facilitating the sharing and development of resources among members."[11] In addition to maintaining a listserv, the nonprofit allows its members to exchange advertising copy, training materials, organizational bylaws, and advice on handling particular retail issues. By 2007, it claimed a membership of 143 cooperatives, more than one-fourth of those operating in the United States. A similar organization, the National Cooperative Grocers Association (NCGA), formed in Iowa in 1999; its membership includes cooperative retailers within the food sector. Though the two organizations remain separate, in 2007 the CGIN took over management of the NCGA.

Cooperatives that formed in the 1990s and into the twenty-first century generally did not adopt the minimalist form of organization, the common model of the 1970s. Patterns of institutionalization took place throughout this field. Many of the established urban cooperatives, and several of those outstate, began major renovation and/or relocation projects that required significant resources: planning, consulting, and capital investment had become standard needs. The few new entrants to the market emerged following longer incubation periods, more fully formed in their organizational and physical structures from the start. Over time, as the cooperative no longer felt like a new-wave phenomenon, there developed a larger shared understanding of what one *should* look like to potential cooperators and patrons. This field of supporting organizations encompassed a wider set of actors—distributors, consultants, accountants, and financiers—all of whom had a stake in the continued success of individual organizations. Of all of these intermediary organizations, perhaps the development agencies played the largest role in helping to standardize procedures for creating, maintaining, and expanding cooperatives.

In 1985, a Minnesota support organization formed as Cooperative Development Services (CDS), a nonprofit based in both St. Paul and Madison, Wisconsin (another major regional center of cooperative organization), providing fee-based consulting services. Its board of directors included representatives from food co-ops in Minnesota and Wisconsin, and its current chair represents a Minneapolis bank. The CDS created a fiscal analysis tool that it calls Common Cooperative Financial Statements, which allows member cooperatives to submit sensitive financial information that other organizations can then consult to compare their situations to those of other cooperatives and thereby make better-informed decisions about how to allocate resources.

Cooperative accounts of many of the renovations they have undertaken—and most of the relocation stories—describe their financing sources as a mix of internal fund-raising and private investment. Several refer to the National Cooperative Bank, originally chartered and funded by the U.S. Congress in 1978 as the National Consumer Cooperative Bank. In 1980, its first year of operation, most of its $10 million in loans supported natural foods cooperatives. In 1981, after Congress and President Reagan threatened to cancel its charter, legislation was passed dictating that it become a private financial institution, and it organized itself as a cooperative organization. It adopted its current name in 1985 to mark its transition from the public to the private sector.

The Northcountry Cooperative Development Fund is another entity within this organizational field. Founded in 1978 as a cooperative, it collected funds from other cooperatives and interested parties to spur the development of co-ops in all business sectors. Still in operation today, it takes as its mission "investing in economic democracy through cooperative enterprise." Its current funders include several philanthropic organizations, such as the McKnight Foundation and the Family Housing Fund, as well as the U.S. Department of Agriculture and Department of Housing and Urban Development. As of 2014, it maintained assets of more than $1 million. In recent years, it created the "Kris Olsen Traveling Cooperative Institute" to assist in training for those involved in worker cooperatives. It was, of course, named for the Minnesotan who had spent so much time and energy promoting co-op development during the 1970s through the auspices of the All Cooperating Assembly, formed in response to the Twin Cities Co-op Wars to help promote the cause of cooperation among cooperatives.

## Cooperation among Cooperatives

After 1980, the pace of cooperative formation slowed considerably. In the Twin Cities metropolitan area, no new organizations formed, and a few began to dissolve. Over the next seven years, eight of the twenty-three co-ops shut down. The failure of some co-ops could be attributed to the success of others nearby. In the South Lyndale neighborhood, the Wedge Community Co-op moved from the basement of an apartment building to the former site of a small convenience store. Its membership and sales grew, but, as they did, nearby co-ops failed to retain enough active participants to fill the volunteer hours required to maintain storefront operations. Though the organizations might not have explicitly competed against one another, the member-patrons made their own market decisions.

In chapter 2, I mentioned the original principles of the Rochdale Pioneers. While these were taken as useful guidelines, they were not received as gospel. The International Co-operative Alliance, a voluntary alliance providing guidance and lobbying for many contemporary new-wave co-ops, has adopted and adapted and simplified these principles to include:

Voluntary and Open Membership
Democratic Member Control
Member Economic Participation
Autonomy and Independence
Education, Training and Information
Co-operation among Co-operatives
Concern for Community

Adherence to these principles provides one explanation for the success of this community of organizations.

Most new small businesses in America last no longer than four years. Less than 10 percent last a decade. The population of Minnesota cooperatives, however, defied this trend. Outside the Twin Cities, only five of thirty-six cooperatives failed to make it through the end of the 1980s. Though some consolidation took place in this population, almost three-fourths of the Minnesota co-ops that survived through 1980 stayed in business beyond the turn of the twenty-first century.[12]

One explanation for their longevity is that Minnesota's new-wave cooperatives cooperated with one another but avoided becoming too intimately tied to one another's fortunes. During the growth era of the 1970s, they successfully fostered the emergence of several ancillary organizations that provided aid and assistance without putting any individual collective at undue risk. In so doing, the co-ops managed to avoid some of the dangers of federalization that had stunted earlier cooperative movements. (Perhaps some lessons from the National Grange were instructive in this regard.) They were also creating the organizational infrastructure for a growing organic food industry. One primary vehicle used to achieve this end was the delivery truck, helping to centralize the supply of natural and organic foods to a decentralized collection of collectives.

Many of the leading figures in the early organizations helped found cooperatives based on their strong political and cultural inclinations. They certainly perceived the cooperative community as a social movement, and they strove to help others form new organizations that would strengthen that movement.

When the People's Warehouse first went into business, it operated from a rent-free warehouse that belonged to the University of Minnesota. In the early years, this distribution center dealt in information along with grocery products. As Craig Cox described it, "The volunteers who regularly gathered there to load and unload trucks exchanged news and gossip and became liaisons from their local co-ops to the larger movement."[13] The network developed in the Twin Cities metro region served outstate cooperatives as well. Dave Gutknecht, the early cooperative activist who found his niche in distribution, described the scope of this first distributor:

> The People's Warehouse [in the early 1970s] was serving a multi-state region in many retail and buying clubs in a similar kind of way— starting out quite small, some of them stayed buying clubs, some of them got a storefront up and running, but from Duluth to Sioux Falls to Iowa City, all around, is the region where similar things were happening. The metro area just has more people, so there were more co-ops, but very much the same thing was happening throughout the region.

The presence of a strong, central, urban core of co-ops also helped support and steady the distribution network to keep the larger community of cooperatives functioning.

> I think it was essential—pretty much across the board the in-town co-ops, the metro co-ops were larger in sales volume than the outstate co-ops, so I would say that was really critical. Plus, because the volume was larger and it was more cost-effective to service those closer-by co-ops it kind of balanced out the fact that we didn't know much about cost analysis and try to figure out how much we were actually spending to send a semi to Owatonna for a $500 order. We didn't have that sophisticated level of business acumen.

Over time, the People's Warehouse and its successor, DANCe (the Distributing Alliance of the Northcountry Cooperatives), tightened their fiscal operations. "I actually think it forced them to be a little more sophisticated as there were more customers and more volume . . . [serving the outstate co-ops] helped the volume, certainly, but basically it required the distribution arm to be more organized," said Gutknecht.

As the growth of (and even the conflicts among) of the early Twin Cities cooperatives demonstrates, distributors remained vital, at the center of the organizational field throughout the 1970s. Distributors ensured that the stores actually had something to sell, allowing for a more consistent experience for members who shopped at these retailers. They also helped form the infrastructure of the organic food industry at a time when neither the federal government nor mainstream agribusiness provided support.

Distribution networks did not simply flow outward from the Twin Cities. In both Duluth and Winona, two of the few rural communities that started new-wave cooperative storefront operations prior to 1975, obtaining goods to sell was an even greater challenge; starting a co-op meant much more than simply finding a cheap storefront. Michael Doyle described how some of Winona's Famine Foods members organized the Great River Warehouse distribution house to complement, not compete with, the People's Warehouse:

> We bought a small truck, and we then went around to the various producers and bought stuff that we took to the Twin Cities co-ops, and then actually got from them the orders for the smaller co-ops and buying

clubs in southeastern Minnesota, northeastern Iowa, and southwestern Wisconsin. . . . There's a cooperative [in a town which] also had an organic apple orchard and produced cider and other products. Then there was the Clayton goat cheese organic dairy, so there were a number of these different producers that were associated with the "back to the landers" . . . we formed a circuit around and then we pulled together the products, so that would help the People's Warehouse truck not return empty.

Additional cooperative distributors, such as the Common Health Warehouse Co-op Association in Duluth (1975–1977), opened outside the metro area. In Iowa City, Iowa, Blooming Prairie Cooperative Warehouse served as another important distributor of natural and organic foods. Founded in 1974 and operating as a cooperative itself, it saw its sales grow from $2 million in 1980 to $20 million in 1990.[14]

These distributors formed relationships with suppliers and provided product consistency. As they demonstrated the demand for and the viability of organic food retailing, agribusiness eventually took notice. The organic sector emerged as a profitable market niche, and it attracted the attention of other retailers, distributors, and producers, none of which necessarily shared the ideologies of the early activists or cooperative members. The push for federal regulation of organic food unfolded in the 1980s and '90s, and larger corporations began to acquire many of the founding companies in the organic food industry. The process accelerated following the congressional passage of the National Organic Foods Act, and most of the early cooperative distributors disappeared.

Gutknecht described the current, co-op-less distribution landscape:

What we found at the distribution level is that scale is very important because over time, the co-op distributors around the country, which there were twenty-five or more in one stage, gradually either merged or simply went out of business in order to address this question of scale, because someone else could provide the retails with comparable products at a better price if they had better scale. So the trend was thriving retails but declining distributors, increasing consolidation as they went from twenty-five to twenty to fifteen to ten, and then by around 2002 the last of our co-op distributors merged or was sold to a private distributor.

By this time, the new-wave co-ops had shifted to a business model of strategic purchasing alliances to secure the best terms for their products, purchased from these (now) mainstream agribusiness distribution ventures. None of these current distributors caters specifically or exclusively to cooperative stores. In 2002, the members of one of the last large cooperatively organized distributors, Blooming Prairie, decided to disband, selling to United Natural Foods, Inc., of Dayville, Connecticut. By this time, Blooming Prairie had become the largest-volume distributor of natural and organic foods in the Midwest, with more than $130 million in annual sales to 2,700 customers. In 2005, United Natural Foods also acquired the Roots & Fruits Cooperative, a worker-owned distributor of organic produce that had operated in Minneapolis since 1978. The brand was subsumed under United Natural Foods' Albert's Organics division. Every major regional distribution company founded to support new-wave cooperative product lines had been acquired by the larger mainstream agricultural corporate actors.

Many of the organic and natural food products now sold by cooperatives are supplied by the large companies the cooperative movement had challenged in earlier periods. And yet, these stores still thrive. While the organic food industry had been maturing, the cooperatives had been evolving as well.

## Beyond the Minimalist Organization

In a 1981 *Moving Food* article, John Noller illustrated the relationship of cooperatives to natural/organic foods, aptly describing the co-ops' lack of retailing prowess:

> During the late 1960s and into the 1970s, selling natural foods afforded an effective entry strategy for groups of cooperators with commitment to cooperative principles but little capital or experience in the grocery business. Natural foods have been and will continue to be a growth sector in the industry; but in many market areas there were no natural food retailers, and those that existed usually operated small stores with high margins. Inexperience in merchandising natural foods was less a handicap for new co-ops than it would have been in merchandising meat or conventional groceries, since merchandising natural foods had not yet been developed into a science. Finally, many of the members

of the new cooperatives associated natural foods with cooperative principles and were willing to contribute underpriced management or labor to the cooperative.[15]

Earlier in this book, I suggested that many of the cooperatives that formed in the 1970s were minimalist organizations, requiring the fewest possible resources to both start up and continue their operations. Over time, many began to create specialized roles within their organizations.

When the cooperatives had few mainstream market competitors for natural food, they had the luxury of running relatively loose business operations that relied on a forgiving attitude among their patrons. Most followed the model of the worker collective, with little or no hierarchy beyond the coordinators who often received a small monetary compensation for taking on extra duties. Key members stepped forward to assume essential roles without any particular recognition for their efforts, and crises developed if they stopped fulfilling these functions. The co-ops associated the principle of democratic participation with egalitarian duties, refusing to implement a hierarchical or managerial system they saw as ideologically opposed to their larger goals. Idealism and adrenaline kept things going for a while, but over time the lack of hierarchy resulted in a loss of accountability. The primary stumbling block was the challenge of developing effective management in an environment characterized by democratic control.

Unfortunately, several cooperatives found that a loose management structure created bureaucratic holes and left key tasks unfulfilled. Throughout the nineteenth and twentieth centuries, stories about the rise of cooperative movements generally ended with descriptions about improper fiscal management leading to their demise. That danger lurked for the new-wave cooperatives as well. Scott Beers, who served as a manager at the Whole Foods Co-op near the Minneapolis Institute of Arts, later became an accounting consultant to a number of the area's cooperatives. In 1980, he provided an analysis for the *Scoop*, evaluating the current state of the cooperative organizations in the Twin Cities:

> History has shown that the two major stumbling blocks to the growth and stability of co-operatives are lack of capital and lack of management expertise. The history of the "new wave" co-op movement is no

exception. Having grown remarkably in size, number, and variety over the past ten years, we now stand at a crossroads. We can no longer function solely on our idealism and the strength of our convictions. We need to develop a more solid foundation and we need to build it from among ourselves.[16]

Three decades later, when I spoke with Beers, he reiterated many of these sentiments, telling me that one constant barrier to success was co-ops' inability to obtain business loans to purchase equipment or expand operations:

We couldn't go to a bank and get $500 to borrow, to buy a freezer. Because the banks couldn't identify who was the owner; who was going to be the responsible party here? And, frankly, the books and records weren't sufficient that you could see that we had profits, that we were going to be able to pay it. So, it was probably right at the time.

Though minimalist organizations can exist using few resources, they still may need specialized skills. How the cooperatives dealt with the lack of management experience often had a strong influence on how they handled their financial matters.

Very few financial records exist from this time period in the public records, but one document from the archives of the All Cooperating Assembly serves as the best indication of how the different organizations began to diverge. Responding to a survey that asked for membership totals and monthly sales, twelve Twin Cities co-ops supplied information (see Table 7). A comparison of just two of these organizations, Southeast and the Wedge, presages the different paths each would take in the coming years. Though the Wedge claimed just three times as many members as Southeast, it reported more than ten times the amount of sales. Members from each of these cooperatives also provided an in-depth analysis of their current situations in the *Scoop*, illustrating how one retained features of the minimalist organization while the other was preparing to leave this status far behind.

Writing in 1978 about the fall (and later rise) of the Southeast Co-op in a neighborhood close to the University of Minnesota and characterized mainly by an ever-changing population of students, Allan Malkis stated:

*Table* 7. **Membership, Sales of Select Twin Cities New-Wave Co-Ops, 1978**

| *Cooperative name* | *Members* | *Monthly gross sales ($)* | *Sales/member* |
|---|---|---|---|
| East Calhoun | 40 | 12,000 | 300 |
| Linden Hills | 450 | 16,000 | 36 |
| Mill City Co-op | 50 | 12,000 | 240 |
| Northside Food Community | 350 | 45,000 | 129 |
| Northeast | 350 | 13,000 | 37 |
| Northside | 80 | 6,000 | 75 |
| Powderhorn Co-op | 100 | 13,000 | 130 |
| Seward Co-op Grocery & Deli | 500 | 47,000 | 94 |
| Southeast | 100 | 7,000 | 70 |
| Wedge Community Co-op | 300 | 75,000 | 250 |
| West Bank | 275 | 80,000 | 291 |
| Whole Foods | 100 | 17,000 | 170 |
| *Totals* | *2,595* | *343,000* | *132* |

*Source:* All Cooperating Assembly report on cooperatives sales, March 1978. Kris Olsen, collector, Minnesota Food Cooperatives Records (St. Paul: Minnesota Historical Society).

*Notes:* The ACA periodically requested reports from all of its members to track the growth of cooperative sales. Such reports were completed by the co-ops' management and submitted voluntarily.

> In 1975, when I joined Southeast, there was no structure in the organization of the store. The prevailing philosophy was basically communal and anarchistic; if people wanted to see the co-op survive, they would turn out and volunteer, if not, then it would cease to exist. There were no coordinators, no work groups, no managers, no Board of Directors, no collective. There were 100 or more members who came in and volunteered once a month or as often as they could to do whatever needed to be done. Time slots existed for volunteers, but it was a matter of chance if they were filled or not.[17]

This loose style of management also applied to procurement: "mushrooms, produce and other goods were brought in by anyone with the time and means to go get them." One of the remarkable features of contemporary food distribution systems is the almost constant availability of products in nearly any store throughout the nation throughout the year. Any grocery store that had a seemingly random stocking routine would sorely test the patience of today's patrons. These business practices did not stem from a lack of interest or loyalty to the co-op on the part of its worker-members, according to Malkis. Instead, he wrote, they

> reflected a commitment to the idea that people were capable of organizing themselves spontaneously if they were truly committed to a task. When the commitment wore off and original members moved out of the area, the problems of transient members and lack of incentive began to sap the energy of the co-op. As a consequence of these attitudes towards organization, Southeast rejected the alternative of hiring a paid staff to run the store. The lack of money also aided in this decision, but the primary reason was not financial but ideological.

When I spoke with Malkis, he still referred to the Southeast Co-op's primary challenges as related to attracting and retaining the proper skill sets. "None of us who were doing the management had a great deal of business background. Accounting and bookkeeping were minimal. And nobody had much training in how to run a business."

The Wedge also experienced crises related to its management structure, but they took on a completely different character. The Wedge moved into a new building in June 1979 and experienced increases in both memberships and sales. Ironically, success posed enormous challenges to its mode of collective management. Gail Graham wrote in a 1980 *Scoop* article that "the way we manage the Wedge has changed over the years, but the changes have been more accidental than purposeful." Explaining why the co-op failed to develop an effective management structure that could deal more successfully with its higher operating expenses, she described how hard it was to continue making meaningful decisions and implementing them using the organizational style that had worked years earlier:

> Technically those in attendance at a collective meeting had the power to make binding decisions. Actually, those decisions carried little weight. The rules and customs within which we had traditionally operated required everyone's participation for decision making to be accepted as legitimate. . . . We saw our problem as structural, for we were trying to run a participatory democracy without requiring full participation.[18]

Looking back, Graham told me that it was the gradual transition from collective management to a management team that ultimately helped the Wedge thrive. She also pointed out that democratic and participatory management, "the big things that the co-ops did, are much more normal in business today." Just as the cooperatives modified their practices as they increased in scale and scope, some larger corporations are now mimicking some of the models that helped employees feel more invested and involved in the organization's mission and products.

Over time, cooperatives had to determine whether and how they would modify their organizational structures to accommodate their particular situations. Some experimented, others asked for help, and some simply disappeared. In some ways, the impressive longevity of so many of the 1970s cooperatives masks a different reality: while ten of the fifteen earliest Twin Cities cooperatives—those founded in the heightened political atmosphere that preceded the Co-op Wars—were still in business after 1980, only six survived another decade. The majority of co-ops that lasted into the twenty-first century were founded post-1975, and most of them underwent significant changes as they matured. The two primary steps for reforming the cooperatives were, first, moving away from volunteer coordinators and instead hiring (and paying) someone to serve as a general manager, and, second, possibly restructuring from a worker-collective model to a consumer-cooperative model that didn't require the storefront to rely exclusively on volunteers. By 1990, only two of the twenty Twin Cities co-ops retained the worker-owned model. The consumer-cooperative model allowed for a greater expansion of the membership base and shifted the basis for participation from volunteerism to patronage. It is not without reason that many activists from those early years lament the changing of the season. Shifting the emphasis of these stores from the modeling of participatory democracy to the provisioning of natural, organic foods dramatically changed the character of these stores.

# Conclusion

# CONTEMPORARY LEGACIES

In October 2008, Minnesota's governor signed his name to the following proclamation:

> WHEREAS: The people of Minnesota have a proud heritage of working together for mutual benefit; and
> WHEREAS: The philosophy of working together has promoted community well-being and improved our quality of life; and
> WHEREAS: Producer, consumer, and worker cooperatives have provided opportunities for people to work together; and
> WHEREAS: Minnesota leads the nation in both the overall number of cooperatives and in memberships in cooperatives; and
> WHEREAS: Cooperatives in Minnesota have a rich history, spanning the Grange mercantiles of the 1800s, through the Finnish cooperative stores, to the new senior housing cooperative industry that began 25 years ago.
> Now, THEREFORE, I, TIM PAWLENTY, Governor of Minnesota, do hereby proclaim the month of October 2008 as: "Co-op Month" in the state of Minnesota.

In doing so, he continued a tradition that dated back to 1924, when the members of the Co-operative Trading Company (founded in 1911 by a group of Finnish immigrants), in Waukegan, Illinois, chose to set aside one month for a period of intensive promotion of cooperative organization. In 1948 Republican governor Luther W. Youngdahl, at the request of the Minnesota Association of Cooperatives, made Minnesota the first state to proclaim October as "Co-op Month."[1]

In 1964, U.S. Secretary of Agriculture Orville Freeman—another former governor of Minnesota—first proclaimed a national Co-op Month along with an actual theme: "USDA Helps Build a Better America." For the next seven years, the government sponsored Co-op Month events, revolving around such themes as "Partners in American Life" (1965), "A National Asset" (1967), and "Progress through People" (1969). Cooperatives have enjoyed a long (and occasionally contentious) history in our nation, so in many ways it shouldn't be so surprising that they played yet another important role in the history of the organic food industry. Even though this economic model endures, however, this should not suggest that it has remained static. Cooperatives remain relevant to contemporary society because they still address issues that are important to conscious consumers: they promote cultural change, they embed social values into the products they sell, and they allow individuals to participate in projects of social justice through the seemingly minor purchasing decisions we all make every day.

## Continued Projects of Social Change

I opened this book by describing a visit to Philadelphia's Mariposa Co-op, where one had to be a member in order to have the privilege of shopping in its cramped quarters. A few years later, when Mariposa moved from its humble yet charming storefront (where the presence of more than twenty customers presented serious navigational challenges in the aisles) to its new, spacious abode, many of its members mourned the end of an era. I saw the same process play out when the Mississippi Market in my hometown of St. Paul not only moved but expanded by constructing three brand-new stores across the city. One board member lamented to me in confidence that she abhorred the co-op's transition toward becoming a "real" supermarket that looked like all of the other large grocery stores in town. However, those concerns paled in comparison to the anxiety created a decade earlier when Whole Foods announced a store just five blocks away from the Mississippi Market. Where one might have expected cheers of victory—organic food was going mainstream—fears that increased competition might harm the cooperative suggested that something else was at stake.

Contemporary cooperatives, however, share more than an historical connection with those original stores that were founded decades ago; they still possess a complex social mission pursuing a difficult project of social change. How can we help people not just eat better food but also develop a different relationship with their natural, social, and business environments? Whole Foods represented economic competition as well as a deliberate co-optation of the feel-good values co-ops had helped attach to the purchase of organic foods, but without the community participation and mobilization that tied consumers emotionally and through "sweat equity" to their co-op.

The growth of the organic food market in the last decades of the twentieth century followed the same patterns of agricultural industrialization described in chapter 2. The major success stories in corporate agribusiness once again involved input substitution, replacing manual labor with mechanized production methods. Centralized decision making went hand in hand with the consolidation of production, processing, marketing, and distributing organizations. As larger mainstream agricultural companies took over organic distribution networks, they also sought to consolidate their hold on the companies that produced these products. The scale of acquisition is perhaps best demonstrated in Figure 27, Philip Howard's 2016 graphic outlining the top 100 acquisitions of formerly independent companies by larger corporate concerns. Several organic product lines that have become fixtures in organic sections and in the minds of consumers are now wholly owned subsidiaries of the biggest market players in the grocery industry: Boca burgers (Kraft), Odwalla juices (Coca-Cola), and Muir Glen canned tomatoes (General Mills) are just a few examples.

So, if agribusiness has embraced, at least in part, the practices and products cooperatives formed to promote and consumers have demanded enough of the stuff to make it commonplace to find relatively inexpensive organics in every Super Target in the country, why do cooperatives, even those that sell organic food, still matter?

When I began to study the organizations that promoted organic food and cooperative retailing, I wanted to demonstrate how organic food served as a selective incentive to attract and retain members for these market-based social movement organizations. I suspected that the loss of that quasi-monopoly had forced the co-ops to professionalize and refine their missions. In the prevailing narrative, the 1970s new-wave cooperative movement experienced astronomic growth, then suffered retrenchment and decline, with the number of co-ops dwindling dramatically. As

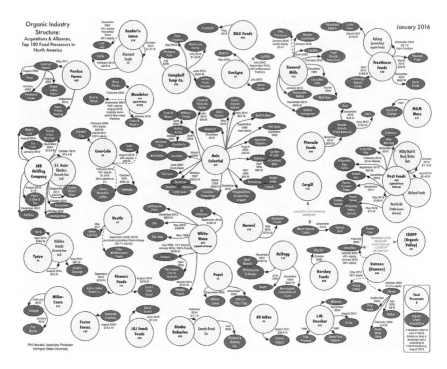

*Figure 27.* Philip Howard's graphic depiction of organic food company acquisitions by the top 100 food processors in North America, 2016. Reprinted with permission of the author.

Cox wrote in *Storefront Revolution*, his definitive history of the Co-op Wars, "the movement died" after the co-ops lost some of their revolutionary zeal.[2] It is certainly true that some of the Minnesota organizations were shuttered over the two decades following that standoff.

My evidence shows, instead, that this population remained strong even as it began to lose its quasi-monopoly on the retailing of organic food. During the 1970s, the focus of these organizations shifted from changing larger social structures to promoting food products consciously grown to provide both environmental benefits and better nutrition for consumers. A larger organizational field developed around the storefront operations, helping them to solidify distribution networks that concentrated on purveying natural and organic foods. They appealed to select individuals' desire to pursue social change without requiring

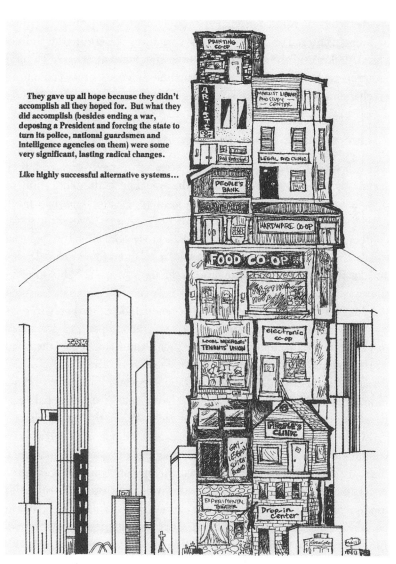

They gave up all hope because they didn't accomplish all they hoped for. But what they did accomplish (besides ending a war, deposing a President and forcing the state to turn its police, national guardsmen and intelligence agencies on them) were some very significant, lasting radical changes.

Like highly successful alternative systems...

*Figure 28.* In 1980, the editorial cartoonist Pete Wagner contemplated the legacy of the alternative movements and the organizations they had created in the previous decade. He made a point of including this cartoon in the published collection of his work titled *Buy This Book.* Reprinted with the permission of the artist.

a large sacrifice—shoppers would pay a bit more and perhaps forgo the greater selection offered by chain stores. Though their primary purpose no longer centered on changing social structures, the co-ops did address Steven Lukes's third dimension of power: the internalization of cultural preferences. In short, they created structural supports as they capitalized on changing social values in a growing base of consumers.

## Consumer Products with a Social Conscience

Though organic food and new-wave cooperatives never divorced, they seemingly agreed to an open relationship. The commodification of organic food and its wider embrace by agribusiness could not take place until it was perceived as a product worthy of exchange beyond the social context in which the consumer transaction was embedded with social values. Prior to the enactment of any state regulations that provided guidance or standards regarding the use of the term "organic," this appellation was placed on certain food items only after negotiation between the producer and the retailer. That is, organic food existed only in relationships of trust amongst market players: the cooperative store had to negotiate the meaning of "organic" with the farmers and then had to communicate this understanding to consumers, effectively creating demand. In this early, perhaps precapitalist orientation of the organic food industry, the exchange was entirely dependent on personal relationships between buyers and sellers at each point in the supply chain.

Once seen as a marginal (and temporary) fad that appealed only to countercultural hippies and utopian environmentalists, organic food grew into a major market niche in which mainstream (or "conventional") producers and retailers played an increasing role. Until the 1990s, health food in general (and organic food in particular) was widely perceived in popular culture as virtuous but unpleasant in a culinary sense. As Samuel Fromartz put it in *Organic, Inc.: Natural Foods and How They Grew*, "health food historically meant bug-eaten organic produce, hardy beans and grains, and badly prepared tofu—their health quotient rising as palatability declined."[3]

As organics became more mainstream and more of the largest agribusiness corporations developed their own organic lines or purchased existing organic processing companies, earlier arguments against organic food based upon unsupported health and viability claims have disappeared. A new critique has emerged, suggesting that industrialized organic agriculture was incompatible with earlier cultural understandings of what "organic" could, should, or did mean. Certainly the emergence of the Whole Foods Market empire was well noted by leaders of the new-wave cooperatives. Smaller grocers were also well aware of the increasing market share captured by the corporate giants Natural Selection Foods and Grimmway Farms as they acquired competitors and placed other growers under contract to supply them with organic products. Outside the regulatory debates surrounding the National Organic Standards program, however, public critiques of the mainstreaming of organic food were largely absent from the popular press prior to 2000.

Contemporary critiques of the newly industrialized organic food industry generally focus on a small set of questions about organic food that have little to do with production methods. They relate to the social and economic relations embedded in the market transactions, the size of the company, the location of the foodsheds, and the motivations of the actors. Encouraging conventional farmers to grow organically and convincing conventional retailers to sell organic foods were longtime goals of the organic movement. Why, then, are these successes also seen as troubling? This is what Julie Guthman, a professor of sociology at the University of California, Santa Cruz, called "The Paradox of Organic Farming." In her analysis of the organic farming sector in California, she concludes that the promise of organic farming faded as it rapidly replicated what it set out to oppose: industrialized agriculture.

Cooperatives played a major role in preserving the integrity of the "organic" label when the USDA was crafting its final set of national standards in the 1990s. The department's first proposal, released in 1997, allowed food products to be certified as organic even if they were not produced from organic seeds, even if they involved the use of "bio-sludge" as a fertilizer (trust me, you don't want to know more), and even if they were irradiated as a sanitization treatment. These three different processes were decried as contrary to the very spirit of organic production, and cooperatives led the way in informing consumers about their acceptability in the standards. After receiving more than 275,000 comments, most of them speaking out against these three items, the USDA subsequently removed them from the "final rule" released in 2002. An obituary for the cooperative and organic activist Eric Kindberg published in *Cooperative Grocer* provides an example of the activism cooperators undertook on this issue:

> He taught folks how to write effective public input and how to get to the National Organic Standards Board meetings. When the 1997 Proposed Organic Rule was published, he and others wrote an analysis of the rule and created a public comment form that was distributed on the internet, in retail stores, and even under car windshield wipers. This outreach generated thousands of public comments, resulting in a completely rewritten 1997 Rule. The current National Organic Program has been greatly shaped by public input, encouraged by Eric.[4]

Cooperatives matter in part because the concept of organic food still matters. Although I have not delved into the specific practices spelled out in regulatory guidelines that qualify a particular product for certification, consumers care about organic food because it embodies the values they share about sustaining their larger society. The critiques raised by Steiner, Howard, and Rodale in the mid-twentieth century still strike a chord. Most people genuinely want their food to be raised with respect for the land, recognizing that the pollutants generated by agriculture and the degradation of the soil will have long-lasting impacts for the future viability of our planet. Most people want the farmers growing our food to be economically self-sufficient, free from dependence on larger corporations for the artificial inputs to properly feed the soil. And most people want purer food that provides true sustenance for their bodies, devoid of carcinogens. For now, those principles are embodied in this social construct of organic food, and most people expect them to be incorporated into the regulations that define the certified label.

The population of cooperative grocery stores has also evolved. And not everybody is happy with how many of the formerly minimalist organizations have grown into multimillion-dollar enterprises, some with tens of thousands of members. (Full participation at a Lakewinds members meeting would require booking one of the Twin Cities' sports arenas.) Many conduct their sales in newly constructed, purpose-built stores that rival those of the national chains (and, of course, of their competitor Whole Foods). More than one board member told me off the record that they miss the old days when their co-op felt, well, less corporate.

The cartoonist Pete Wagner—who has long held the view that editorial cartoons should have a point rather than just restate the headlines— expressed disappointment with how the cooperatives had changed. If he were to write a new book, he would actually "be voicing my disappointment over how they [food cooperatives] have become nothing but expensive boutiques that only the rich and near-rich can afford unless they want to spend 80 percent of their income on food. We are in the struggling lower middle class, and we were spending that much until stores like Aldi and Trader Joe's and Fresh Thyme came along offering some organic staples at more reasonable prices."[5] In an ironic twist of economic fate, the growing popularity of organic food continues to put price pressures on these commodities, and cooperatives once again suffer by comparison to some of the larger retail giants that can buy in great quantities and negotiate discounts.

*Figure 29.* Lakewinds Co-op, which traces its origins to a buying club that operated out of a church basement in the early 1970s, now has more than 20,000 members shopping at three different suburban locations south and east of Minneapolis. This store in Richfield opened in 2014, requiring a $1.8 million investment. Photograph by the author.

*Figure 30.* The Hampden Park Co-op is one of only three of the original pre–Co-op War Twin Cities cooperatives still in operation. Unlike the Seward Co-op and the Wedge Community Co-op, both of which chose expansion routes and began moving into larger venues in the 1990s, Hampden Park still retains much of its original small-store approach appropriate to its neighborhood and clientele. Its building still sits on the corner. Photograph by Bill Lewis.

I get it. While many of the original early-1970s cooperatives managed to stay in business for decades, most chose to shut down their operations in the face of increasing competition—some from neighboring cooperatives that embraced expansion models—and continued financial pressures. In 2007, many in this community lamented the closing of the thirty-seven-year-old North Country Co-op, accurately calling it the end of an era. Workers cooperatives always faced challenges to their ability to maintain commitment and enthusiasm, and some of the drama and tension was part of the charm that got lost in the transition to a consumer cooperative model. And I know that pointing out the much smaller reach of those cooperatives in terms of their member/customer base won't satisfy the current critics. As Table 7 indicates, in 1978 the twelve co-ops that responded to the ACA survey reported a total of 2,595 members, a fraction of the roster for many single contemporary stores. Expanded square footage and increased membership did necessitate a change from the workers collective model, limiting the potential of the stores' participatory democracy structure. It does mean that a lot more organic food is being sold, of course, but there's no denying that most of today's co-ops are strikingly different from those from the past.

Still, I am reminded of Svetlana Boym's discourse on nostalgia, a way of both remembering and forgetting something we don't have in the present moment:

> I would define it as a longing for a home that no longer exists or has never existed. Nostalgia is a sentiment of loss and displacement, but it is also a romance with one's own phantasy. Nostalgic love can only survive in a long-distance relationship. A cinematic image of nostalgia is a double exposure, or a superimposition of two images—of home and abroad, of past and present, of dream and everyday life. The moment we try to force it into a single image, it breaks the frame or burns the surface.[6]

I was never part of that early cooperative scene in the 1970s, but I also know the thrill (and I'm familiar with that nostalgia) of collectively creating a new scene, of filling a structural and cultural void, of trying to run a business while staying true to one's self. In the early 1990s, my brother Andy and I teamed up with our friend John Pucci to open a small, independent coffee shop named "Motor Oil Industrial Coffees," next door to the Speedboat Art Gallery in St. Paul. Financed primarily by cash advances on my Discover card, we relied on sweat equity and the benevolence of countless volunteers to serve coffee, bagels, and soup to the aficionados of punk and zine artists in the Twin Cities. It was an exciting, exhilarating, and exhausting endeavor—and in the end it required too much personal sacrifice to be sustainable. It's hard to create a lasting institution based upon opposition to the mainstream forces of society, especially if the values you promote become widely shared. But the memories live on—at least the ones that help me forget how hard it was to be constantly living on the edge.

There are still, of course, many co-ops in Minnesota (including in the Twin Cities) retaining a smaller footprint even if they're not renting space in a corner-store location, where the cashier learns your name by the third time you have shown up and the breakdown of the dairy cooler still gets talked about for days. But I don't believe that the continued relevance of the contemporary cooperative is tied to resisting the urge to grow or to the cheaper provisioning of organic food. I have suggested these social movement market organizations arose in the 1970s to promote a shift in internalized cultural preferences, to encourage a conscious consumerism that focused on sustaining local and agriculture food economies. There is still much work to be done.

In what may present the next front in the fight for food, many activists have turned toward raising awareness around local provisioning. The cover story of a 2007 issue of *Time* magazine urged people to "Forget Organic. Eat Local." Its author claimed, "Organic adherents take it on faith that the way food is grown affects its nutritional quality. But advocates of local eating are now making another leap, saying what happens after harvest—how food is shipped and handled—is perhaps even more important than how it was grown."[7] In November 2007, the New Oxford American Dictionary announced that it had chosen "locavore" as the word of the year. Beating out "colony collapse disorder" and "social graph," the relatively recent term "was coined two years ago by a group of four women in San Francisco who proposed that local residents should try to eat only food grown or produced within a 100-mile radius. Some groups refer to themselves as 'localvores' rather than 'locavores.'"

The concept was not entirely new—we see many precursors to this in "back to the land" movements throughout the twentieth century, especially in the writings of Wendell Berry during the 1960s—but in a period of rapid globalization the appeal of the "local" took on new urgency in the twenty-first century. Gary Paul Nabhan's 2002 memoir *Coming Home to Eat: The Pleasures and Politics of Local Foods* predated the coinage of the term "locavore" by several years and came on the heels of the nutritionist Joan Dye Gussow's 2001 memoir *This Organic Life*. Both of these authors are part of a long tradition of authors and scholars promoting the values of local food sources. The local food movement (also referred to as "regional food" or "food patriotism," emphasizing foodsheds or bioregions) has been described academically as a "collaborative effort to build more locally based, self-reliant food economies—

one in which sustainable food production, processing, distribution and consumption is integrated to enhance the economic, environmental and social health of a particular place."[8] It is considered part of the broader sustainability movement. Proponents of local food emphasize different aspects associated with particular culinary, ecological, economic, geographic, and social boundaries.

It has become very fashionable in contemporary grocery stores of any kind to display idyllic pictures of farmers working their fields, tending to their livestock, or presenting their bounty in their cupped, outstretched hands. In many co-ops, however, those images are not just stock photos—they actually depict the local farmer whose products are on the shelves beneath them. New-wave co-ops have excelled in "buying local" since their outset, in large part because they had to; when organic food was not widely available, the co-ops often had to forge relationships with local growers to provide that produce. If cooperatives continue to pursue one of the primary Rochdale principles—education—they might convince future potential patrons that it is not just what you buy that matters but also where it comes from.

## Private Commerce, Public Benefits

Cooperatives (in general) exist at a nexus between for-profit and nonprofit firms, and they share features with both. As the members of consumer cooperatives can play several roles simultaneously, these organizations have the ability to pursue multiple goals in the market and social realms. Just like for-profit enterprises, cooperatives participate in competitive economic markets, and they cannot repeatedly spend more than they take in without facing dissolution. This applies to every business sector in which they appear, including agriculture, housing, banking, retail, and medicine. Cooperatives must also return annual dividends to their members based on the past year's business performance.[9]

A consumer cooperative in particular aims to be a *corrective* to market failures; again, these could be predatory behaviors by existing for-profit companies or the unavailability of a product consumers want. The patrons of consumer cooperatives already play two roles when they make purchases, acting as both customers and owners. But for members of cooperatives engaged in a project of social change, they can also be actors within a social movement. The market failure that prompted the formation of Minnesota's consumer cooperatives was a lack of available natural and organic foods in a community. The original member-owners were not motivated to challenge the pricing structure of for-profit ventures. The goods they desired were steeped in a reform-oriented social movement, full of positive cultural connotations promoting sustainable agriculture.

One reason that Minnesota's new-wave cooperatives succeeded was their focus on products that eschewed brand names and excessive packaging. Whether or not these food items were organic, the attempt to present them as slightly less commodified consumer goods helped the cooperative differentiate itself from other market organizations. Consolidation within the organic food industry has resulted in many of the largest agribusiness companies selling mass-marketed, brand-name products with just as much packaging as conventional items, and cooperatives now have little choice but to sell these products in their stores. However, because of both their smaller retail footprints and a legacy of self-service, bulk-bin shelving practices, cooperatives are in a better structural position to continue providing a shopping experience perceived as an alternative to the mainstream supermarket.

Certainly, most customers who purchase organic foods do so for personal reasons related to health, flavor, or exotic consumerism. These products have become an important component of ethical and political consumption, and purchasing them from a co-op—particularly now, when they are often also available in more mainstream groceries and supermarkets—is associated with a sense of virtue. Promoting organic food through its purchase in local consumer cooperatives helps promote sustainable agriculture and a set of social values.

The assumption that human beings operate as *Homo economicus* ignores the cultural meanings associated with market transactions. Yes, consumers generally make purchasing decisions that involve economic gains (or smaller economic losses), but even if this is a primary consideration of cooperative participants, it is probably not their only one. It is also possible for individuals to advance their own interests in other realms without doing so at the expense of others. In fact, pursuing a personal desire without harming somebody else could be seen as an act of righteousness.

New-wave cooperative grocery stores gave individuals just that opportunity, allowing them to participate more actively in local consumer markets and to promote increased production of natural and organic food products. This organizational form differs from that followed by other actors in the ethical retailing industry by its "no-profit" orientation. Unlike Whole Foods, which posted profits of $507 million in 2016, net earnings from a cooperative support its local economy and its member-owner patrons.

In this sense, the new-wave cooperative remains a type of social movement organization, albeit one that does not explicitly seek to change the larger social *structure*. Its immediate goal is to attract and retain members in order to remain viable in the economic marketplace. It works to educate potential members about the virtues of natural foods and emphasizes members' power to participate more actively in the consumer market. To overcome internalized *cultural* preferences for cheaper foods more readily available at lower prices in supermarkets, the cooperative must absolutely sell that veneer of righteousness and consumer power. If, as I have attempted to demonstrate in this book, these organizations emerged to fill a market void and provide a retailing venue for organic food, there is no strictly logical reason for most of them to exist any longer. Whole Foods has at least one store in every major metropolitan market, proclaiming itself "the world's leader in natural and organic foods, with more than 350 stores in North America and the United Kingdom."[10] Most mainstream supermarkets have also attempted to take advantage of the fastest-growing market niche in the grocery sector. There is little chance that, if it had not gotten a thirty-year head start, the new-wave cooperative movement would survive today.

So it is against the odds that these organizations continue to attract new members and open new stores. This can only be a result of how the new-wave co-op lets people participate in a project of social change without taking a large personal risk. Most contemporary food co-ops in Minnesota no longer require members to volunteer on a weekly or monthly basis, as was the case in the 1970s.[11] By law, all members must purchase a share in the organization, typically $100 or less, but they can sell their share back should they choose to leave the cooperative. (And in the 1970s, shares in a Minnesota new-wave co-op typically cost three to five dollars.)

Cooperative activism has certainly involved calls from some quarters to reform the larger social structure. The attitudes of the Cooperative League of the U.S.A. in the 1910s promoted such an agenda, as did the activities of the Co-op Organizers in the Twin Cities during the 1970s. As Henry Hansmann, a Yale University law professor with expertise in alternative economic enterprises, has noted, one appeal of cooperative economic activity remains its *oppositional* orientation:

> In the popular mind, it is common to attribute the development of cooperative enterprise, and consumer cooperatives in general, to peculiar patterns of culture or ideology that have little to do with the underlying costs and benefits of the cooperative form. Cooperatives are the peculiar institutions of Scandinavians, it is said, or of individuals with a peculiarly strong political antipathy to capitalism.[12]

This public perception is at odds with the widespread use of the cooperative form in so many American business sectors, with agriculture, law, health care, supermarket and hardware retailing among them. As Hansmann noted, "The pattern of customer-owned enterprise that we observe, however, strongly belies such notions. . . . Nobody could accuse the banks that belong to the MasterCard cooperative of being anticapitalist." It isn't the organizational form that is a radical idea; it is the use to which it is put that matters.

Cooperatives remain relevant because they continue to present themselves as social movement organizations, even if most no longer pursue loftier aims of restructuring the American economy by replacing free-market capitalism with cooperative business ventures. In fact, those two concepts are not mutually exclusive, as the cooperatives have demonstrated so well over the past forty years. These businesses thrived *within* the capitalist system, not in spite of it. By providing a low-risk opportunity for consumers to articulate a desire for social change, however, they have been able to expand their domain of concerns. Patricia Allen, director of the Center for Agroecology and Sustainable Food Systems at the University of California, Santa Cruz, published an article in 2000 with her student Martin Kovach, "The Capitalist Composition of Organic: The Potential of Markets in Fulfilling the Promise of Organic Agriculture," in which they observed:

There is a clear tension between the hope of green consumerism and the power of market dynamics. Along with the progress in organic farming practices, the growing market for organic food, and political changes, there are questions about the "real" as opposed to symbolic power of green consumerism.

They also stated, "Advocates of organic agriculture claim that it will help preserve the environment, improve people's health, and create better conditions for agricultural workers."[13] Certainly those goals have not yet been achieved. But social movements are rarely in the position to declare victory and go back to the farm; their primary challenge involves maintaining interest and attention to their issues as they strive for progress, not perfection, in their pursuits.

When new-wave cooperatives formed in the 1970s to meet the needs of a youthful constituency interested in nutrition and ecology, they had three appealing features, any one of which could have attracted new members: political ideology, community, and "good food." Many who stayed involved refer to the democratic and transformational attributes that resulted from this particular organizational form. Reflecting on the Co-op Wars in his book *Storefront Revolution*, Craig Cox wrote, "the co-op movement was not built on food policy or even on economic issues—the foundation of this movement was constructed from an almost religious belief in the value of personal and community empowerment."[14] Cooperatives channeled the energies of antiestablishment activists into local concerns, conveniently focused on the daily operations of stores, bakeries, and warehouses.

This book has explored how new-wave cooperatives have existed as examples of a unique organizational form for more than four decades in the state of Minnesota. Throughout my research, I have attempted to avoid delving into the reasons that any particular co-op might have survived (or failed), preferring to examine the population as a whole. I believe this is the only way to evaluate them properly, because none existed in isolation. Cooperation among cooperatives was, after all, one of the most ardently held of the Rochdale principles. Each co-op not only was aware of its compatriots but also worked alongside them to help create a stable distribution network through which to buy and sell products not available in mainstream outlets. In so doing, they helped create a market infrastructure for organic foods that eventually went beyond this particular organizational field. The spirit of "cooperation among cooperatives" occasionally did not present itself as well as the cooperatives might have hoped, but even during some of their darkest hours—the forcible overtaking of the People's Warehouse is a glaring example—the groups did not retreat into isolationist stances. If anything, the conflicts they endured brought out some of their unique qualities: the impulse to share information among supposed competitors, a willingness to question internal and external structures, and the desire to live up to a set of stated ideals. In the end, Minnesota's consumer co-ops have focused on the provisioning of natural foods as a primary identity, complementing their participatory democracy. As it moved into the twenty-first century, the cooperative movement remained strong, and new organizations and storefronts have opened across the country.

The goal so many worked toward (even when their efforts seemed less than hopeful) has been achieved; organic food has now achieved mainstream acceptance. Even so, cooperatives thrive. Following a twenty-year period of organizational stability, at least ten new natural/organic food cooperatives have opened in Minnesota since 2000, most of them large-scale operations requiring hundreds of thousands of dollars of financing. The continued relevance of cooperative stores within the organic marketplace suggests that their identity as a particular type of organization—albeit one closely associated with a particular product—has remained key to their survival. By merging a focus on benefits for the individual member-owner, including both an opportunity to contribute to local economic stability and the provisioning of healthier food products, cooperatives remain competitive while still supporting their founding principles. And by emphasizing "cooperation among cooperatives," they have helped to create an organizational field to support the distribution of organic food products even beyond their own brick-and-mortar boundaries. The social change many championed when this movement began more than forty years ago—the hope that they could challenge the dominance of prevailing agricultural paradigms—has been realized without leading to the irrelevance of co-ops.

New-wave cooperatives have successfully shifted internalized cultural preferences regarding the type of food we consume. In a consumer era that has begun to emphasize green technologies and local provisioning of products, cooperatives are poised to publicly question and debate how their practices line up with their ideals, occasionally struggling to make ends meet but always trying to transform consumer behavior in a market economy that has all too often celebrated competition over cooperation.

# ACKNOWLEDGMENTS

THIS BOOK BEGAN as a dissertation project at Princeton University. I had set out to provide a comprehensive history and analysis of the organic food industry. Fortunately, my advisers convinced me to consume this meal one bite at a time. Since I kept running into cooperative grocery stores as an important link between the industry's early years and its contemporary reach, I decided to focus on how this organizational form became so strongly associated with this particular product.

I will always owe many thanks to my advisers at Princeton—Paul DiMaggio, Robert Wuthnow, and Miguel Centeno—for their continued advice and their support of this research. Paul in particular offered invaluable comments on multiple versions of this manuscript, and all three forced me to think more precisely about the organizational realities facing cooperatives in the capitalist market. Bob's vast knowledge of American historical and cultural trends helped me understand how concurrent movements often intersected in novel ways that became apparent only later. Miguel challenged me to tell an interesting story and gave me a great deal of encouragement to speak to a wider audience beyond the narrow subfields of our discipline. They have all been excellent role models as scholars and mentors, and they have inspired me to grow in those capacities.

Princeton's sociology department is an outstanding center for scholarship, and the administrative support staff of Blanche Anderson, Cindy Gibson, and Donna DeFrancisco dispensed invaluable help to navigate the various bureaucracies of the institution. Princeton's Program in American Studies provided additional financial support while I researched the origins of the organic food industry in America, and I received professional improvement funds from Winona State University to complete this manuscript.

The staff at three research institutions lent me assistance to explore their archives: the Center for Cooperatives University of Wisconsin–Madison, Wilson Library at the University of Minnesota–Twin Cities, and the Gale Family Library at the Minnesota Historical Society in St. Paul. The Kris Olsen collection of 1970s Minnesota co-ops documents, archived at the Gale Family Library, was indispensable in my research; Heidi Heller and Jenny McElroy were particularly helpful in locating photographs and providing permissions to reproduce them, while Eric Mortenson expertly turned them into high-quality digital images. The MHS is truly a treasure of our state. I am also indebted to the work of Florence Parker, a staff member at the U.S. Bureau of Labor Statistics from 1920 to 1952, who served as an advocate for consumer cooperation and, importantly, helped the bureau publish a wealth of statistics on these organizations for three decades. My analysis in chapters 2 and 3 relies heavily on the information found in those bulletins, and I would have a far less interesting story to tell without them. The same is true for my engaging interviewees, who generously shared their histories.

This work centers on the cooperative spirit observed through the creation of countercultural market organizations. Throughout this process I have been blessed with examples of this ethos in many different realms. I found the support of Terry Boychuk, Michal McCall, Jack Weatherford, and Clay Steinman at Macalester College instrumental in introducing me to the field of sociology. Macalester faculty members Karin Aguilar-San Juan, Terry Boychuk, Ruthann Godollei, Joanna Inglot, Kiarina Kordela, and Peter Rachleff generously discussed aspects of this project with me. Graduate students at Princeton University who helped me include my valued friends Nina Bandelj, Wendy Cadge, Marion Carter, Eszter Hargittai, Kieran Healy, Erin Kelly, Brian Steensland, and Steven Tepper. As I completed my thesis, I joined a strong and supportive "accountability group," and James Gibbon in particular has been receiving (if not reading) daily reports from me for many years. I am grateful for all of the encouragement and support I have received from him and the other members.

Many fine colleagues at the University of St. Thomas, Hamline University, Grinnell College, and Winona State University helped me learn pedagogical skills as well as the importance of finding the proper balance among teaching, service, research, and my personal life. In particular, I have had the pleasure of working with Jennifer Chernega, Karla Erickson, Susan Ferguson, Meg Wilkes Karraker, Peter Miene, Mark Norman, Aurea Osgood, Sharon Preves, and David Speetzen, who all provided much guidance and encouragement in their roles as department chairs, advisers, colleagues, and friends. Lenny Russo, my esteemed chef, is a tireless proponent for local, organic, and sustainable food, and I hold him in high regard.

Several editors and writing coaches provided both support for the writing process and comments on various drafts of this manuscript, including Jessica Matteson at the University of Minnesota, Susan Callaway at the University of St. Thomas, and Judy Hunter and Mark Baechtel at Grinnell College. Letta Page and Jon Wallace reviewed entire later versions with keen eyes and answered countless questions regarding stylistic conventions; Jeri Famighetti provided the final review and corrected numerous stylistic mistakes. Any remaining errors, of course, are my responsibility.

This book exists only because Jason Weidemann at the University of Minnesota Press saw its potential and offered his encouragement, support, and much patience to help me pursue the project to its conclusion. The Press assembled an excellent production team, including assistant production and design manager Rachel Moeller and Neil West, Brenda West, and Katie West of BNTypographics West; I appreciated the production team's choice of Janson Text as the primary font. Gabriel Levin, Jason's editorial assistant, was also instrumental in the preparation of the final manuscript.

I thank my family for their support, including both of my brothers, Andy Upright and Kelly Upright, and especially my late mother, Carol Upright. Although she passed away before I completed this book, she always let me feel her pride in my past accomplishments and potential for the future. Finally, I extend my greatest thanks to Ruthann Godollei, who persevered with me throughout the writing of this manuscript and the advancement of my career. She has served as an excellent role model for including our passions for scholarship, teaching, and the pursuit of social justice in everything we do. My admiration for Ruthann knows no bounds, and I would not be where I am or who I am without her.

# APPENDIX

This appendix includes the names for all Minnesota new-wave cooperatives formed between 1971 and 1999, organized by the city in which they operated and noting the year in which they first opened (and possibly closed). When their names changed over the years, the most recent name is listed first, with previous names listed in parentheses.

The initial list of Minnesota new-wave cooperatives was derived from various directories published between 1973 and 1994. These include the following:

Co-op Directory Association. 1977. *Food Co-op Directory*. Albuquerque, N.M.: Co-op Directory Association.

Co-op Directory Association. 1980. *Coop Directory 1980*. Albuquerque, N.M.: Co-op Directory Association.

Ronco, William. 1974. *Food Co-ops: An Alternative to Shopping in Supermarkets*. Boston: Beacon Press.

Keller, George. 1994. *1994 National Co-op Directory*. Brooks, Maine: Co-op News Network.

Additional information came from articles in the *Scoop*, a trade magazine published between 1976 and 1980 by the All Cooperating Assembly, available in the archives at the Minnesota History Center, St. Paul, Minnesota.

| City | Cooperative Name (Previous Name) | Years Active |
|------|----------------------------------|--------------|
| Afton | Afton Village Co-op | 1993–1995 |
| Albert Lea | Wintergreen Food Co-op | 1976– |
| Anoka | Anoka Food Co-op | 1977–2003 |
| Bemidji | Harmony Food Co-op | 1977– |
| Big Lake | Great River Co-op | 1978–1985 |
| Blue Earth | Rainbow Food Co-op | 1979– |
| Brainerd | Crow Wing Food Co-op | 1979– |
| Brooklyn Center | Northwest Community Co-op | 1979–1985 |
| Buffalo | Buffalo Family Foods | 1980–1988 |
| Burnsville | Valley Natural Foods Co-op | 1977– |
| Cambridge | City Center Market | 1976– |
| Dawson | Western Prairie Food Co-op | 1992– |
| Duluth | West End Neighborhood Food Co-op | 1978–1981 |
| ——— | Whole Foods Co-op | 1971– |
| Ely | Northwoods Whole Foods Co-op | 1978– |
| Grand Marais | Cook County Whole Foods Co-op | 1976– |
| Grand Rapids | Cove Whole Food Co-op | 1976– |
| Hackensack | Countryside Co-op | 1976– |
| Hastings | Spiral Food Co-op | 1978– |
| Houston | Root River Market Co-op | 1999– |
| Isle | Mille Lacs Area Food Co-op | 1977– |
| Lengby | Good Foods Store | 1978–1992 |
| Litchfield | Natural Foods Co-op/Market | 1980– |
| Little Falls | Heartland Foods | 1976–1984 |
| Long Prairie | Everybody's Healthfood Market | 1978– |
| Mankato | Community Food Store | 1976–1982 |
| Marshall | Family Food Co-op | 1977–1992 |
| Minneapolis | Beanery | 1972–1978 |
| ——— | Bryant Central | 1973–1977 |
| ——— | East Calhoun | 1977–1995 |
| ——— | Ecology Cooperative | 1971–1973 |
| ——— | Elliot Park Co-op | 1980–1983 |
| ——— | Good Grits Neighborhood Non-Profit Store | 1975–1979 |
| ——— | Linden Hills Food Co-op | 1976– |
| ——— | Mill City Co-op | 1972–1985 |
| ——— | North County Co-op Grocery | 1971–2007 |
| ——— | Northeast Whole Foods Co-op | 1973–1978 |
| ——— | Northside Food Community | 1974–1979 |
| ——— | Powderhorn Co-op | 1973–1995 |

| | | |
|---|---|---|
| ———— | Seward Co-op Grocery & Deli | 1971– |
| ———— | Southeast Co-op | 1979–1986 |
| ———— | Wedge Community Co-op | 1974– |
| ———— | West Bank Co-op Supermarket | 1972–1988 |
| ———— | Whole Foods | 1971–1983 |
| Minnetonka | Lakewinds Natural Foods | 1982– |
| Morris | Pomme De Terre Food Co-op | 1975– |
| New Brighton | New Brighton Food Co-op | 1976–1981 |
| New Ulm | New Ulm Food Co-op | 1994–1998 |
| Northfield | Prairie Foods | 1980–1984 |
| Oak Center | Oak Center General Store Food Co-op | 1978– |
| Ortonville | Granary Food Co-op | 1986– |
| Owatonna | Harvest Food Co-op | 1979– |
| Red Wing | Whole Valley Food Co-op | 1978–1987 |
| Rochester | Rochester Good Food Co-op | 1983– |
| Sandstone | Kettle River Trading Post Co-op | 1978–1989 |
| Silver Bay | Friends and Neighbors Co-op | 1981–1987 |
| St. Cloud | Good Earth Food Co-op | 1973– |
| St. Paul | Capital City Food Co-op | 1979–1994 |
| ———— | Hampden Park Food Co-op | 1973– |
| | (Green Grass Grocery) | 1973–1979 |
| | (SAP TOO) | 1979–1990 |
| ———— | Merri-Grove Co-op | 1976–1982? |
| ———— | Mississippi Market Food Co-op | 1980– |
| ———— | North End Community Co-op | 1977–1983 |
| ———— | Selby Community Food Store | 1971–1982 |
| ———— | St. Anthony Park Foods | 1972–1990 |
| ———— | Westside Food Co-op | 1977–1981? |
| St. Peter | St. Peter Food Co-op & Deli | 1979– |
| Stillwater | River Market Community Co-op | 1977– |
| | (Valley Food Co-op) | 1977–2008 |
| Virginia | Natural Harvest Whole Food Co-op | 1979– |
| Wayzata | St. Luke Community Co-op | 1978–1982 |
| Wells | Glass Jar Food Co-op | 1983–1990 |
| Willmar | Kandi Cupboard | 1980– |
| Windom | Plum Creek Food Co-op | 1980– |
| Winona | Bluff Country Co-op | 1972– |
| | (Famine Foods) | 1972–1992 |

# NOTES

## Introduction

1. During the 1970s, a similar confusion about the proper use of the "natural" label took place in federal regulatory circles, but both the Federal Trade Commission and the Food and Drug Administration deemed the term too nebulous to regulate.

2. Before the 1970s, Minnesota also played host to a large number of mostly rural consumer cooperatives that formed between 1920 and 1940. Few of these remain in existence today, but new-wave cooperative activists embrace them in their historical accounts.

3. Throughout this work, I shall generally refer to the dominant value orientation of the cooperatives as "ethical consumerism." Others have referred to this concept as "political consumerism," but this shifts the focus toward the larger structures of society rather than toward the personal motivations and moral underpinnings of the individual. In many ways, the Co-op Wars was a battle between these two conceptions of how one's purchasing dollar has a lasting impact in a movement for social change.

## 1. The Cause of Organic Food

1. In March 2012, the Mariposa Co-op moved down the street from its narrow, 500-square-foot storefront on Baltimore Avenue to an expansive space in a formerly abandoned bank building. The renovations cost more than $2.5 million, and it took more than four years to acquire the funds, design the new store, and complete the construction. When it relocated, it also changed most of the policies that had characterized its membership for almost forty years. Shopping was no longer restricted to members, and the work requirement was eliminated. It also began accepting cash for purchases, and members no longer

had keys for after-hours access. One of my brother's metal grills constructed for the old location, however, did find a home in the new store.

2. Quoted in Sanderson (1976). In addition to stocking canned goods, the CO was also pushing the People's Warehouse (and thus the cooperatives themselves) to start selling sugar. At this time, most of the natural foods advocates eschewed all forms of granulated sugar, advocating for honey as the sole sweetener to be used in cooking and baking.

3. As I mentioned in the Introduction (but will reiterate once again), the term "organic" did not become a regulatory term—one relating to labeling and certification regimes—until late in the twentieth century. In these early chapters, I often refer to natural, organic, and sustainable food regimes without making fine distinctions among them. Throughout much of the twentieth century the meanings of these terms did not remain fixed, and in fact attempts to define them legislatively resulted in fierce debates and regulatory turf wars. I will occasionally use the term "eco-foods" as a catch-all for products produced and consumed with a greater awareness of how they impact both the natural and the human biological systems. In part, my loose nomenclature reflects the usage of the periods we are investigating as well as the ambiguity of what "organic" could or should mean in the larger market.

4. The order of the elements N, P, and K was proposed by the National Fertilizer Association in 1928 and adopted by the Association of Official Agricultural Chemists in 1930 (Mehring, Adams, and Jacob 1957). Modern mixed fertilizers indicate the percentage of their NPK nutrient contents with designations such as 10–15–10.

5. Quotation from Nobelstiftelsen (1964). Haber's Nobel Prize was perhaps appropriate since the award was funded by the estates of a dynamite industrialist. Haber had devoted additional research during the war to the effects of poison gas, overseeing the Germans' first use of chlorine gas at Ypres, Belgium, where more than 67,000 people died. He also developed the first mass-production gas masks with absorbent filters.

6. Statistics from Nelson and Parker (1990). The 1900 Census of Agriculture reported that the scientific management of farms was encouraged by the USDA, which had helped to "so [educate] the farmers of the country that intensive farming is now practiced to a much greater extent than formerly, and the careful and scientific use of fertilizers is everywhere becoming more general. These facts, combined with the gradual exhaustion of the soil in the older parts of the country, have created an increasing demand for commercial fertilizers" (U.S. Census Bureau 1902).

7. See Ordish (1976, 43–46). In 1476, cutworms were taken to court in Berne, Switzerland, pronounced guilty, excommunicated by the archbishop and

then banished: a rare example of pesticidal justice in both the profane and the divine realms.

8. See Ordish (1976). His delightful work *The Constant Pest: A Short History of Pests and Their Control* provides some very interesting accounts of creative pesticide use prior to the eighteenth century. One class of pesticides developed between the two world wars of the twentieth century was based on cyanogens, a nitrogen-based chemical compound. An early pesticide known as "Zyklon A" had been banned by the Treaty of Versailles because of its potential use in the production of poison gas. Zyklon B was developed by Fritz Haber before he was forced to emigrate by the Nazis because of his Jewish heritage. Initially promoted as an insecticide, this gas was later employed in the gas chambers of concentration camps. The German company IG-Farben (founded by Carl Bosch, the other half of the Haber-Bosch nitrogen-fixation process) held the patent on Zyklon B, and it later employed 83,000 slave laborers from Auschwitz during World War II. Fourteen of the twenty-three members of IG-Farben's board of directors would be sentenced to prison terms at the Nuremburg trials for crimes against humanity.

9. Müller would receive the Nobel Prize in Physiology or Medicine in 1948 for his discovery of DDT's effectiveness in fighting typhoid and related diseases. In his presentation speech, Professor G. Fischer related the following story about the chemical's effectiveness and persistence: "In 1945, when DDT was still relatively untried, I met an English Major in Germany who told me he had treated the window pane of his room with DDT since he was plagued by masses of flies. After the DDT solution had been sprayed on, the flies died and lay in heaps on the window ledge. The following morning a German soldier entered and thoroughly cleaned the window. When the Major noticed this he couldn't help crying 'Goodbye my DDT!'. But this farewell was uncalled for. In spite of the thorough cleaning, the window pane retained its deadly action on the flies. This little story amply illustrates how persistent DDT is and how small the dosage required" (Nobelstiftelsen 1964).

10. See David Goodman et al. (1987) for an extended discussion of input substitutions. Fitzgerald's *Every Farm a Factory* (2003) presents a compelling argument that the industrialization of farming operations involved much more than the acceptance and adoption of technological advances; an all-encompassing logic of scientific management was adopted by academics, bankers, economists, and government officials. "The offices, bureaus, and departments in the USDA, designed to serve as conduits between the state and its farmers, were also the means to quantify, rationalize, and standardize farm activity so that it could be understood and controlled from a distance" (34).

11. Quotation from Loomis and Barton (1961, 18–19).

12. Statistics from the National Agricultural Statistics Service (2009, 9).

13. Call and Throckmorton (1918, 3). Throckmorton later became the dean of agriculture at Kansas State University and an advocate of input substitutions rather than methods of soil preservation based on the practices described earlier. In 1951, he wrote an article titled "The Organic Farming Myth," in which he said: "In recent years there has grown up in this country a cult of misguided people who call themselves 'organic farmers' and who would—if they could—destroy the chemical fertilizer industry on which so much of our agriculture depends. These so-called organic farmers preach a strange, two-pronged doctrine compounded mainly of pure superstition and myth, with just enough half-truth, pseudo-science and emotion thrown in to make their statements sound plausible to the uninformed" (1951, 21). Kansas State University later named its Plant Sciences Center building in his honor.

14. Steiner (1974, 64) and Pfeiffer and Heckel (1940, iii). Debates continue within the biodynamic movement on issues such as "the effects of planting dates and lunar positions on the yield of carrots," as evidenced by a 1998 article in issue 230 of the journal *Biodynamics*.

15. Wrench (1945, 128). While Lord Curzon's project continued for the next twenty years, his second term as governor general ended abruptly in 1905 due to rising hostility directed at his partition of Bengal into two regions, one of which would become the independent nation of Bangladesh in 1947.

16. Howard (1924, 36). At this time, many natural sources of nitrogen were actually exported in the form of various oil-seeds, food products, and animal hides and bones. Nitrogen that was imported to the region was primarily routed to Java and the Straits Settlements. Had synthetic nitrogen fertilizers been more accessible and affordable to the farmers in Howard's region of inquiry, his further studies in natural methods of nitrogen retention might never have taken place. Howard adopted a similar approach to solving other agricultural problems by examining the source before proposing a solution: "*Insects and fungi are not the real cause of plant diseases but only attack unsuitable varieties or crops imperfectly grown. Their true role is that of censors, pointing out the crops that are improperly nourished. . . .* In other words, the pests must be looked upon as Nature's professors of agriculture" (quoted in Rodale 1945, 30, emphasis in original).

17. The "rudest of the arts" quotation is from Lawes, Gilbert, and Masters (1883, 290), while the second is from Howard (1924, 36).

18. Howard (1940, 195–96, emphasis added).

19. Rodale grew up in New York City afflicted by a number of ailments, including dizziness, colds, and chronic headaches. His early education was in accounting, and for a time he served as a tax auditor for the federal government.

Rodale later went into the electrical equipment business with his brother and moved his business to Emmaus in 1930. The Rodale Manufacturing Company, which produced wiring devices and electrical connectors, was a major success, allowing the brothers to accumulate millions of dollars despite the ongoing Great Depression. These fortunes supported J. I. Rodale's activities for the rest of his life. Carlton Jackson's (1974) biography, *J. I. Rodale: Apostle of Nonconformity*, provides an interesting account of his life.

20. Throckmorton's 1951 essay vilifying organic production techniques appeared to directly oppose Rodale's efforts to popularize the concept. Throckmorton wrote, "Strange as it may seem, those who attack the use of fertilizers have little or no reason to use them, as they usually aren't making their living by farming. Many of them are folks who garden or farm for recreation" (21).

21. As the 1950s progressed, Rodale became increasingly disenchanted with scientific communities, an attitude that corresponded to his growing public stature as a well-known but marginal and cranky public figure. Nevertheless, Rodale's effect on the sustainable agriculture movement cannot be underestimated. As a marketer, he used the word "organic" in a way that was nothing short of brilliant, as it usurped an existing term in the sciences that had, even in the cultural realm, a reference to living matter. For all of his refusal to take political stances, he successfully cast the opponents of his project as "inorganic," against life. Given his long history of lackluster publishing success, this single contribution to the movement was a brilliant marketing ploy. Beyond simple nomenclature, Rodale also pointed out one possible avenue for social movement success, by appealing to consumers without imposing any larger system of beliefs.

22. Secretary Flemming's quotation from Callahan (2011, 245). The secretary's announcement was based on the recently passed "Delaney Clause" of the Federal Food, Drug, and Cosmetic Act. Formally the Food Additives Amendment of 1958, this section declared that the FDA could not approve the use of any food additive that had been demonstrated to cause cancer in laboratory animals. While the amendment did not cover pesticide use on raw foods, it applied to processed foods, since concentrations can increase dramatically, representing an unintended "additive." Although the EPA attempted in 1988, during the Reagan administration, to exempt the use of pesticides and other additives that posed a "de minimus" risk to humans, this change was later challenged by the National Resources Defense Council and overturned by the Ninth Circuit Court of Appeals. The ironically named "Food Quality Protection Act" of 1996 specifically exempted pesticides from the Delaney Clause.

23. Hunter (1962).

24. Erskine (1972).

25. Margolius (1971, C1).

26. "Boom in Organic Foods" (1972, A18).

27. Rodale Press (1971, BR19); Berry (1971, 25, emphasis in original).

## 2. Twentieth-Century Cooperatives

1. Massachusetts Bay Colony quotation from Knapp (1969, 6). Alexis de Tocqueville ([1840] 1969), in his work *Democracy in America*, made particular mention of the tendency to form associations, wryly claiming that "Americans of all ages, all conditions, and all dispositions, constantly form associations. . . . As soon as several of the inhabitants of the United States have taken up an opinion or a feeling which they wish to promote in the world, they look out for mutual assistance; and as soon as they have found another out they combine" (513).

2. Quotation from Brown (1944, 23).

3. See Knapp (1969) for a thorough treatment of cooperative development in the United States. Throughout the history of early American cooperatives, one often sees a pattern of immediate interest and success, followed by rapid expansion and then financial failure. In this respect, the Union Cooperative Association No. 1 was a trendsetter in several ways.

4. Quotations in this section are from National Grange (1874), including the two stated principles. The National Grange is still an active organization based in Washington, D.C., claiming 240,000 members in 2007, with branches in more than 2,000 municipalities. Though it no longer plays a major role in any economic markets, it does serve important social functions for its members.

5. The "pell mell" quotation is from Buck (1913, 275). Florence Parker wrote extensively about the National Grange in her 1956 work, *The First 125 Years: A History of Distributive and Service Cooperation in the United States, 1829–1954*, published by the Cooperative League of the U.S.A.

6. Hood (1933). Note that, as with the later 1992 law authorizing the USDA to create national organic standards, these laws governing cooperative associations were considered an issue of "marketing" for the agricultural industry.

7. Parker (1956).

8. Kallen (1976, 257).

9. Cummings (1897, 266).

10. Bailey (1911, 220).

11. Margaret Digby's 1933 work *Digest of Co-operative Law at Home and Abroad* provides a good comparative assessment of the diverse legal environment facing cooperatives at this time.

12. For those who are truly interested in the politics of how government bureaucracies create and protect their turf as they confront different presidential administrations, Joseph P. Goldberg and William T. Moye's 1985 *The First Hundred Years of the Bureau of Labor Statistics* is actually quite an interesting read.

13. Quotations in this and the next two paragraphs are from Parker (1923).

14. In many of these rural areas, agriculture would have been the largest employment sector, but these data specifically exclude farmers' cooperatives unless they also had a retail component.

15. Parker (1943b, 1).

16. Response rates had improved substantially between the 1920s surveys and those conducted in the '30s. If anything, the decreases in organizations, membership, and sales were probably even more pronounced.

17. Flexner and Ericson (1957, 2). As I demonstrate in chapter 3, similar issues of consistent categorization presented challenges for enumerating more contemporary cooperatives as well.

18. Rao (2009, 7), emphasis in original.

19. Rao (2009, 10).

20. Jasper (1997, 264), emphasis in original. In the wake of the Supreme Court's *Obergefell v. Hodges* ruling allowing same-sex marriage nationwide, several states have proposed "religious freedom" laws permitting individuals employed in business enterprises and local governments to refuse service to LGBTQ+ couples. The strongest pressure applied to governors, convincing many of them to veto such legislation, has come from professional sports leagues threatening to refrain from future competitions and economic participation in these states.

21. While I wish I could take credit for coining the term "buycott," I first ran across this term when reading an analysis by Gendron, Bisaillon, and Rance (2009) exploring the social action dynamics of the Fair Trade movement. Calling such organizations "social economic movements," they write, "We present it as a new generation of the social movement, not in its essence as such but more through its methods of action, which involves different tools that have become refined and diversified over the years. Boycotting campaigns have been replaced by *buycotting* strategies (see Micheletti, 2003), based not only on the education and awareness of consumers but also on measures of traceability and labeling" (72). The term has thus been in use for more than a decade.

22. North American Students of Cooperation (1991, 7).

23. Rao (2009, 12), emphasis in original.

24. International Cooperative Alliance, http://www.ica.coop/coop/princi ples.html.

## 3. Resistance and Persistence

1. My early conception of what "organic" meant in this paragraph was admittedly simplistic and crude, and it makes me think about how our parents

used to tell my vegetarian brother to just pick the meat out of the chili and stop complaining. Since that time, I have learned that this simplistic definition not only is widely shared but also serves as a very convenient summation of the underlying ideology. The actual practices required to grow organic food on a larger scale (as well as the regulations governing organic label certification) are certainly much more complex, but in this work I'm much more concerned with the *cultural* understanding of this term.

2. All data pertaining to 1970 city populations, land masses, education, and income in this chapter and in chapter 4 derive from Vol. 1, part 25 ("Characteristics of the Population: Minnesota") of the *1970 Census of the Population* (U.S. Bureau of the Census 1973).

3. Keillor (2000, 5).

4. Before the 1970s, Minnesota also played host to a larger number of mostly rural consumer cooperatives that formed between 1920 and 1940. Few of these remain in existence today, and, though new-wave cooperative activists embrace them in both their historical accounts and their contemporary listings, these organizations did not adopt the countercultural attitudes expressed during the 1970s, nor did they emphasize natural or organic foods in their stocks of supplies.

5. The *Cooperative Grocer* publication continues to this day, under the auspices of a national trade association, the Cooperative Grocer Network. Even a cursory examination of article titles in its archives provides a good sense of the issues faced by these organizations as the organic foods industry matured and achieved widespread acceptance by larger agribusiness companies and the consuming public. In particular, one can trace the evolution of computing technology in small storefront operations, as authors first gave advice on whether to purchase a computer, then explained how spreadsheets worked, and later commented on integrating point-of-sale systems and, finally, business websites.

6. Interview with Dave Gutknecht, December 4, 2009. Throughout the rest of this book, I will include one note the first time I introduce the subject of an interview; all future comments attributed to that person should be assumed to be from the same interview unless stated otherwise.

7. Interview with Gail Graham, January 19, 2010.

8. Blooming Prairie was itself purchased by United Natural Foods in 2002, marking the end of cooperative ownership in this distributorship lineage. Graham became a board member for United Natural Foods, which serves as one of the major suppliers to many contemporary cooperatives.

9. Curhan and Wertheim (1972, 28).

10. "Food Shoppers Buy Together," *Business Week* (1970, 99). Zwerdling's exaggerated claim about thousands upon thousands of co-ops was included

in a 1979 edited volume titled *Co-ops, Communes & Collectives: Experiments in Social Change in the 1960s and 1970s*, which is nevertheless an excellent collection of studies and analyses collected when the movement was still fresh and vibrant.

11. Hillestad (1979). The concept of a "minimalist organization" is described in more detail by Terence Halliday, Michael Powell, and Mark Granfors (1987), including the "liability of newness" concept referenced later. They suggest two additional key dimensions that differentiate the minimalist from the non-minimalist organization: reserve infrastructures and propensity for adaptation. Perhaps ironically, minimalist organizations have *greater* access to supplemental organizational infrastructures, because everyone involved in the operation of the business understands that it cannot operate completely self-sufficiently. Members pool their resources. Operating as a collective, many early activists involved in the new-wave cooperative movement understood that they needed to contribute their talents or labor as the need arose. These tasks could have included providing legal counsel, helping with the accounting, or cleaning out the produce cooler. However, though these services help sustain the business, the minimalist organization defines many of them a priori as extracurricular, structurally unnecessary to continue operations. Minimalist organizations also exhibit a higher tendency to adapt to changes in the market environment; they appear least susceptible to organizational inertia as a controlling factor inhibiting transformation. Because group members have invested less (both financially and emotionally) in the organizational or physical structure, they do not have the same reluctance to alter their business model in response to external stimuli.

12. Interview with Michael Doyle, July 30, 2009.

13. "Hearthstone Co-op Re-Opens," *Scoop* (1979, 5).

14. Personal correspondence with Steven Schwen, July 3, 2009.

15. Unless specified otherwise, all of the unattributed financial records and newsletter excerpts in this and the remaining chapters are from the "Minnesota Food Cooperatives Records" archives collected by Kris Olsen at the Minnesota Historical Society.

16. Halliday et al. (1987, 457).

17. Lakewinds Community Cooperative (2011), www.lakewinds.com.

18. Despite the state law, for the purpose of brevity I shall continue to use the term "cooperative" even for those legally designated as "cooperative associations."

19. Sharp and Copeland (1976, 9). As chapter 4 demonstrates, the timing of these legal incorporations was not random; the events surrounding the Co-op Wars brought new attention to such matters. In the years after 1980, the founding

dates correspond much more closely to SOS filings and often preceded official opening dates by several months. This in itself can be seen as a step toward greater institutionalization of this organizational form and community.

20. I found most cooperatives willing to supply the most basic information, although several were wary about providing any detailed financial records. Combined with the lack of operational data for many of the failed organizations, a complete analysis based on these characteristics is not possible.

21. This longevity of rural grocery cooperatives is even more remarkable given that many of the towns in Minnesota have seen traditional grocers, whether independent or chain, forced out of business when big-box stores like Walmart or its bulk-buying venture, Sam's Club, established a foothold in the area. I know many very guilty-feeling liberals in outstate areas who are loath to admit that they shop at Walmart and quickly point out that it's become the only option within a reasonable distance of their homes. That co-ops have been able to hold out—whereas Piggly Wiggly could not—seems to reinforce the political and even emotional investment communities make in rural co-ops.

22. Belasco (1989, 273).

23. Hansmann (1980) assumes that the primary appeal of a cooperative lies in its ability to help consumers navigate a hostile market. Ware (1989) takes a similar economic approach to explain the existence of cooperatives in competitive markets, arguing that they strive to achieve goals similar to those of for-profit companies.

24. Mitchell (1959, 663); Stevenson (1965, 406); Soper and Watt (1965, 415); Duscha (1972, SM34). The USDA, long aligned with the interests of both larger farming enterprises and the businesses that supplied them, remained opposed to anything remotely promoting organic food production throughout the 1970s. In 1979, however, the USDA formally acknowledged the desire of growers to learn more about organic farming when Bob Bergland, President Carter's Secretary of Agriculture, directed the USDA to study the organic movements in Europe and Japan. This represented the first (and, as it turned out, the only) foray into organic agricultural research independently initiated by the USDA. Bergland commissioned the study after visiting one of his Minnesota neighbor's recently converted organic farm, where the secretary found the "soil had improved, with crop yields up, production costs down and animals healthier" (Wells 1980, C3).

25. "The 'Organic' Craze," *New York Times* (1971, D37).

26. Heinz (1972, 47).

27. Nixon (2016).

28. Epstein (1972, 235); Hildebrand (1972, 945).

29. Mayer (1973, L5); Mayer and Dwyer (1977, 112); Fosburgh (1974, 146).

30. Technically speaking, as will be discussed later, a cooperative is *not* a nonprofit organization. Hansmann contrasts the functions of the nonprofit company and the cooperative association: "The typical cooperative is a limited-profit enterprise so far as investors of capital are concerned; earnings in excess of the amounts distributable to investors must be reinvested or returned to patrons. Thus cooperatives bear a certain resemblance, on the one hand, to nonprofits, and, on the other hand, to regulated-rate-of-return organizations such as public utilities" (1980, 889). I think we can forgive the cooperative activists, however, for suggesting that they are not operating their stores in order to maximize revenue.

31. *Co-op Handbook Collective* (1975, 42).

32. "Food Shoppers Buy Together" (1970).

33. See Sommer (1982) for one example of a writer attributing the rise of cooperatives to a desire for cheaper health food. Zwerdling (1979) attempted to provide statistics to document the growth, but as stated earlier his figures were not based on a more rigid definition of a cooperative as a formal business organization.

34. Personal correspondence with Tori Reynolds, July 29, 2009.

35. Even though the legislative power of individual states to override federal legislation is structurally limited by the Constitution's Commerce and Supremacy Clauses, actions by the states have been critical in filling legislative voids and in providing models for regulation that can then be taken up by actions at the federal level. As Bones stated in a review of organic food certification laws, "The absence of strong federal action in regulating food has allowed the states to exercise significant authority" (Bones 1992). Oregon was the first state to pass a law governing the labeling of organic foods, enacting its legislation in 1973. California adopted a comprehensive set of organic labeling requirements in 1979. By 1991 an additional twenty-one states had followed Oregon's lead and also created such standards regulating the labeling of organic foods.

36. Phenix and Evechild (1975, 1).

37. Sharp and Copeland (1976); Bobbie (1976); Hubbuch (1975); Plowshare Farms (1975).

38. Gutknecht (1990, emphasis added).

39. Noller (1981).

40. Haveman and Rao (1997, 1607).

41. Haedicke (2017, 134).

42. Raasch-Gilman (1994, 1).

## 4. Dissent among the Dissenters

1. The University of Minnesota campus straddles the Mississippi River. Most of the older academic buildings reside on its east bank, known as the "East Bank." The West Bank served as an expansion to the campus, with major urban renewal building projects taking place in the 1960s and '70s. The People's Center included a health clinic (which continues to serve lower-income community members to this day) and the West Bank Community Union.

2. All three of these outstate co-ops remain in business to this day.

3. Interview with Allan Malkis, August 11, 2010.

4. Interestingly, the 1972 presidential election ballot in Minnesota also contained the names of five minor-party candidates: Louis Fisher for the Industrial Government Party, Linda Jenness for the Socialist Workers Party, Gus Hall for the Communist Party, Dr. Benjamin Spock for the People's Party, and John Birch Society member John Schmitz for the American Party. Except for Schmitz, these minor candidates all promoted far-left political agendas. Though they received a combined total of less than 2.5 percent of the votes nationwide and in Minnesota, the leftist candidates also underperformed in most of the neighborhoods surrounding the early cooperatives. In the combined precincts around the North Country cooperative, for example, these candidates were selected by voters on only 8 of the 380 ballots cast. Though residents of these areas had decidedly liberal political views, they also demonstrated a pragmatic approach to social change in voting.

5. I conducted a formal statistical analysis of these data, taking into account all of the variables mentioned here and using a binomial logistic regression for the 169 cities in Minnesota with populations greater than 2,500. With an $R^2$ value of .71, the analysis showed that for each 1 percent increase in the amount of support that McGovern received over Nixon for his strongest ward in any given city, it became 13 percent more likely that a cooperative would form in that city between 1971 and 1975.

6. The distinction between a worker- and a consumer-owned cooperative does have implications for the constituents of these organizations (emphasizing participatory democracy), but, in practice, the difference had less meaning for the new-wave cooperatives. Most of the earliest operations (prior to 1975) began as worker-owned businesses, then shifted their focus once they had attracted enough patrons they could recruit as members. Most of the later groups founded themselves explicitly as consumer cooperatives. Even worker-owned cooperatives might allow nonmembers to purchase goods, albeit at higher prices or without the benefit of a member discount.

7. As mentioned in chapter 3, one early cooperative activist had urged me to focus on the collective aspect of cooperatives rather than concentrate on a

few key personalities. The events of the Co-op Wars included several individual clashes between key cooperative activists, including allegations of physical assault and property damage. In this section I pay more attention to the ideological arguments and organizational changes put forth by the combatants; Cox's work provides a more detailed and gripping account of this period.

8. Cox (1994, 39–40).

9. Comeau and Haugen (1975).

10. Phenix and Evechild (1975).

11. Garwick, Biseanze, and Long (1975, 1).

12. Cox (1994, 71).

13. Sanderson (1976).

14. Cox (1994, 108).

15. Tilly and Wood (2009, 3). See Tilly (1978, 1995, 2006) for explorations of cross-national historical social movements on a larger scale. *Regimes and Repertoires* (2006) is especially useful for describing the relationships between tactics and goals. It is also worth noting that, towards the end of his life, Dr. Martin Luther King Jr. had shifted from "classic" civil rights issues to ones emphasizing economic justice. He was assassinated in Memphis after spending the day supporting black sanitation workers who were on strike, one of his many later efforts in his "Poor People's Campaign."

16. Lukes (2004, 19), emphasis in original. When considering how the state might wield this first dimension of power in areas of food production or consumption, we might recall the Supreme Court case *NFiB v. Sebelius* (567 U.S. 519 (2012)) about the constitutionality of the Affordable Care Act. Several questions posed by the justices pondered whether the government could force citizens to eat broccoli.

17. Lukes (2004, 27). While Lukes proposed these three dimensions as novel conceptions in *Power: A Radical View*, his third dimension echoes the concept of "false consciousness" described by Karl Marx more than one hundred years earlier. When the preference structures of the elite are internalized by the masses, one of the biggest challenges for social movement activists involves lifting this veil and providing a new perspective on nearly every aspect of an individual's life.

## 5. Developing Organic Market Infrastructures

1. I performed a binomial logistic regression analysis to isolate the most important factors in this second wave of cooperative formation in Minnesota's cities with populations greater than 2,500. For those who are well versed in this form of statistical analysis, you might be impressed that the $p$-value was less than .001 for the influence of a 1940s cooperative in any given city.

2. Gersten (1987), emphasis added.

3. Jenson (1986).

4. Leverton (1974).

5. Felien (1975), emphasis added.

6. Burchard (1972).

7. Rao (2009, 12), emphasis in original.

8. Personal interview with Lori Zuidema, December 4, 2009.

9. Even after the first national organic standards were proposed in 1997, Secretary of Agriculture Dan Glickman stated explicitly that this was merely a marketing term that did not imply any health or environmental benefits.

10. I highly recommend Julie Guthman's *Agrarian Dreams: The Paradox of Organic Farming in California* for a detailed study about how California farmers pushed for certification regimes in their state. Guthman studies the development of organic standards from the producers' point of view, arguing that the implementation of the 2002 national organic standards actually represented a step back for this movement.

11. Cooperative Grocer Information Network (CGIN) (1998).

12. According to an oft-cited Dun and Bradstreet report from 1996, "Businesses with fewer than 20 employees have only a 37% chance of surviving four years (of business) and only a 9% chance of surviving 10 years." The fact that more than 75 percent of the co-ops operating in 1980 were still in business thirty years later suggests these operations do not follow norms of mainstream capitalist enterprises in more ways than one.

13. Cox (1994, 40).

14. When the members of the Blooming Prairie Cooperative Warehouse chose to sell their operations to United Foods, one term of the sale allowed for the organization to create a new nonprofit organization. The Blooming Prairie Foundation now offers grants to those who help fulfill its new mission: "to further the health of the people and the planet and the cooperative business model by supporting development, research, and educational efforts in the organic industry and the cooperative community."

15. Noller (1981).

16. Beers (1980, 11).

17. Malkis (1978, 5).

18. Graham (1980, 5).

## Conclusion

1. Youngdahl, who is probably more revered in Minnesota for creating the Minnesota Governor's Fishing Opener in the same year—a tradition that

has also continued to this day—later served as a judge on the U.S. District Court for the District of Columbia. One of his proudest legal achievements involved a dispute with Senator Joseph McCarthy, challenging the constitutionality of prosecuting Johns Hopkins University professor Owen J. Lattimore on charges that he had lied about being a communist sympathizer.

2. Cox (1994, 137).

3. Fromartz (2006, 238). This book, *Organic Inc.*, along with Philip Conford's *The Origins of the Organic Movement*, provide very compelling accounts about the histories, ideologies, and philosophies of early organic activists and the industrialization of this agricultural sector.

4. Bowman (2009).

5. Personal correspondence with Pete Wagner, February 18, 2019.

6. Boym (2016). In this excellent exploration of a very contemporary malady, Boym suggests that nostalgia "appears to be a longing for a place but is actually a yearning for a different time—the time of our childhood, the slower rhythms of our dreams. In a broader sense, nostalgia is a rebellion against the modern idea of time, the time of history and progress."

7. Cloud (2007).

8. This definition of a community food system was written by the UC Sustainable Agriculture Research and Education Program, quoted in Feenstra (2002, 100).

9. I have suggested that cooperatives exist in a market space between two supposed binaries: for-profit and nonprofit enterprises. Interestingly, the Minnesota legislature passed statute 304A in 2016, creating a new class of business category known as a "public-benefit corporation," one that expressly states in its articles of incorporation that it is dedicated to providing "a net material positive impact from the business and operations of a general benefit corporation on society, the environment, and the well-being of present and future generations." As of July 2017, eighty-five companies had registered with the state as public-benefit corporations; each has to file an annual report stating how it is contributing to the greater good of society (Prather 2017). This designation is not merely a marketing label. It helps redefine a company's fiduciary responsibility to its investors, allowing it to undertake activities that might not benefit solely the financial bottom line.

10. Whole Foods Market (2019).

11. Potential liability issues have constrained the desire of some cooperatives to require volunteering. The store might face increased costs to provide insurance for the volunteers. It might also have to report the value of any compensation (in terms of member discounts) to the Internal Revenue Service, requiring a member to pay taxes on the privilege of providing free labor.

12. Quotation from Hansmann (1996,166–67). Minnesota, of course, was settled during the nineteenth century, in large part by Scandinavian immigrants, and their role in making this state a "cooperative commonwealth" is explored in great detail by Steven Keillor.

13. Allen and Kovach (2000, 221).

14. Cox (1994, 5).

# BIBLIOGRAPHY

Allen, Patricia, and Martin Kovach. 2000. "The Capitalist Composition of Organic: The Potential of Markets in Fulfilling the Promise of Organic Agriculture." *Agriculture and Human Values* 17: 221–32.

Bailey, L. H. 1911. *The Country-Life Movement in the United States*. New York: Macmillan.

Beers, Scott. 1980. "Setting Coop Foundations: North Country Development Fund." *Scoop*, September, 11.

Belasco, Warren J. 1989. *Appetite for Change: How the Counterculture Took on the Food Industry 1966–1988*. New York: Pantheon Books.

Berry, Wendell. 1971. "Think Little." In *The Last Whole Earth Catalog*. Edited by Stewart Brand, 24–25. Menlo Park, Calif.: Nowels Publishing.

Bobbie. 1976. "Northfield Co-op." *Scoop*, April–May, 11.

Bones, Gordon G. 1992. "State and Federal Organic Food Production Laws: Coming of Age?" *North Dakota Law Review* 68: 405–44.

"Boom in Organic Foods." 1972. *Washington Post*, March 4, A18.

Bowman, Cissy. 2009. "In Memory of Eric Kindberg." *Cooperative Grocer*, April.

Boym, Svetlana. 2016. *The Future of Nostalgia*. New York: Basic Books.

Brown, William Henry. 1944. *The Rochdale Pioneers: A Century of Cooperation*. Manchester, England: The Co-operative Union Ltd.

Buck, Solon J. 1913. *The Granger Movement*. Cambridge, Mass.: Harvard University Press.

Burchard, Hank. 1972. "The Great Hunt for the Puny Potato." *Washington Post*, February 28, C1.

Call, L. E., and R. I. Throckmorton. 1918. "Bulletin No. 220: Soil Fertility." Manhattan: Agricultural Experiment Station, Kansas State Agricultural College.

Callahan, Joan R. 2011. *50 Health Scares That Fizzled*. Santa Barbara, Calif.: Greenwood Publishing Group.

Cloud, John. 2007. "Eating Better Than Organic." *Time*, March 2.

Comeau, Rebecca, and Bob Haugen. 1975. "The Beanery Paper." Unpublished manuscript. Kris Olsen, collector, Minnesota Food Cooperatives Records. St. Paul: Minnesota Historical Society.

Conford, Philip. 2001. *The Origins of the Organic Movement*. Edinburgh: Floris.

Cooperative Grocer Information Network (CGIN). 1998. "CGIN Bylaws." http://www.cgin.coop/about/bylaws.

Co-op Handbook Collective. 1975. *The Food Co-op Handbook: How to Bypass Supermarkets to Control the Quality and Price of Your Food*. Boston: Houghton Mifflin.

Cox, Craig. 1994. *Storefront Revolution: Food Co-ops and the Counterculture*. New Brunswick, N.J.: Rutgers University Press.

Cummings, Edward. 1897. "Co-operative Stores in the United States." *Quarterly Journal of Economics* 11: 266–79.

Curhan, Ronald C., and Edward G. Wertheim. 1972. "Consumer Food Buying Cooperatives: A Market Examined " *Journal of Retailing* 48: 28–39.

de Tocqueville, Alexis [1840] 1969. *Democracy in America*. Translated by George Lawrence. New York: Harper Collins.

Digby, Margaret. 1933. *Digest of Co-operative Law at Home and Abroad*. London: P. S. King & Son, Ltd.

Duscha, Julius. 1972. "Up, Up, Up—Butz Makes Hay Down on the Farm." *New York Times*, April 16, SM34.

Epstein, Emanuel. 1972. "A Blind Spot in Biology." *Science* 176: 235.

Erskine, Hazel. 1972. "The Polls: Pollution and Its Costs." *Public Opinion Quarterly* 36: 120–35.

Feenstra, Gail. 2002. "Creating Space for Sustainable Food Systems: Lessons from the Field." *Agriculture and Human Values* 19: 99–106.

Felien, Ed. 1975. "What's Happening in the Co-Op Movement?" Unpublished manuscript. Kris Olsen, collector, Minnesota Food Cooperatives Records. St. Paul: Minnesota Historical Society.

Fitzgerald, Deborah Kay. 2003. *Every Farm a Factory: The Industrial Ideal in American Agriculture*. New Haven, Conn., and London: Yale University Press.

Flexner, Jean A., and Anna-Stina Ericson. 1957. *Consumer Cooperatives*. U.S. Bureau of Labor Statistics Bulletin No. 1211. Washington, D.C.: U.S. Government Printing Office.

"Food Shoppers Buy Together." 1970. *Business Week*, December 5, 99.

Fosburgh, Lacey. 1974. "Organic Food Myth Dispelled." *New York Times*, March 10, 146.

Fromartz, Samuel. 2006. *Organic, Inc.: Natural Foods and How They Grew*. Orlando: Harcourt.

Garwick, Kris, Michael Biseanze, and Judy Long. 1975. "A Recap on 'Jeb' and 'Emma's' Response to the Beanery Paper." Unpublished manuscript. Kris Olsen, collector, Minnesota Food Cooperatives Records. St. Paul: Minnesota Historical Society.

Gendron, Corinne, Véronique Bisaillon, and Ana Isabel Otero Rance. 2009. "The Institutionalization of Fair Trade: More Than Just a Degraded Form of Social Action." *Journal of Business Ethics* 86: 63–79.

Gersten, Ross. 1987. "Building a Cooperative Community." *Cooperative Grocer*, February–March, 6–9.

Goldberg, Joseph P. and William T. Moye. 1985. *The First Hundred Years of the Bureau of Labor Statistics*. U.S. Bureau of Labor Statistics Bulletin No. 2235. Washington, D.C.: U.S. Government Printing Office.

Goodman, David, Bernardo Sorj, and John Wilkinson. 1987. *From Farming to Biotechnology: A Theory of Agro-Industrial Development*. Oxford: Basil Blackwell.

Graham, Frank Jr. 1970. *Since Silent Spring*. Boston: Houghton Mifflin.

Graham, Gail. 1980. "Three Co-ops Work to Develop Democratic Decision Making." *Scoop*, September, 6, 11.

Gussow, Joan Dye. 2002. *This Organic Life : Confessions of a Suburban Homesteader*. White River Junction, Vt.: Chelsea Green Publishing Co.

Guthman, Julie. 2004. *Agrarian Dreams: The Paradox of Organic Farming in California*. Berkeley: University of California Press.

Gutknecht, Dave. 1990. "Interview: Organics Growth a Continuing Wave—but Where Are the Co-ops?" *Cooperative Grocer*, October–November, 5–7.

Haedicke, Michael A. 2017. *Organizing Organic: Conflict and Compromise in an Emerging Market*. Stanford, CA: Stanford University Press.

Halliday, Terence C., Michael J. Powell, and Mark W. Granfors. 1987. "Minimalist Organizations: Vital Events in State Bar Associations, 1870–1930." *American Sociological Review* 52: 456–71.

Hansmann, Henry B. 1980. "The Role of Nonprofit Enterprise." *Yale Law Journal* 89: 835–901.

Hansmann, Henry B. 1996. *The Ownership of Enterprise*. Cambridge, Mass.: Belknap Press of Harvard University Press.

Haveman, Heather A., and Hayagreeva Rao. 1997. "Structuring a Theory of Moral Sentiments: Institutional and Organizational Coevolution in the Early Thrift Industry." *American Journal of Sociology* 102: 1606–51.

"Hearthstone Co-op Re-Opens after 2 Months." 1979. *Scoop*, January, 5.

Heinz II, Henry J. 1972. "Nutritional Illiteracy." *New York Times*, June 14, 47.

Hildebrand, Joel H. 1972. "Organic Gardening." *Science* 177: 944–45.

Hillestad, Sharon. 1979. "Hasting Co-Op Will Open Early Next Year." *Scoop*, January, 3.

Hood, Robin. 1933. "The American Situation." In *Year Book of Agricultural Co-operation 1933*. Edited by The Horace Plunkett Foundation, 117–28. London: P. S. King & Son, Ltd.

Howard, Albert. 1924. *Crop-Production in India: A Critical Survey of Its Problems*. London: Oxford University Press.

Howard, Albert. 1931. *The Waste Products of Agriculture: Their Utilization as Humus*. London: Oxford University Press.

Howard, Albert. 1940. *An Agricultural Testament*. London: Oxford University Press.

Hubbuch, Ray. 1975. "Farming Anyone?" *Scoop*, August–September, 3.

Hunter, Marjorie. 1962. "U.S. Sets Up Panel to Review the Side Effects of Pesticides: Controls Studied—Kennedy Finds Work Spurred by Rachel Carson Book." *New York Times*, August 31, 9.

Jackson, Carlton. 1974. *J. I. Rodale: Apostle of Nonconformity*. New York: Pyramid Books.

Jasper, James M. 1997. *The Art of Moral Protest: Culture, Biography, and Creativity in Social Movements*. Chicago: University of Chicago Press.

Jenson, Cheryl. 1986. "Market Niche in Vacationland." *Cooperative Grocer*, February–March, 11–12.

Kallen, Horace Meyer. 1976. *The Decline and Rise of the Consumer: A Philosophy of Consumer Cooperation*. New York: Arno Press.

Keillor, Steven J. 2000. *Cooperative Commonwealth: Co-ops in Rural Minnesota, 1859–1939*. St. Paul: Minnesota Historical Society Press.

Knapp, Joseph Grant. 1969. *The Rise of American Cooperative Enterprise: 1620–1920*. Danville, Ill.: Interstate Printers & Publishers.

Lakewinds Community Cooperative. 2011. "Who We Are." http://www.lake winds.com/store/Who-We-Are-W15C0.aspx.

Lawes, John. B., Joseph Henry Gilbert, and Maxwell Tylden Masters. 1883. *Agricultural, Botanical and Chemical Results of Experiments on the Mixed Herbage of Permanent Meadow: Part II. The Botanical Results*. London: For The Royal Society of Trèubner and Co.

Leverton, Ruth M. 1974. "Organic, Inorganic: What They Mean." In *Shopper's Guide: The 1974 Yearbook of Agriculture*. Edited by Jack Hayes, 70–73. Washington, D.C.: U.S. Government Printing Office.

Loomis, Ralph A., and Glen T. Barton. 1961. *Productivity of Agriculture*, vol. 1238. Washington, D.C.: U.S. Department of Agriculture.

Lukes, Steven. 2004. *Power: A Radical View*. Houndmills, Basingstoke, Hampshire; New York: Palgrave Macmillan.

Malkis, Allan. 1978. "The Phoenix Rises Again." *Scoop*, December, 5–6.

Margolius, Sidney. 1971. "'Unfit for Human Consumption'." *Washington Post*, December 9, C1.

Mayer, Jean. 1973. "Nutrition Questions and Answers: Demineralization of the Bone." *Washington Post*, June 3, L5.

Mayer, Jean, and Johanna Dwyer. 1977. "'Organic' Foods: Are They Better?" *Washington Post*, June 5, 112.

Mehring, A. L., J. Richard Adams, and Kenneth Donald Jacob. 1957. *Statistical Bulletin No. 191: Statistics on Fertilizer and Liming Materials in the United States*. Washington, D.C.: U.S. Department of Agriculture.

Mitchell, Helen S. 1959. "Don't Be Fooled by Fads." In *Food: The Yearbook of Agriculture 1959*. Edited by Alfred Stefferud, 660–68. Washington, D.C.: U.S. Government Printing Office.

Nabhan, Gary Paul. 2009. *Coming Home to Eat the Pleasures and Politics of Local Foods*. New York: Norton.

National Agricultural Statistics Service. 2009. *2007 Census of Agriculture*. Vol. 1: *Geographic Area Series*. Washington, D.C.: U.S. Department of Agriculture.

National Grange. 1874. "Declaration of Purpose of the National Grange." St. Louis, Missouri.

Nelson, Lewis B., and J. Harold Parker. 1990. *History of the U.S. Fertilizer Industry*. Muscle Shoals, Ala.: Tennessee Valley Authority.

Nixon, Alex. 2016. "Kraft Heinz Aims to Boost Sales with New Products, Cross Branding." *Tribune-Review*, June 6.

Nobelstiftelsen. 1964. *Nobel Lectures in Chemistry*. Vol. 1: *1901–1921*. Amsterdam, New York: Published for the Nobel Foundation by Elsevier Pub. Co.

Noller, John. 1981. "Slow Chain Coming." *Moving Food*, January–February, 30–35.

North American Students of Cooperation. 1991. *Organizer's Handbook*. Ann Arbor, Mich.: NASCO.

Ordish, George. 1976. *The Constant Pest: A Short History of Pests and Their Control*. New York: Scribner.

"The 'Organic' Craze." 1971. *New York Times*, February 7, D37.

Parker, Florence E. 1923. *Consumers' Cooperative Societies in the United States in 1920*. U.S. Bureau of Labor Statistics Bulletin No. 313. Washington, D.C.: U.S. Government Printing Office.

Parker, Florence E. 1927. *Cooperative Movement in the United States in 1925 (Other Than Agricultural)*. U.S. Bureau of Labor Statistics Bulletin No. 437. Washington, D.C.: U.S. Government Printing Office.

Parker, Florence E. 1931. *Consumers', Credit, and Productive Cooperative Societies, 1929*. U.S. Bureau of Labor Statistics Bulletin No. 531. Washington, D.C.: U.S. Government Printing Office.

Parker, Florence E. 1935. *Consumers', Credit, and Productive Cooperation in 1933*. U.S. Bureau of Labor Statistics Bulletin No. 612. Washington, D.C.: U.S. Government Printing Office.

Parker, Florence E. 1938. *Consumers' Cooperation in the United States, 1936.* U.S. Bureau of Labor Statistics Bulletin No. 659. Washington, D.C.: U.S. Government Printing Office.

Parker, Florence E. 1943a. *Activities of Consumers' Cooperatives in 1942.* U.S. Bureau of Labor Statistics Bulletin No. 757. Washington, D.C.: U.S. Government Printing Office.

Parker, Florence E. 1943b. *Consumers' Cooperatives in the United States in 1941.* U.S. Bureau of Labor Statistics Bulletin No. 725. Washington, D.C.: U.S. Government Printing Office.

Parker, Florence E. 1944. *Operations of Consumers' Cooperatives in 1943.* U.S. Bureau of Labor Statistics Bulletin No. 796. Washington, D.C.: U.S. Government Printing Office.

Parker, Florence E. 1945. *Operations of Consumers' Cooperatives in 1944.* U.S. Bureau of Labor Statistics Bulletin No. 843. Washington, D.C.: U.S. Government Printing Office.

Parker, Florence E. 1946. *Operations of Consumers' Cooperatives in 1945.* U.S. Bureau of Labor Statistics Bulletin No. 890. Washington, D.C.: U.S. Government Printing Office.

Parker, Florence E. 1948. *Consumers' Cooperatives and Credit Unions: Operations in 1946.* U.S. Bureau of Labor Statistics Bulletin No. 922. Washington, D.C.: U.S. Government Printing Office.

Parker, Florence E. 1949. *Consumers' Cooperatives: Operations in 1948.* U.S. Bureau of Labor Statistics Bulletin No. 971. Washington, D.C.: U.S. Government Printing Office.

Parker, Florence E. 1951. *Consumers' Cooperatives in 1949: Operations and Developments.* U.S. Bureau of Labor Statistics Bulletin No. 1013. Washington, D.C.: U.S. Government Printing Office.

Parker, Florence E. 1952. *Consumers' Cooperatives: Operations in 1950.* U.S. Bureau of Labor Statistics Bulletin No. 1049. Washington, D.C.: U.S. Government Printing Office.

Parker, Florence E. 1956. *The First 125 Years: A History of Distributive and Service Cooperation in the United States, 1829–1954.* Chicago: Cooperative League of the U.S.A.

Pfeiffer, Ehrenfried, and Frederick Heckel. 1940. *Bio-Dynamic Farming and Gardening: Soil Fertility, Renewal and Preservation.* New York: Anthroposophic Press.

Phenix, Chuck, and Nancy Evechild. 1975. "A Response to the Beanery Paper." Unpublished manuscript. Kris Olsen, collector, Minnesota Food Cooperatives Records. St. Paul: Minnesota Historical Society.

Plowshare Farms. 1975. "Farmers Meeting, March 8–9." *Scoop,* 16.

Prather, Shannon. 2017. "New Class of Minnesota Business Invests in Doing Good." *Star Tribune*, July 29.

Raasch-Gilman, Betsy. 1994. *A History of North Country Co-op*. Minneapolis: North Country Co-op.

Rao, Hayagreeva. 2009. *Market Rebels: How Activists Make or Break Radical Innovations*. Princeton, N.J.: Princeton University Press.

Rodale, J. I. 1945. "Pay Dirt: Farming and Gardening with Composts." New York: Devin-Adair.

Rodale Press. 1971. "If You're Ready to Try Organic Gardening This Year." *New York Times*, February 21, BR19 (advertisement).

Rudd, Robert L. 1964. *Pesticides and the Living Landscape*. Madison: University of Wisconsin Press.

Sanderson, Linda. 1976. "Ideological Differences May Lead to Charges against Co-op Members." *Minneapolis Tribune*, January 15, 1B.

Sharp, Kathy, and Tom Copeland. 1976. "Goings On . . ." *Scoop*, April–May, 9.

Sommer, Robert. 1982. "Consumer Co-ops: Alternative Economic and Social Units." *Alternative Lifestyles* 5: 109–17.

Soper, Edna W., and Bernice K. Watt. 1965. "Question, Please." In *Consumers All: The Yearbook of Agriculture 1965*. Edited by Alfred Stefferud, 407–16. Washington, D.C.: U.S. Government Printing Office.

Steiner, Rudolph. 1974. *Agriculture: A Course of Eight Lectures*. London: Rudolph Steiner House.

Stevenson, Eugene H. 1965. "Nutrition Nonsense." *Consumers All: The Yearbook of Agriculture 1965*. Edited by Alfred Stefferud, 402–7. Washington, D.C.: U.S. Government Printing Office.

Throckmorton, R. I. 1951. "The Organic Farming Myth." *Country Gentleman*, September, 21, 103, 105.

Tilly, Charles. 1978. *From Mobilization to Revolution*. Reading, Mass.: Addison-Wesley.

Tilly, Charles. 1995. *Popular Contention in Great Britain, 1758–1834*. Cambridge, Mass.: Harvard University. Press.

Tilly, Charles. 2006. *Regimes and Repertoires*. Chicago: University of Chicago Press.

Tilly, Charles, and Lesley J. Wood. 2009. *Social Movements, 1768–2008*. Boulder: Paradigm.

U.S. Bureau of the Census. 1973. *1970 Census of Population: Characteristics of the Population*. U.S. Department of Commerce. Washington, D.C.: U.S. Government Printing Office.

U.S. Census Bureau. 1902. *Twelfth Census of the United States, Taken in the Year 1900. Agriculture: Part I: Farms, Live Stock, and Animal Products*. Vol. V. Washington, D.C.: U.S. Census Office.

Van den Bosch, Robert. 1978. *The Pesticide Conspiracy*. Garden City, N.Y.: Doubleday.

Ware, Alan. 1989. *Between Profit and State: Intermediate Organizations in Britain and the United States*. Princeton, N.J.: Princeton University Press.

Wells, Patricia. 1980. "Organic Farming, British Style, Pays Off." *New York Times*, October 1, C3.

Whole Foods Market. 2019. "About Whole Foods Market | Wholefoodsmarket .Com." http://www.wholefoodsmarket.com/company/.

Wrench, Guy Theodore. 1945. *The Wheel of Health*. Milwaukee, Wis.: Lee Foundation for Nutritional Research.

Zwerdling, Daniel. 1979. "The Uncertain Revival of Food Cooperatives." In *Co-ops, Communes & Collectives: Experiments in Social Change in the 1960s and 1970s*. Edited by John Case and Rosemary C. R. Taylor, 87–111. New York: Pantheon.

# INDEX

*Page references in italics refer to images or figures.*

106–12, 172–78; new-wave
cooperative grocery stores and,
71–75, 105–12, 123–26, 129–
33; origins of, 23–24; public
perceptions of, 7–8; skepticism
of, 107–12; social change and,
194–205; supporting organizations
for, 178–82
Organic Food Producers Association
of North America, 117
Organic Foods Production Act, 2
*Organic Gardening and Farming
(OGF)*, 38–39, 70, 113
Organic Growers and Buyers
Association (OGBA), 113, 178
Organic Grower's Cooperative, *181*
*Organic Inc.* (Fromartz), 198
organizational infrastructure,
cooperatives' development of,
184–87
*Organizer's Handbook*, 72
*Origins and Legacies: The History of
the Cooperative Movement* (ACA),
120

Parker, Florence, 59–64, 81, 83, 95,
162
People's Bakery, 127
People's Center, 232n1
People's Pantry, 127
People's Warehouse (Minneapolis):
Co-op Wars and, 21–22, 139–40,
144–45, 147, 150, 163, 222n2;
demise of, 163; expansion of, 127;
founding of, 5; history of, 14–15,
184–85
*Pesticide Conspiracy, The* (van den
Bosch), 41
pesticides: growing concern over,
39–46; history of, 39–40, 222n7,

223n8; industrial agriculture and,
27–28
*Pesticides and the Living Landscape*
(Rudd), 41
Pfeiffer, Ehrenfried, 35
Phenix, Chuck, 143–44
Philadelphia Contributionship for
the Insurance of Houses from Loss
by Fire, 49
Policy Review Board (PRB), 145, 150
political activism: co-op formation
and, 93–94, 129, 132–37, 157–59,
164–71; Co-op Wars and, 137–50;
in Minnesota, 232n4. *See also* social
movements
Pomme de Terre Food Co-op (Morris, Minn.), 102–3, 123–24, 137
Powderhorn Co-op (Minneapolis),
128, 136
Powell, Michael, 229n11
power: cooperative movement
challenges to, 79–81, 105–6,
125; Co-op Wars as challenge to,
150–56; first dimension of, 151–
52, 233n16; hot causes and cool
mobilization and, 156–59; second
dimension of, 152–53; third
dimension of, 153–56, 233n17
*Power: A Radical View* (Lukes),
151–56, 233n17
Prairie Dog Store, 103
*Prevention* magazine, 39, 70
producer cooperatives, 49
public-benefit corporations, 235n9
public opinion, environmental issues
and, 41–46

racism: consumer cooperatives and,
59, 61–63, *62*; new-wave food
co-ops and, 140–41

CRAIG B. UPRIGHT is associate professor of sociology at Winona State University.